Democracy and the Ten Commandments

Democracy and the Ten Commandments

The Politics of Limited Government in the Bible

Robert Kimball Shinkoskey

RESOURCE *Publications* · Eugene, Oregon

DEMOCRACY AND THE TEN COMMANDMENTS
The Politics of Limited Government in the Bible

Copyright © 2016 Robert Kimball Shinkoskey. All rights reserved. Except for brief quotations in critical publications or reviews, no part of this book may be reproduced in any manner without prior written permission from the publisher. Write: Permissions, Wipf and Stock Publishers, 199 W. 8th Ave., Suite 3, Eugene, OR 97401.

Resource Publications
An Imprint of Wipf and Stock Publishers
199 W. 8th Ave., Suite 3
Eugene, OR 97401

www.wipfandstock.com

PAPERBACK ISBN: 978-1-4982-9009-8
HARDCOVER ISBN: 978-1-4982-9011-1

Manufactured in the U.S.A.

Scripture quotations throughout are from the King James Version.

For a Return to Rule of Law

Contents

Introduction | 1

PART I

1. Democracy and Captivity in the Ancient Near East | 8
2. Organizing a New Government at Sinai | 14
3. Moses' Theory of Self-Government | 26
   A Closer Look: Priesthood in the Bible | 36
4. Moses as Executor of the Law | 41
5. The Molten Calf: A Gold Mine of Political Information | 56
6. Deuteronomy and Democracy | 67
7. Judges Follow Precedents Set in the Wilderness | 75
8. People and Elders in Government | 79
   A Closer Look: Three Crowns of Jewish Government | 94

PART II

9. Civic Concerns and Secular Focus of the Bible | 97
10. Bible Literature as Propaganda for People's Government | 102
11. Early Science and the Gods: Putting Political Content Back into Bible Vocabulary | 110

PART III

12. Ten Oppressions In Egypt, Ten Solutions in Israel | 118
    A Closer Look: Separation of Cult and Crown in Ancient Israel | 122
13. The First Two Commandments: Organizing Government | 131
14. Third and Fourth Commandments: Organizing and Regulating the Economy | 153
15. Fifth, Sixth, Seventh, and Eighth Commandments: Limiting National Government and Empowering Local Government | 167
16. Ninth and Tenth Commandments: Mandating Justice and Literacy, Citizenship and Public Health | 199

Epilogue | 209

Appendix I: Comparison of Government Charters of Ancient Israel and the United States | 213

Appendix II: A Note on the "Public Display" Controversy | 222

Bibliography | 225

Name Index | 231

Subject Index | 235

Introduction

MODERN CHRISTIAN CHURCHES WOULD have us believe that ancient Israel suffered greatly in captivity in Egypt, and yet, not one of the ten new laws accepted at Mt. Sinai had to do with correcting that suffering. Lost to the usual thinking is the idea that the Ten Commandments might have been intended for and understood by the Israelite people as articles for the organization and operation of government. Christians say that those ancient laws are best interpreted as individual morality, community ethics, and good religion. Political notions, civic laws, secular precepts . . . are distasteful to churches whose pastors rule over quiet Sunday communion, and shun the roar of Monday through Saturday traffic.

A reasonable reading of the fourth commandment law on six days of work and one day of rest is that it established basic labor conditions in ancient Israel. St. Thomas Aquinas, on the other hand, saw the (Protestant) fourth commandment setting aside a Sabbath day not in terms of relief from rigorous slave labor in Egypt, but as a way to "set apart some time for the things of God."[1] Understandably, the "things of God" are the things of the church: the rituals, private beliefs, moral teachings of a group of Christian disciples. St. Thomas believed that the purpose of the law was "the repose of the mind in God."[2] We see it here as the repose of the body in freedom—a public, non-denominational law for labor relief and occupational choice. Modern Catholic theologians follow the path outlined by Aquinas. Coauthors Dauphinais and Levering, for example, indicate that together the job of "the Mosaic law or Torah and the new law of Jesus Christ" is to "make

---

1. Aquinas, "The Moral Precepts of the Old Law," 52.
2. Ibid., 54.

us fit for heaven."[3] We argue here that the laws were fashioned to make man fit for earth.

It is not just one commandment that is commandeered for limited use, however. Aquinas finds that the third (Protestant) commandment prohibiting taking the name of God in vain "prohibits perjury . . . blasphemy . . . false teaching."[4] Two of this list are offenses against true Catholic religion. The actual civic content of the third commandment, which we will see below is considerable, is greatly diluted by such an interpretation.

In fact, complex civic laws like the Ten Commandments are seen as a simple religious catechism that Church fathers can teach like an elementary school curriculum. Aquinas opines: "The precepts of the Decalogue are concerned with matters that the mind can grasp instantly."[5] It is the contention of this book that those laws are so rich and formidable that it has taken 3,000 years, and a great deal of Biblical science, even to get to the doorstep of an able understanding of their meaning. Catholic theologians and Protestant reformers have impeded the process as much as helped.

Luther, for his part, made the commandments into a support for his doctrinal reforms. He saw the law against idolatry in a narrow way, as a Jewish cultic requirement, rather than in a broad cultural and social vein. He wrote, "The sectarian spirits have misunderstood also with respect to the images, for that too pertains only to the Jews."[6]

John Calvin, who steered further away from the Catholic church than Lutherans did, nevertheless still held to the long Christian tradition about the private religious focus of the commandments. He reminded his Reformed followers: "In the First Table, God instructs us in piety and the proper duties of religion, by which we are to worship his majesty."[7] Like Aquinas, he believed that the Decalogue was deliberately simplified, ready-made for use to instruct the ignorant in right versus wrong: "God spoke in a gross and uncultured manner in order to accommodate himself to the great and small and the less intelligent."[8]

Calvin did not have much regard for the implications of the Decalogue in terms of civil government. Out of his twenty chapters on administration of the two kingdoms, civil and church, he wrote nineteen chapters on

---

3. Dauphinais and Levering, "Law in the Theology of St. Thomas Aquinas," 48.
4. Aquinas, "The Moral Precepts of the Old Law," 59.
5. Ibid., 55.
6. Luther, "How Christians Should Regard Moses," 76.
7. Calvin, *Institutes*, 377.
8. Calvin, *Sermons*, 153.

church government and only one on civil government.⁹ For example, Calvin dismissed the prospect of viewing the fourth commandment as civil labor law with a quick flick of the wrist: "It was not [God's] principal aim for there to be one day a week in which people ceased to work in order to catch their breath."¹⁰

The particular "take" modern Christians have on the Ten Commandments has been, given such encouragements by Church leaders, predictably simplistic, anachronistic (based on modern ideas), and self-serving. The first commandment against having other gods is seen as a law promoting worship, and usually according to a specified denominational creed. A Reformed church commentator writes, "Worship God alone . . . Take pleasure in God."¹¹ The second commandment against images is a law against the making of a physical idol of God, and perhaps, then, attributing powers to a dumb object. The same commentator summarizes the meaning of this law thusly: "Do not try to depict God visually."¹² The third commandment against taking the name of God in vain is seen as a prohibition on cussing, or mocking God.

The fourth commandment relating to the Sabbath is seen as a law promoting church attendance and worship. The fifth commandment promoting honor of mother and father is seen as a law specifying respect for one's elders. The sixth commandment against killing is seen as a simple prohibition of murder. The seventh commandment against adultery is a law against sleeping around with others while married. The eighth against stealing is a law against shop-lifting, or rougher forms of theft. The ninth against false witness is a law against lying. The tenth against coveting works best as a curriculum aid for sermons about the psychology of individual thoughts and desires.

Unfortunately, the question must be asked, does this tidy little list of personal moral/religious admonitions really provide adequate solutions to the sorts of political, economic, and military problems confronting a tribal confederation as it begins to function as an actual Middle Eastern nation? After all, a similar moral code had long existed in Egypt in the form of the Book of the Dead, but that did not seem to stop political and economic oppression there at all. Where in this interpretation of the Ten Commandments is the law on the functions of government, election of leaders, division of powers, economic activity and taxation, human rights? Ultimately,

9. Burgess, "Reformed Explication," 91.
10. Calvin, *Sermons*, 112.
11. Burgess, "Reformed Explication," 97.
12. Ibid.

such a light-weight interpretation of the commandment law gives religious leaders tremendous latitude to opt out of active participation in society altogether, or bend with the prevailing winds of government, whether those winds blow in the interests of ordinary people or not. Is this what the ten commandments was actually meant to do? To allow political whatever, whenever?

This book has two objectives. The first is to outline the history of democracy in the ancient world, to show how Israel's earliest history (Abraham, Isaac, Jacob) fit into that broader story, and to show how Israel's experience in Egypt conditioned the type of government she turned to once outside of Egypt. The second is to show how Israel's foundational law and her early government traditions after ratifying that law, set up an enduring government system of the type we know today as a democratic republic—a system of consensual government . . . a society based on power to the people and limited national government.

The experiences of oppression in Egypt inspired the reforms that the Israelites ratified as their constitutional law. Neither Israel in Egypt, nor Israel in Canaan, existed in a historical vacuum. The twelve tribes had to deal with political, military, social, economic, cultural and religious forces around them. They ratified a law that was intended to serve as the guiding light for government through periods prosperous and poor, religiously diverse and religiously orthodox. That law specified, simply, that the people should decide, all of the people. The founding fathers of the Israelite confederation took great pains to see that future generations did not fall under the spell of bright promoters who would ask that power be turned over to a wealthy class, or a single ruler. They did not want a society in which a smarter, or quicker, or more brutal party cornered the market or the power. They did not want the people to fall prey to promoters promising quick individual prosperity at the expense of the neighbor or by alliance with wealthy nations in the world around them. Their constitution specified slow, painstaking processes for individual self-improvement and national improvement. Early governmental laws and traditions enacted pursuant to the original ten laws guided the society capably for several hundred years. In time, however, Israel's citizens traded away their right to govern themselves locally for a system of hereditary monarchy and highly centralized government that brought wealth to the few and denied education and opportunity to the many. The citizenry traded rule of law for unhampered rule by political celebrities.

The Christian church today has refashioned historical reality, kidnapped it really, by re-making ten commandment law to serve selfish, though at times well-intentioned, interests. The church has de-politicized, de-intellectualized, de-humanized, and misinterpreted the original civic law of the land of Israel, and, in the process, their own Old Testament scripture. Early Jewish rabbis may have done something similar, too, when they turned the public law of Israel into private law to regulate life revolving around the synagogue after the great dispersal from Palestine in the first century. In the process, all seem to have left out not only some of the trimmings of the tradition, but the main course itself. They have contented themselves to regulate theological belief and congregational solidarity without much thought for constitutional theory, government organization, and community action.

This mis-telling of the actual civic history of the Bible peoples has not gone without significant negative consequences for medieval and modern society. Christianity has committed so many abuses in the name of their frail interpretation both the Old and New testaments that Generation X and Millennial Generation young people today can hardly contain their distaste for what their ancestors have wrought in the name of religion. Historically, Christianity has supported the divine right of kings, priestly theocracy, economic oligarchy, imperial war-making, repression of human rights, misogyny, slavery, and utopian cult activity under the leadership of exploitative leaders, all on the basis of a sloppy and sordid interpretation of the Ten Commandments. In fact, the Ten Commandments are unalterably opposed to all of these practices.

On the other hand, some Christian sectarians believe the Bible supports a view that God is interested in church activity rather exclusively and is willing to leave political activities to the unbelievers. When religious groups dare to assert themselves in the civic realm, they do so without much solid understanding of what positions they should actually take.

The Bible is an elegant historical record of a people and a society interested in everything under the sun, including science, education, good government, social justice, private land, inheritance, health and welfare, personal liberty, family success, peace and happiness. Those people chose to go about the business of making a new nation by setting up a particular form of government and dedicating that system of government to a national deity. This is something that virtually every other nation in the ancient Near East did. The only real difference between Israel and other nations was that their tribes and their chosen leader, Moses, favored democratic republicanism and real freedom for the people, after having lived for so long without it in Egypt. The god they honored in the process was a God of both considerable citizen rights and considerable citizen responsibilities. The national leader and government were not to be the only parties with rights and responsibilities like Ramses and his cronies in Egypt. Every person was to be an empowered governor in Israel.

Students of the Old Testament who see some political content in the scripture have formulated an interpretative approach that can be called "theo-politics." This is a step in the right direction, but it still leaves the Bible in the hands of the theologians rather than inviting the political and legal scientists to play a co-leading role. One such theologian is James Barr. James Barr starts his article on "Politics and the Bible" with the statement "The Bible is not a purely religious book; its pages are full of kings and empires, armies and wars, cries for justice."[13] He then offers five "great architectonic images of political life" in the Bible, each of which describes a portion of the "look and feel" of the civic tradition of the Bible, including the New Testament. Barr's theo-politics serve as a useful starting point for launching us into the full breadth and depth of political science in the Bible.

The first image or impression of civic life is the "theocratic" image, the idea that God is in charge of government and politics. He indicates that this is "perhaps the most influential such image." Barr's first political image is certainly reflected in the actual language of the Bible, the ancient way of verbally expressing life as it was known then. God directs such civic details as what kinds of animals are safe to be eaten, and whether interest can be charged for the loaning of money. God makes new legislation and decides cases at court. Barr writes, "Direct divine instructions for state and politics exist enshrined in the Bible." Almost everything is attributed to God, as if God were individually orchestrating each natural law like gravity on earth, the motions of heavenly bodies, the falling of rain and the growing of crops like some kind of omnipotent conductor.

The second great political image is the "alien state" portrayal of culture. Israel is set apart from other nations, and has set about the task of being a "holy" people. (Deut 26:19) This interpretive view can be read as setting up a sort of religious xenophobia or exceptionalism, whereby God perennially favors Israelites as a kinship group, either for their particular obedience to religious law or their great spirituality.

The third political model found in the Bible is the prophetic image of society. In this view, it is the task of the church—the inheritors of the prophets' legacy—to protect against shortcomings and injustices in society. The prophetic model seems to allow a little room for coexistence with the theocratic model. If divinely appointed kings do not provide occasional benefits and reforms, and if class distinction between the rich and poor gets too marked, the prophets can then try to de-legitimize the kings.

The fourth model of Biblical government is the "eschatological" image. According to this view, a new world is coming, or aborning, or periodically

---

13. Barr, "Politics and the Bible," 599.

possible. (Mark 12:1–30) War and evil, the twin woes of both the founding politicians and the prophets, will ultimately be banished. (Isa 2:4, 11:1–9; Rev 21:1–5)

The fifth model is the image of migration. In this view, the church are a pilgrim people, going to whatever place God might direct so that they can build an ethical, democratic society which draws its primary sustenance from the land. Abraham and Moses set the early example, and Jews and Christians, including Puritan settlers in New England and Afrikaners in South Africa, have followed that example to find peace and self-determination since then. (Heb 13:14)

The final political image that stands out in the Bible is that of "liberation." The Exodus is one of the dominating events of the Bible's Old Testament story, and the struggle against Roman imperialism and over-lordship of a once independent land is a key aspect of the New Testament story. The goal is release from economic slavery, intellectual repression, and oppressive taxation. The church must stand up with the poor, oppressed, and marginalized of society, and advocate for reform, or overthrow an evil regime.

The image that we present in this book is one of a constitutional republic, where kings are replaced by citizens and their laws, at least during Israel's first several hundred years. This is a story of civic salvation . . . happiness and prosperity through local and national independence from autocracy. We downplay the idea of theocracy here, and even contradict it with our discussions on separation of priestly and princely power. We distance ourselves from the second political image, that of Israel as a special nation. We maintain every democracy in the ancient Near East was quite special. We see a crucial role for prophets, but underline their function as constitutional specialists, cultural renewal activists, and political party organizers. They don't spend much time in church.

The eschatological image of the final reign of good is hard to comprehend in view of the Bible's portrayal of evil and political danger as never-ending forces in the world. We see merit in the migration image, but see the migration of the mind from slavish complacency to citizenship action to be a bigger movement touted by the Bible than a geographic one. We find the liberation image wanting as far as explaining exactly what the people are wanting freedom from and in pointing out how certain broad constitutional laws provide answers to the specific oppressions. This liberation image is getting warmer, but still assumes non-believers must be encouraged to know what is right politically and act upon it.

Part I

1

Democracy and Captivity in the Ancient Near East

It is important to understand that the Bible's story of freedom-seeking people and their devastating slide into captivity at the hands of a once friendly neighboring nation was likely one of many such stories in the ancient world. This particular story apparently was just better documented and achieved a greater degree of notoriety than most. We are able to take this view after coming to an understanding that the natural political condition of neighboring tribes in the ancient world was peaceful cooperation between the tribal groups and democratic self-determination within each group. When an autocratic or aggressive war lord seized tribal leadership and ran roughshod over the tribe and its neighbors, the tribe saw even more clearly that the traditional way of limited leadership was better. When a large or powerful city-state took root in the ancient Near East, small tribal groups often took flight to avoid taxation and control. Alternately, they threw in their lot with the king and hoped he would make good on promises for a good life for them. Things were sometimes good for a period, but things were often bad for intolerable periods of time. In the view of the ancient tribes, powerful central government did not work very well. And that view took root over a very long period of time and in many places. It was not a sudden phenomenon.

Political anthropologists have found evidence of democratic group behavior in the long period before written history. In the very early period, hunter-gathers limited the power of the band leader and insisted upon inclusion in decision-making. However, with the development of city-states, some city leaders began to tax their people and build police forces to suppress dissent and standing armies to extend their predatory behavior outward.[1]

Larger societies flourished in lowland cities, but smaller and more democratic groups flourished in and about the cities when central power waned and where relatively inaccessible highland areas were available which could sustain unmolested family and clan life. This pattern is suggested in the Genesis narrative about democratic life in Eden in the beginning. Eden, an idyllic site located in a forested highland area (a river flows out of the site), is host to innocent socio-economic family life not affected at first by violence, and characterized by both farming and herding.

Geographers and historians of the ancient Near East describe periods of expanding and contracting imperial power. Kings captured and sometimes relaxed control over peripheral territories and people. Palestine was a good example of such a peripheral territory. Archeology of the late Bronze and early Iron Age periods in Palestine shows a roll-back of traditional hegemony in the area during the period of Judges in the Bible, beginning around 1200 BCE, the time when the bulk of Israelites arrived in Canaan. The Israelite tribes lived in relative peace and independence until around 700 BCE, when a great foreign power, Assyria, finally pressed heavily into the area. After Assyria, came Babylon, Greece, and Rome. Each invasion affected the lives of Israelites. In between came smaller irritations from the likes of Amalek, Midian and Philistia.

Outside Palestine, smaller, anti-autocratic societies flourished in Syria, Anatolia (modern Turkey), and Persia as well. These areas were overrun by imperial societies frequently but often held to local political institutions "above every other bond of loyalty."[2] Before the advent of the strong king Cyrus, Persian chief magistrates, for example, were temporary rulers. Each served as "the head of the principal of seven dominant clans, and ruled the nation in continual consultation with the leading clansmen."[3] This and other free soil domains demonstrated remarkable staying power throughout history. For example, indigenous, egalitarian, small-scale communities on the border between Sudan and Ethiopia have successfully survived in that buffer zone for the past three thousand years.[4]

1. Boehm, "Pre-Classical Democracy – Prehistory," 29–31.
2. Frankfort, *Kingship and the Gods*, 337.
3. Ibid., 338.
4. Gonzales-Ruibal, *Archaeology of Resistance*.

The literature of the Bible is filled with vocabulary related to suffering from both external aggression and, at times, local oppression. The Bible uses a great number of words related to distress, harm, oppression, abandonment, exploitation, aggression, bondage, and exile, and an equally large number of words expressing relief, wellness, redemption, restoration, enfranchisement, peace, release, and return, when self-government and peace were re-established. Before the Exodus from Egypt, the Hebrews "cried" out loud to express their sadness. Once in Canaan, they lived under regular threat from nearby alien tribes. The Hebrew word "yr" translates as "fear" and can be found numerous places in the Bible in verb, adjective and noun form. The word "lqh" translates as "take" or "capture," and many other words like it are found in numerous places as well. English words used to translate Old Testament vocabulary related to war summarize the process of conflict and/or capture and are poignantly indicative of great ordeal and suffering. Such words include smite, pluck up, tear, blast, cut down, waste, stroke, dashed to pieces, rip open, hew down, heap, waste, cut out, sweep, tread down, thresh, winnow, besiege. Many words also reflect the idea of fleeing from such devastation and living in exile from one's homeland. In an earlier work this author wrote, "The words used to communicate these critical events can be grouped into a chronology reflecting the all-too-painful cycle of events detailing political, economic, and social captivity repeated over and over again in the history summarized by Deuteronomistic and Chronicalistic historians." The Bible's frequent body counts do not resemble the triumphalist victory poems of Near East kings and do not demonstrate that the Israelite God had a lust for murder and mayhem. Those body counts are published in order to give credence to the illegitimacy of autocratic political practices of those who do the killing, or the failings of a people who all-to-often give up peace-loving democracy in favor of lust for blood and treasure.[5]

The narratives in both testaments stress the never-ending battle of democratic society for survival in the wake of imperial activity, and local government oppression. The books of Exodus and Revelation are but more expansive and more deeply critical versions of earlier Mesopotamian and Egyptian accounts of citizen discontent with the self-important courts of monarchy, like the Mesopotamian story of Gilgamesh and the Egyptian story of Sinuhe. Greek stories of Illiad and Odyssey, and the Roman story of Romulus and Remus sound a similar note as well. The end result of experience with oppression is reversion to governmental processes that limit the powers of the national leader. Tribal groups throughout the region seemed to have remained poised to recoup political freedoms at a moment's notice.

5. Shinkoskey, *Biblical Captivity*, 10, 19–23.

Henri Frankfort, speaking of Egypt, mentions "the ease with which . . . provinces become independent under their own chiefs whenever central power weakened." They kept local government institutions at the ready for such an eventuality. In other places, local home rule was an ongoing tradition. Frankfort points out that the oldest political institution in ancient Mesopotamia was the assembly, or electorate, of all free men. They "left power to deal with current matters in the hands of a group of elders . . . in times of emergency they chose a 'king' to take charge for a limited period." The Hittite governor/king reported to a council of nobles which could curb or reverse his actions, as was the case in Mitanni and smaller Syrian states.[6] This was the governing pattern of the Israelite tribes in Canaan for the first 300 years as well.

One pair of authors write that the biblical book of Genesis is a "rich source for . . . political terminology and constitutional ideas."[7] Genesis, for example, corroborates the results of scientific study of early societies of the ancient Near East, like Sumer in Mesopotamia. Bible patriarchs like Noah and Abraham re-established democratic governance in places where they could, like elders did during the inter-dynastic periods in Egypt and Mesopotamia. The Bible's patriarchs, portrayed essentially as humane political leaders, made covenants or constitutions with their people to govern according to law and likely to make policy and take action only according to the consent of the people. Abraham's constitution, for example, required the leader and the people to tolerate those tribes and city states nearby who allowed them to govern themselves, and took issue with those that did not. (Gen 12:3) When Abraham raised an army, in addition, it is extremely likely he had the consent of the militia and their families for the task of rescuing Lot. (Gen 14:14) He did not conscript them against their wishes as strong kings were wont to do. Although the Bible does not explicitly say so, patriarchs like Abraham, Isaac, and Jacob were likely elected, or at least subject to removal if they did not govern according to popular will. In fact, Jacob's sons and their followers frequently disregarded the advice of their tribal patriarch and implemented their own (often misguided) policies by right of common consent. The bulk of the Israelite people disregarded Samuel's advice discouraging a stronger central government and went with the majority view of the elders, who clearly were excited about the possibility of new power, wealth, and security for themselves and their clans. (1 Sam 8:19–20)

Before Israelite democracy took root outside of Egypt, earlier democracies functioned in Canaan and Phoenicia and during the Old Hittite

---

6. Frankfort, *Kingship and the Gods*, 17, 215, 338.
7. Elazar, and Cohen, *Jewish Polity*, 45.

period in Asia Minor. A growing body of archaeological and textual evidence points to democratic activity in ancient Phoenicia during the period 1600 to 400 BCE, a fact that the Bible itself corroborates when speaking of Israel's historical friendship with Tyre. Phoenicia was ruled for periods by "judges" ("suffetes"), who were elected, term-limited chief magistrates. Popular elements such as rule of law, equality, free speech, individual rights were also in evidence.[8]

One pre-eminent indicator of democratic functionality then, as now, was the separation of church and state, or perhaps more pertinently, separation of priest and palace, shrine and state, sacred and secular spheres of government. The Mesopotamian monarch Urukagina was a politically "progressive" usurper of private property, which he then placed in the public domain, like early twentieth century American presidents. Urukagina, in a complicated series of maneuvers during his term of office, either separated the priestly function from the statecraft function, or, more likely, fused it more closely together, depending upon which researcher one favors. The point made here does not depend upon a definitive answer, as we are only concerned to show that the issue was an important one for the ancients.[9]

Indeed, Akhenaten in Egypt reduced the property and privileges of the priesthood of Amun-Re as a means of establishing his own priesthood in power.[10] A back and forth shifting in power from priestly governing groups to secular governing groups, or a dabbling of one sector of social power in the perquisites of the other, was typical both of monarchic and limited government societies throughout ancient as well as medieval times. This is evidenced by Bible stories about Abimelech, Gideon, Saul, Uzziah, Josiah and others, the Cluniac struggles in Europe, and the church/state struggles on the American continent in the modern period.

The Bible demonstrates, and history outside Palestine corroborates, that ultimately the power to regulate religion falls under the purview of the people or the ruling families and their chosen forms of government. For example, if the people and their government leaders do not want iconic public religion and heavy involvement of government in private religion, they don't have to have it. Moses demonstrated that good government plays a role in religion, but only a limited one, when during his inaugural term as chief executive of ancient Israel he administered the first laws governing the investment of the clergy. Moses gave the public priesthood to Aaron, which required broad secular duties as well as the quite narrow religion-related

---

8. Stockwell, *Secret History*, 35–48; Stockwell, *History of Democracy*, 75–79.
9. Mieroop, *Ancient Near East*, 45; Nissen, *Early History*, 147–48.
10. Murname, "Egypt, History of (Dynasties 18–20)," 350.

duty of trying to obtain God's blessings for the nation. Once this was done, various clergies formed up under the Israelite constitution granting free religious worship in the nation. Political power over the fundamental flavor of religion in the nation was demonstrated later at the time of the secession of the northern tribes from the southern in Israel. Jeroboam authorized two national chapels in the north to compete with the one in Jerusalem. But aside from exercising the power to spank religion into the diverse forms it has in ancient nations, tribal confederations of democratic types knew how to stay out of the way of sacred beliefs in their populations the world over. In India, for example, executive magistrates were charged with upholding the privileges of the priestly Brahman class, but were not charged with organizing their affairs or governing them.

2

Organizing a New Government at Sinai

THE PATTERN OF ONGOING fear of aggression and oppression in the ancient world, together with the hope for some kind of sophisticated avoidance of it, find a suitable mirror in the story we outline in this chapter. The Bible's glimpse into the daily grind of ancient autocratic government is priceless and inspiring and pregnant with meaning for modern political humankind.

The story of Israel in captivity in Egypt is told in the book of Exodus. The story, however, begins in Genesis, where the jealous brothers of Joseph sell him into slavery to Midianites. He finally ends up in Egypt, working his way up the royal court hierarchy. Joseph's father and brothers and their households are eventually drawn to Egypt to avoid a plague, and live there seemingly pleasantly for a couple hundred years, until the House of Seti comes to power. The book of Exodus opens as the Israelites have grown numerous and Seti worries that they are upsetting the delicate balance of political power in support of the dynasty. He subjects Israel to great harassment and persecution. Pharaoh Seti conscripts the Israelites into his public building program and, then, in order to put a stop to their proliferation, he directs the Israelite midwives to kill every male child born among the Jews. The midwives find a way to sidestep the order at least for a time. When the slaughter of the innocents finally begins in earnest, Moses' mother Jocheved places him in a basket on the Nile river and luckily Pharaoh's daughter finds it and adopts the child. Moses grows up in and around a court of royalty, but is forced to flee the country when he comes to the rescue of an oppressed Hebrew, kills an Egyptian man and is found out.[1]

---

1. For a vibrant summary of the details of the first two chapters of Exodus, see Hazony, *Dawn*, 76–78.

Organizing a New Government at Sinai

Moses basically does a political internship in the house of a Midianite democratic leader, his future father-in-law Jethro, and returns to Egypt after a conversation with a God whose voice comes out of a burning bush. Moses goes to Pharaoh and essentially argues that a distinctive cultural sub-grouping within Egypt like the Hebrews should have the right to decide their own worship practices and not be forced to conform to the king's wishes even if they have been conscripted into public labor en-masse. Moses orchestrates the appearance of a number of devastating plagues, each of which inch Pharaoh closer to letting Israel go. After perhaps several years of wrangling with Pharaoh, the Hebrews slip out of the town of Goshen on a three-day pilgrimage ostensibly to worship their new God, but likely to bind themselves together into some kind of political covenant as a people and perhaps make a run toward the ancestral home in Canaan. When Pharaoh reneges on his promise to let them go and sends his army out to find and exterminate or capture them, they escape across the Reed Sea, perhaps at low tide, and Pharaoh's troops become mired, defeated, and destroyed.

While we have given it basic socio-political structure, what is missing from this thumbnail sketch are numerous other essential political details that the text provides if one is willing to dig for them, details that turn the Exodus event into a believable, real life historical memory by those who chronicled it, rather than a religious fantasy full of mystery and miracle. For example, the form of local or tribal government of the Hebrews under long-term Egyptian rule likely involved a certain level of self-government, which is suggested by the presence of elders ("zakenem"). (Exod 3:16, 4:29) Moses may have initiated the election of these elders, or merely motivated their activation from dormancy. Ramses II usurped the local government power elders would expect to have even in Egypt and put it in the hands of Egyptian taskmasters ("sarei misim") and Israelite "officers" ("shoterim"; Exod 5:6) in the employ of Pharaoh. These officers report to the taskmasters.[2] (Exod 5:14) Moses sidestepped these court party operatives and organized the elders as a policy body and went with them to confront Pharaoh. (Exod 3:16–18)

Israel seems to have begun to coalesce into an autonomous political group even before leaving Egypt, perhaps under the direction of the elders. For example, the elders enacted a policy of circumcision as a sort of indication of belonging to a new style of community. (Exod 4:25) They also marked their doors with the blood of the paschal lamb, which can be interpreted as delineating a type of territorial boundary between the Hebrews and the Egyptians, a sort of good ghettoization of the community,

---

2. Elazar, and Cohen, *Jewish Polity*, 53.

and a demonstration of the ability to implement localized public policy apart from policies established by Pharaoh. The arrangements for celebration of the Passover (Exod 12–13) suggest a certain autonomy of family units ("batei av," households) within the overall political structure. This was a foreshadowing of the Fifth Commandment law enshrining family government and local home rule in Israel.[3]

Other aspects of the political constitution negotiated and ratified at Sinai and the tradition resulting from it are foreshadowed early on as well. Firstly, Moses acted as statesman, or constitutional party organizer and functionary, in his early dealings with the people, not as lawmaker. He may have prompted the elders, but they deliberated and decided. He was a capable middle-man between the elders and Pharaoh, but could have had no success at all with Pharaoh without the elders' consensus backing him up. Secondly, Moses did not come out of the membership of the senior tribe, that tribe (Rueben) with the most wealth and political authority. He came rather from the Levite tribe, who were associated with the educated elite both in Egypt and in the new Israel. This is an indication that knowledge rather than money or status would play the most important role in Israel's new government. Moses was not even the firstborn in his own family. One set of authors astutely remark, "The clear implication is that already the right to wield authority in the polity of the "Bnei Yisrael" did not pass through inheritance. Beyond that . . . leadership must be confirmed by popular acclaim."[4] Moses' qualification for leadership was not blood, but ability. In particular he was well trained in history and science, and particularly political science. Moses was the people's choice, not the gentry's choice. He was endowed with an ethical spirit (Exod 5:20-23), not a wealthy spirit, and represented the concerns of the great bulk of the people, not the concerns of the few. (Exod 5:1-21)

Moses was capable of serving in any one of several kinds of leadership capacities in the new confederation. However, he had certain weaknesses common to ordinary human beings that created opportunities for others to help him govern, and even encouraged them to try to supplant him. Due to lack of public relations and verbal communications skill, Moses shared both the task of negotiation with Pharaoh and leading the executive branch of government in the wilderness with Aaron. But "sharing" does not even begin to tell the whole story of the requirements for leadership in constitutional Israel. Together, Moses and Aaron demonstrated not only the sophistication of the Hebrew educated elite and the possibilities of teamwork, but also the

3. Ibid., 54, 56.
4. Ibid., 54.

absolute need for separating the creative sacred function from the grinding secular function in the governing structure and in society. This early dual executive department leadership precedent foreshadowed the horizontal separation of national government powers enshrined at Sinai soon after. It also suggested a certain limitation of the power of the chief executive so that it was checked by a parallel political power on the national level. But the Hebrew people through their elder councils demonstrated something just as important as national separation of powers—the readiness of the people to assume self-government.

One of the evidences of the idea that Moses and the Israelite people self-consciously constructed a constitution dealing with the usual social, economic, political, legal and international matters of an ancient Near East government while encamped at the foot of Sinai was simply that they needed one at that moment in time. They had lived for a long time under a strong national regulatory environment in Egypt, but now in the wilderness had no regulation of their lives at all on any level. They needed a way to organize government, and a way to define and empower acceptable activities of daily living. They needed domestic law in order to regulate marriage, divorce, child-rearing, and inheritance. They needed economic law to guide hired labor, and buying and selling. They needed laws to define and encourage good citizenship and to promote public health, and laws to regulate relations with other tribes and nations. Also, they wanted to be able to speak and worship freely. They wanted reasonable boundaries to be set both guarding, promoting, and, in some cases, limiting speech and action in the new nation. They intended to set those boundaries quite far to "the left", that is, in favor of liberality. Even though they wanted extensive and real freedom, they still needed government structure, and also a legal enforcement mechanism to police their society, however.

Politically, the Israelites needed to be able to answer the most basic of political/constitutional questions: by what authority do they set up their government?[5] We mentioned above that the standard solution in the ancient Near East about authority was that the wealthy were born to rule politically. That did not hold sway in Israel since neither Moses nor Aaron seemed to have any particular wealth. Authority reportedly came from heaven, after Moses' remarkable encounter with the spirit of heaven in Midian. But authority even more obviously came from the common people whose stripes on their backs taught them what they wanted and whose oral histories of their ancestors reminded them where freedom could be put into practice.

---

5. Walzer, et. al., *Jewish Political Tradition*, xxl.

What we are saying here is that the people could see the finish line from the start. Available land in Canaan, they hoped, along with educated (prophet and priestly) leadership, migration, local self-determination, purity (health), legal education, and the current decline of great power hegemony in the eastern Mediterranean, were giving them an opportunity they were determined to seize. They were in a political state of nature, having the ability to do whatever they wanted. The Reformation-era commentator Spinoza wrote that they had a "natural right over everything that lay within their power."[6] Beyond the question of authority, they needed to decide how they would be organized and led, and which group or groups exercised sovereignty, or final decision-making power. In essence, since they had attained freedom, they now had ability to define power and rights however they wanted. It is critical to an understanding of the entire Bible that the Israelites decided that the people of each individual tribe had the greatest sovereignty. Each tribe could do as it pleased, and this was demonstrated loudly and clearly in the stories about the wilderness and the period of Judges. Early on, Israel planned to divide the land in Canaan according to tribes and they then carried out this plan to the fullest. This policy did not merely imply tribal sovereignty, but assured it by means of the economic power the land afforded each tribal grouping. During the migration, and certainly in Canaan later, the tribes decided on their own if they would support various calls to action by the tribal confederacy. Often they stayed home rather than defend their brother tribes from outside threats. The tribes delegated minimal power to their legislating elders on the national level, and those elders then delegated power to the administrator of the nation to implement the people's policy.

In their earliest moments of migration, the tribes adopted a temporary emergency law until such time as that law could be further elaborated to meet the extended migratory period and settlement situations that would arise in the new land. Moses seems to have used his father-in-law, Jethro, as a consultant in the early stage of the government-forming process. Jethro, for example, helped him organize the migrating camp on a de-centralized basis even before Moses and the camp settle into deliberations to form a permanently de-centralized government at Sinai. The tribes nominated leaders and Moses appointed those leaders according to tribal wishes. (Exod 18:13–27)

Finally, when Israel had put sufficient distance between themselves and Egypt, they negotiated a set of constitutional laws, which they ratified in the form of the Ten Commandments, found now in Exodus 20, or possibly

---

6. Ibid., 43.

an abbreviated or pastoral version of these laws found in Exodus 34. These early precepts were couched in the form of categorical principles. That meant few or no exceptions to the rule. These laws nevertheless allowed for later legislation meant to implement them or snippets of case law meant to interpret them.

The first four articles of government, often termed the First Table, seem to the modern eye to suggest organization of a religion devoted to a specific monotheistic god who pointedly set aside mandatory worship time for himself alone. In fact, not only the first four, but all ten of the commandments are devoted not to religion, but to civic and arguably even secular law. The ten articles follow an ancient Near East secular document format that, as a matter of conventional form, merely calls upon one or more gods to oversee and witness the faithfulness of the parties signing the document. In this case, the document calls on the God of the Exodus to witness the pact made between the people/tribes and the national government and for the people to stick to the governmental principles inspired by the God of the ancestors. That earlier God, called El, had brooded over an earlier democratic experience in Canaan. The "god" references in the first and third commandments (no other gods, and no taking of the name of God in vain) are thus really just part of the usual packaging of the secular contents of such compacts. Those mentions constitute a necessary formality rather than the actual substance of the document. The substance of the first few articles of government, as in any democratic government, is concerned with the organization and operation of civic institutions in the new society and, in particular, power relationships between government units. The first article deals with organization of the national government on the basis of political freedom for all of the people. The third article deals with organization of the economy on the basis of freedom of livelihood and of buying and selling for all of the people.

The mention of what appears to be religious idolatry in the second commandment and what appears to be mandatory church attendance in the fourth commandment rather are better understood quite differently. The second commandment actually deals with organization of and limitation of the executive branch of government and the fourth deals with the basic labor law of the new nation. The first commandment, in addition, constitutes a statement about the parties' expectation of, and hope for, faithfulness in complying with the provisions of the document. The parties wanted the freedoms of the locally-governing tribes to hold up over the long haul. For that to happen, the tribes had to support one another like one neighbor would support another. They wanted the tribes to work together to obtain the necessary land, and even after obtaining the land, to help one another out in maintaining not only possession of the land, but democratic governance of it. The God of Israel witnessed their intent to accomplish these things, but it was clearly in the hands of the people to make them happen.

It is decidedly the case that the Ten Commandment covenant under God did not have the purpose of requiring a specific pattern of religious worship for the confederated parties any more so than for the parties to international treaties. Like the broader agreements between nations, the commandment covenant's purpose was to deal with a much broader scope of civic life. There is nothing in the ten laws about prophets or priests, angels or devils, religious saviors or salvation, nothing of creedal statements of faith or ritual worship using incense and sacrifice. The ten laws are not even necessarily a statement about belief in an anthropomorphic God.

The ancient Near East treaty form was appropriate for use by the migrants out of Egypt since the commandments essentially served as a treaty between co-equal members of a confederation of allied tribes who were not large enough to be actual city-states or great nation-states. It served as a foundational law to oversee the grounding of a new democracy planted in the soil of an ancestral homeland, much as the American Articles of Confederation served the purpose of grounding a new political entity in the soil of the colonial ancestors who came to the New World from Europe. The difference between Israel's experience and the American experience is that Americans did not have to leave their thirteen colonies and then come back to reclaim them. Oppression by a major power crept up on them slowly but surely. Like the Bill of Rights used in conjunction with the American Constitution, the Ten Commandments served to protect religious worship and other democratic human rights. As with treaties among nations, this type of political contract allowed the marshalling of manpower and other resources for social, political, or military causes in defense of others in a local, inter-tribal league when needed.

In the Exodus version of the constitutional treaty between the twelve tribes, God proclaims "I am the Lord your God, a jealous God, who visits the sin of the fathers upon children to the third and fourth generations for my enemies." (Exod 20:5–6) This is similar to the curses, or consequences, usually listed in ancient Near East treaty documents between a more powerful partner and a less powerful one. Leviticus 26 and Deuteronomy 28 contain longer and more elaborate curses which attend upon Israel's dismissal of the terms of the treaty signed between tribes and national government at Sinai. In effect, the taskmaster of the treaty stipulations has been shifted from a blood-thirsty imperial power, to a humane, human rights-oriented heavenly spirit. In the monarchic version of the treaty document, the stronger king vows to punish the weaker one if the weaker does not do his bidding. In the democratic version, the law proposes to hold the people to the stipulations of the treaty—such things as democratic governance, free economic activity, family formation, non-violence, and diligent public health and citizenship activity. If the citizenry do not live up to the level of human socio-political productivity that God believes they can produce, they must make political changes to return to constitutional government or they will be turned over to human imperial conquerors and have to deal with their gods, that is their chariots, their swords, their international bankers, and their insecure kings.

The golden calf incident (Exod 32) tells us a good bit about the main two philosophies of government found in the migrating party, which both have to do with financing government. Recall that Moses was absent from the community for an extended time in communion with Yahweh for the purpose of drawing up the official draft charter of government. He came down the mountain with a proposed set of laws and saw the people had turned over their wealth to produce a golden calf and were partying in celebration of their choice of a city-state or monarchic style government. The calf story memorializes several significant political events: an early attempt to set up the rule of a strongman in place of the rule of law; an attempt to start-up national government without the existence of a constitutional law document; an attempt to give the chief magistrate a big role in the performance of public ritual; and an attempt to set up a national treasury to finance the expansive interests of the section of the electorate represented by Aaron. The last of these story-lines will be reserved for special treatment below in chapter 5.

The standard church view is that the children of Israel incorporated a heathen national church, organized around a molten idol. When Moses returned from the mountain, Aaron's explanation was this: "For they said unto me, Make us gods, which shall go before us: for as for this Moses, the man that brought us up out of the land of Egypt, we wot not what is become of him. And I said unto them, Whosoever hath any gold, let them break it off. So they gave it me: then I cast it into the fire, and there came out this calf." (Exod 32:23–24) The phrase "which shall go before us," however, suggests not so much an organized church as the outcome of the peoples' actions, but a national government symbol or framework which would allow them to go forward as an organized people.

In Moses' view, the political actors have gotten the cart before the horse. Here they are organizing the set-up of an autocratic government and giving that government a national treasury without specifying or limiting its powers in any way. They seem to have chosen Aaron as their first leader, and devoted themselves to a centralized form of government usually symbolized in the Middle East by such a molten icon. Are they trying to set aside the emergency powers given to Moses to lead them on their journey? Are they waiting for Aaron to start making laws for them? Some scholars see this as an attempt by Aaron to replace Moses, or pre-empt the God of the Exodus in the civic affairs of the new culture.[7] We see it here as a struggle over organization and operation of the national government. It is Moses' view that in spite of whatever they believe they have done, they must first write a political constitution, a code of law, for it is his fervent desire that they become a democratic people, which above all means that all people within the realm are subject to the same set of laws and that there will be no special classes of privileged people.

That law code must specify the organization and operation of government, including, likely, a provision spelling out separate and distinctive roles for government and public shrine activity rather than the closely fused role given to those two grand sectors suggested by the golden calf. They also needed a set of minimum political ethical requirements that would guide the civic and cultural behavior of all the people. Once this is done, it would clearly be permissible for someone to step into the shoes of priestly leadership of the national cathedral-type function which virtually every ancient nation had. Moses' own worth as a political "prophet" (organizer, leader) thus hinged upon how he dealt with Aaron and the calf. In fact, Moses argued for toleration and forgiveness of Aaron. He reminded the people that since they were now free of Pharaoh they had better make sure they stay thoroughly free of him and his kind. He thus argued for and won the destruction of the calf. (Deut 9:20)

Moses believed Yahweh expected him to propose an organizational structure to accommodate both the traditional civic/secular functions of national government, and the semi-religious/priestly function of ancient national governments. This bifurcated government system was likely the same structure in place in Midian, where Jethro occupied one of the two separated seats of confederacy-wide power. In fact, Moses was the founder of and inspiration for both sectors of government. How he handles his considerable power at this juncture is a ticklish matter. It was his intent to limit national government power and executive department power within the national government. How could he do so if he kept a hand on both of these poles of power? Together, God, Moses, Aaron, and the elders negotiated a provision whereby Moses would step away from officiating in one of the roles. In doing so, they provided an important degree of separation between public cult and public secular activities. It is telling that he took the mantle of secular leadership for himself, and offered the "ecclesiastical" leadership

---

7. Propp, "Golden Calf," 257.

to Aaron.[8] In doing so, Moses reserved the right to administer the economic and social and political resources of the people, and to adjudicate certain cases needing decision-making in the migrating community. The civil leadership provided a proper foundation and protection for the policies which allow for the organization and operation of the "sacral" arena. If the civil affairs were organized properly, and the laws well conceived and executed, things would go well in the priestly sphere. Priests of the public sector could then lead well in the cultural/educational/healthcare realm, and priests of the private sector would be given freedom to equip their followers for a more spiritual kind of salvation.

Moses, and later David—the two most formidable political leaders in Israel—both set sterling examples of separation of the national priestly sector from the national secular sector for others to follow. They situated the political religion of the land at the mid-point of the scale of possible relations between church and state, that place where government offers public ceremonial recognition of a favored brand of religion—just and democratic religion—without dictating doctrinal substance or content of private worship. For example, Moses implemented the Levite policy whereby politicians could not be priests, and priests could not easily be politicians. Much later on, politicians were still respecting this traditional policy. David stayed out of priestly matters of the sort that Saul got in trouble for meddling in.

As we have suggested above, Moses at Sinai was faced with sorting out four different governmental and government-related roles that he had his hands on in the beginning: military commander/emergency chief magistrate; educated high priest/teacher/government civil servant; judge/adjudicator of disputes; and prophet/revolutionary political party organizer.[9] To this can be added vulnerable, penitent, human being/citizen. Once he gave general direction to the state, economy, and private culture acting in the role of principal architect of the nation, he turned over to Aaron the administration of public ritual matters related to sacrifices, offerings, holiday remembrances, sacred shrines and objects like the ark and tabernacle and its furnishings, and, it turns out, many other functions not related to public ritual. Aaron and his successors would also administer government regulations related to purity, circumcision, and food science, and thus exercise

---

8. We will see that there is very little of the modern churchly priesthood in this ancient priestly civic role.

9. In fact, several authors see the consequent governing structure of early Israel as consisting of four different sets of political actors: chief magistrate/judge/king/secular ruler; priestly officers; prophets; and judiciary/court judges. See Levinson, "First Constitution," 1873; also Halbertal, "God's Kingship,"132. We will have more to say about this organizational structure in a later section.

control over public health activities. He and the Levites would also deal with some judicial matters, and some other secular matters of criminal and civil law, including popular instruction in the law and priestly cities of refuge. He would also handle tax collection and storage ("tithes" and "offerings"), keeping and copying of public records, and administration of Levite employment on the national level.

Moses and his successors would handle political and military organization and operation, including requirements for and exemptions from military service, and regulations regarding service in the field, including spoil and captives. Moses would also deal with citizenship requirements, census-taking, road development and land distribution, international relations, crimes against the state and the constitution, and the appellate judiciary. Economic affairs were handled by landowners, merchants, and herdsmen. The tribe, clan and especially families would deal with administration of humane laws, such as the distribution of assistance to the poor and travelers, creditor-debtor relations, property rights and conveyance, domestic law such as marriage, divorce, and inheritance, and crimes against morality and against the person.[10] In sum, Moses gave away one of the four roles entirely (priestly), kept one for himself (chief magistrate), and shared the other two with others (prophets and judicial personnel).

Israel's system of political government after crossing Jordan was essentially the same as it was at this point of definition in the wilderness. It was a bi-cameral government, consisting of public administration of secular civic affairs at all levels by means of family, local, and tribal public officials called "elders," in tandem with public administration of priestly civic affairs by means of family, clan, and tribal priests, and national high priestly leaders. The judging elders and priests at each level handled both executive and judicial functions pertaining to their spheres, had independent and essentially co-equal authority and served as check and balance on each other. The secular legislative function was handled by a council of elders on local, tribal, and national levels, and was guided by the Ten Commandment charter ensuring legislative branch supremacy on the confederate level, which was set in stone and could not, or should not, be altered. Priests were likely hired by or appointed by secular leaders at all levels, as we see in the story of Micah the clan leader during the period of Judges.

When enforcement of the national charter was neglected or overthrown by cultural practice, executive fiat, or politico-military subjugation by neighboring kingdoms, a renewal- or revolution-minded prince/judge/

---

10. For a general summary in of the laws of Israel in traditional terms, see Kent, *Israel's Laws*, vii–xxvii.

prophet led a political revolt, after which the old confederate charter, or a slightly modernized one, was once again re-enthroned.

This picture of government held true essentially until the time of Solomon, who bypassed "the lineages" (that is, the tribal and clan governments) and enacted a strong central government bolstered by regional federal officeholders beholden to him.[11] He also usurped some of the priestly power, but likely left most of the government of those affairs where they historically resided. There was little or no support for strong executive authority in Israel in the early days. It was not until David and Solomon and Nathan suggested an Israelite form of strong central government and gave it a theologic underpinning that some powerful elements in Israel (aristocratic land owners and priestly families) then came on board. Even the literary prophets accepted one of the symbols of the new centralism (Jerusalem as a light to the world) but they insisted upon a return to government localism and original constitutional law to provide the source of that light.

---

11. Halpern, "Kingship and Monarchy," 416.

3

Moses' Theory of Self-Government

Now we turn to Moses' philosophy for how government should be conducted in Israel. There are three items of theory which Moses and the people embraced early in their experience. The first countered the theory of divine executive department leadership prevalent in kingships of the ancient Near East. The myth current among strong king polities was that the people could not hear the voice of God. Only the king had that prerogative. Israelites had been trained in Egypt to say, "Let not God speak with us, lest we die." (Exod 20:18–19; 19:25, 33:20) But Moses invited the legislative leaders of the people, the elders, to accompany him into God's presence, a place where fundamental government decisions were typically deliberated. (Exod 19:7, 9) Using political language strange to the ear of modern man, Moses taught that common people truly could approach God and "not die." Indeed, ultimately all of the people actually heard the voice of God and participated in the civic debates encouraged by God. God welcomed their participation. In particular, God extended his intimate hospitality to the legislative body and acted through them to make both the constitutional law and statutory law based on the constitution. Moses reminded them just before they entered Canaan, "Did ever people hear the voice of God speaking out of the midst of the fire, as thou hast heard, and live?" (Deut 4:33) While local, small groupings of tribes acting as loose democratic confederations were well known in many places in the Near East, the historian Moses seemed to believe that Israel had perhaps become the first democratic grouping of enough size to rival or earn the respect of city-states in the region.[1] (Deut 4:33, 36; see also 5:24)

---

1. Wildavsky, *Moses*, 106.

A religious philosophy/constitutional theory that says common people can approach and hear from God accompanies a political theory that says common people can approach and hear from the chief magistrate of the land without suffering bodily harm. The magistrate in a democratic society could not be a secluded despot like a strong-arm king. After all, in a democratic society, the leader was just a common citizen entrusted with temporary power to implement the decisions of the elders in a crisis, a public servant who would shortly return to his regular occupational duties. He was not a professional politician like a king and did not practice "monarchic aloofness." Moses, as former court official in Egypt, could approach Pharaoh, but common people could not. Indeed, after many painful negotiating sessions, Pharaoh finally put Moses back into the category of irritable common folk who categorically could not approach without being bidden. After Moses overstayed his welcome, Pharaoh finally let him know he would be killed if he tried to approach again. (Exod 10:28)

In the early Israelite activity in the wilderness, Moses followed good democratic practice by allowing easy access to his administration. In fact, Moses heard virtually every Israelite care and concern personally until Jethro suggested he use some help to handle the great press of issues. Moses' commitment to personal involvement in justice in courts of first jurisdiction is a great departure from the practice of rulers in the ancient Near East, who normally outlawed any unauthorized appearance before the king. (Esther 4:6, 11) In a democratic republic, both God and the presiding elder of the republic are accessible, not hidden away from public sight.

A corollary to this idea of political and judicial openness is the notion that the chief magistrate is a servant of the people, elected by them to serve at their pleasure. If he serves well, he may continue in office. Even much later on during the time of "kings," this idea of servant leadership was still current. The advisers of the strong king Rehoboam tried to reason with him thusly: "If you wilt be a servant unto this people this day, and wilt serve them, and answer them . . . then they will be thy servants forever." (1 Kgs 12:7) Use of the word "answer" in this statement implies that the king should not only be listening to the citizenry, but working hard to give them the answer they desire. The magistrate's job, in one prophet's view, is to "gently leadeth." (Isa 40:11)

The second item of theory associated with Moses' administration is suggested by the government openness we outlined above and relates to consensual government. With regard to policy-making in the confederation, the administrator of the laws must defer to the representatives of the people, the elders. Accordingly, Moses' first political act was decidedly not to approach Pharaoh on his own but to bring together the elders in Goshen and see if they would authorize him to negotiate with Pharaoh. Moses called the elders into session as the executive officer in any democratic republic might do, and then implemented their wishes, their "cries," with regard to first meeting with Pharaoh, later preparing for and leaving Egypt, and, finally, making policy decisions in the wilderness. The people expressed their desire for autonomy, free religion, and economic rights, by figuratively crying their wishes out loud and Moses did his best to fulfill them.

Moses' first act in service of the people's policy wishes, or more specifically, of the policy wishes of the people's legislature, the council of elders, was carrying the message to Pharaoh that they be made free. The second was organizing the physical exodus from Egypt. With these two feathers in the cap of the elders—their successful bending of the leader's will to their wishes—the people next expected, wanted, asserted the necessity of, other acts of service to them by their government. They made clear to Moses that he worked for them, and not the other way around. He carries out their policy wishes, not they his wishes.

Throughout the rest of the Pentateuch (the first five books of the Bible), legislative action by the people and their elder representatives is used to give direction to the executive administrator. Moses' administrative track record in keeping his hands off the legislative power lays down a precedent for legislative department supremacy in the government for several hundred years in Israel. For example, the legislating elders declined the administration proposal to enter and settle Canaan immediately. Moses then complied with their wishes. They demanded that drilling for water take place at Meribah. He ultimately complied, even when disagreeing. When politicians less respectful of the constitutional law than Moses began to usurp the function of the elders during the period of settlement, things went wrong in Israel. A succession of kings who acted like the people worked for them earned the condemnation of prophets like Hosea, who wrote, "All their kings have fallen . . ." (Hos 7:7) The Bible is not bashful about providing examples. Saul's usurpations caused military defeat. (1 Sam 31:1) David's personal initiatives caused a plague. (2 Sam 24:15) Ahab's power grabs caused drought. (1 Kgs 17:1) Zedekiah's strong-arm tactics brought destruction of the temple.[2]

As a result of the constitution-making activity at Sinai, the legislative grouping of elders, and at times the people acting as a convocation of the whole, henceforth either proposed and decided the laws directly themselves or ratified proposals put forward by the administrator of the nation. Initially, the legislative body gave their consent to Moses for a term of office—likely the amount of time it would take to get them safely out of Egypt. He

---

2. Walzer, *Jewish Political Tradition*, 149.

let them know he would do what they wanted . . . help them become a free people. Like an elected leader in any democratic-oriented republican nation, he was destined to be held by the people to keep his policy promises. Once he accomplished the incredibly difficult objective of removing the people beyond the reach of Pharaoh's army, the people extended his term of office, but made it clear it was they who were fully in charge now, not him. Moses could not continue to stay on as leader in the wilderness unless he delivered their needs and wants. Wildavsky writes, "Moses makes promises about a better future."[3] Moses' failure to implement the people's policy wishes ultimately leads to "murmuring," expression of their collective will and/or political discontent with their leader. Whenever things got bad the people forced a vote of confidence or no confidence to determine whether the current government leader should continue.

While out on the road, the multitude asserted discontent with Moses' performance in several ways. They moaned, "What shall we drink" (Exod 15:24); they complained, "Would to God we had died" (Exod 16:2–3); they "chided with Moses." (Exod 17:2) Ultimately, the Bible relates that the people challenged the executive department's performance ten times. (Num 14:22) At the root of such complaints is that Moses has not delivered yet on his political promise to bring them into a land flowing with milk and honey. In fact, they have not even been led to bread and water. They are given only a "light bread" called manna, and are even restricted by executive department policy as to how much they can gather of that each day. They travel without sufficient stocks of water, as we learn from the story of Meribah. Later, Dathan and Abiram charge, "Thou hast not brought us into a land . . . or given us inheritance." (Num 16:14)

The point about the murmurings is not that the people do not love God or accept Moses' divine relationship with God, as theologians and church administrators often assert. The real point is that the chief executive must allow free speech, murmurings about policy matters, without instituting repression. This contrasts with Pharaoh, on the other hand, who grudgingly entertained proposals, usually denied them and instituted repression, and even instituted repression after he accepted proposals. He not only made promises to the Israelites that he did not keep but refused to consult with advisers. He was a political animal in the worst sense, trying to appear to be the good guy. He followed the prevailing winds among the people with respect to the Israelite problem and took a liberal position only when it was

---

3. Wildavsky, *Moses*, 145.

clear they were converted to the Israelite cause. He even tried to take credit for the policy of release rather than give it to Moses.[4]

The third item of democratic theory we will deal with in this section is Moses' assertion that his people are to become a "kingdom of priests." This meant that virtually every adult citizen in society was to be encouraged to attain the educational and political sophistication, and position of respect, that ordinarily only a single individual high priest attains in established government circles in other lands. (Exod 19:6) Any citizen could be an Aaron. In fact, Moses believed any citizen could become a prophet-judge like himself. (Num 11:29) This is somewhat like the saying common in the public school system in 1960s America, "Anyone can become President." In fact, one Rabbinic author wrote in Mishnah Harayot 3:6–8 that even an illegitimate child took a place of political importance over an ignorant high priest.[5] Moses' assertions are a statement of the democratic expectation that every citizen can be, and, in a vigorous democracy, must for a time actually be, a government official at some level. This theory became reality in the grant of considerable governing authority to parents to rule virtually every aspect of not only their children's lives, but the lives of hired workers, servants and others living within the family estate. We will explore this constitutional grant of political power to parents further under the topic of the Fifth Commandment.

Anyone who wanted to enter higher politics could do so, and, if proven to be capable, could become an elder, tribal chief, or national chief judge. Freedom for individuals to be all that they can be was the reason for the Exodus event in the first place. Priests, after all, were merely government civil service functionaries who served these ordinary citizens who become extraordinary political leaders for a period of time. In fact, a guarantee of political enfranchisement of all citizens provided a pathway to social and economic leadership in both tracks of government service: the priesthood, as well as in the civic or secular prophethood. For example, one expert writes, "Anyone could be a priest at a local sanctuary."[6] Abimelech, the son of Gideon, appointed political mercenaries of lowly stature. This proved the point that any citizen had an opportunity to access governing circles. Unfortunately, Abimelech sidestepped the spirit of the tradition, which was to appoint responsible and capable government employees with genuine priestly credentials. (Judg 9:4) The subsequent history of judges and kings

---

4. Wildavsky, *Moses*, 70–102, 95.

5. This is an ironic admission of the viability of the teaching of Jesus in the time of Caiaphas the high priest—Jesus having been illegitimate in the sense of not having a known biological father.

6. Rehm, "Levites and Priests," 305.

showed that ordinary people like the shepherd boy David, and the dresser of sycamore trees, Amos, could rise to great prominence without any association with governing families or any specialized training in priestly, kingly, or prophetic duty.

The expectation of a kingdom of priest-citizens meant that there was to be no caste out of which high public officials were drawn. Any of the thousands of co-equal citizens could be considered for the job of chief executive or assistant chief executive of the land. Jephthah, for example, was a rogue as a young man, but learned the military craft and was asked to lead the nation during crisis. (Judg 11) Such political latitude to select from the population derived from the freedom the people had not only to self-direct their own labor power (Exod 1:13–14, 3:7, 5:6–9) but speak out, worship, and live as they please. (Exod 3:18; 5:3) While there appeared early on to be a limitation on who can be priests, the limitation to one tribe, the Levites, was based upon the idea the Levites were dedicated to legal education. They were a type of lawyer's guild. But it was likely that membership in the Levite tribe was not actually hereditary but based on passing an examination of competence of some type, as in the civil service of most democratic societies.

The priestly line through Aaron owed their "original promotion . . . to their high office . . . not to any superiority in wealth or other accidental advantages . . . (but) to those who were pre-eminently gifted with persuasive eloquence and discretion . . . (for) a strict superintendence of the law," says Josephus.[7] These characteristics were needed because they dealt with "trial of cases of litigation, and the punishment of condemned persons." A similar understanding of the need to pass a type of early civil service examination was prevalent in Greek democracy as well. In Greece, Aristotle described priests as non-partisan government employees handling the law and invoking the favor of the god or gods on the entire city and all its inhabitants, not on one particular type of creedal believers only. In his view, the priesthood was an "appropriate sinecure [ongoing civil service position for the family] for aged citizens of unblemished reputation."[8] Since parents typically were charged with training their young in their own occupations as apprentices, existing priests often trained their own children in the law to become priestly lawyers. Moses knew this, and that is why Moses used such flowery language to describe a grant of continuing priestly authority to Aaron's offspring.

7. Josephus, "Against Apion," 184–89.
8. Aristotle, *Politics*, 1329a, 27–34.

But, while all citizens were encouraged to be educated like priests and take their turn in government service, like priests, it must be mentioned that in the Biblical version of ancient Near East priesthood, priests did not serve as chief magistrates, rulers, or kings, like ancient Near East strongmen priests did in Egypt, Christian priests did during the Middle Ages, and Judaic Hasmonean priests did during the time of the Greek colonial period in Palestine. For Spinoza, there was no theocratic legitimacy or right of legislation given to Mosaic-era priests to rule in both the sacral and the secular sphere. There was separation of cult and state. If a citizen aspired to the role of priest and became one, he had to give up aspiration for service in the fully secular part of government.[9]

Biblical priests and princes were like dual Roman consuls who horizontally demarcated or separated the functions of the national governmental sphere. The chief magistrate was admonished to heed the high priest's oracular findings and not interpose his own, thus usurping the priestly function. (Num 27:21) The chief executive could not meddle in priestly department employment patronage business. For example, the policy decision/oracle about division of priesthood duties between Aaronids and Levites came to Aaron, not to Moses.[10] (Num 18:1–7) Also, the prince (Joshua in this case) had to pay respect to the independent national power of the priest by standing up in his presence. (Num 27:21) He also had to know he was just in a temporary leadership position during good behavior: "That his heart be not lifted up above his brethren." (Deut 17:20) Similarly, the priest was admonished not to try to usurp the province of the civic ruler, but rather to sit on the "right hand" of the magistrate as his chief servant.[11] (Zech 6:11–13) Indeed, government centers for each branch of the national government were in separate locations. For example, during Judges, the political capitol was in Shechem, and the ritual capitol in Shiloh.

In spite of the practical pattern of fathers sometimes apprenticing sons in the priestly profession, what is suggested by Moses' description of the people as a "kingdom of priests" is that there is to be no actual hereditary priesthood at the highest national level in Israel, in the sense usually found in strong central governments in the ancient Near East. The rationale given later on for a hereditary priesthood at the time of the Hasmoneans (well after Jewish return from Babylon) is that fusion of the priestly and princely roles was only to be a temporary (emergency?) situation "until a true

---

9. Walzer, *Jewish Political Tradition*, 168, 194; also see our discussion of the "Levite policy" in part II.

10. Sakenfeld, *Numbers*, 105.

11. Walzer, *Jewish Political Tradition*, 168.

(popular, charismatic, elected) prophet shall arise."[12] (1 Macc 14:25–49) History shows that "temporary" anti-constitutional measures often become permanent. In fact, ongoing Hasmonean great kingship caused a split that gave birth to the democratic-oriented Pharisee movement leading to New Testament Judaism.

The fact that Moses gave Aaron and his sons the priesthood "forever," (Exod 28:1; 29:9) does not particularly suggest an hereditary government office and therefore a caste system in early Israel. Democratic governments like early Israel were so slim and spare in terms of budget appropriations for national offices that it was often necessary for cabinet members to use their own family members to help the government limp along on the national level. This is republican limited government efficiency at work.[13] If priests and Levites were in fact drawn from one genealogical branch (more likely one tribal political branch) of the Israelite family, it was out of convenience, tradition, and almost forced servitude, as there was little glory in the work, in the early days at least. Levites could not hold land and therefore were devoted to poverty and obtaining higher education. Likely their only way to economic success was to opt out of the Levite tribe/tradition altogether. On the other hand, it was possible for non-Levites to be priests, and thus high level government employees. Samuel, from the tribe of Ephraim, became a priest in the house of Eli, for example.[14]

Moses' suggestion that priesthood was to be held in perpetuity in Aaron's family is belied by the fact that Aaron himself lost the job and was forced into retirement as a result of losing the confidence of the people. Luckily, one of his sons was prepared to take on the responsibility, with likely little pay.[15] (Num 20:26) The idea of "forever" in Moses' democratic republic went with the qualification of "during good behavior." The job was also subject to wholesale turnover by way of the next administration's appointments to the government. This happened when the David-era electorate removed the Elide priestly temple dynasty from office. (1 Sam 8:1–5) During the time

---

12. Ibid, 188–89.

13. In the early United States, for example, several of the early presidents of the country used their sons to help manage the affairs of the office, since there was such a small appropriation made for the office of the president. Sons in democratic societies always serve essentially as apprentices in their fathers' jobs, and sometimes learn enough to became qualified and experienced to take on the job themselves. Thus, in early national America some four generations of the Adams family served in high positions in and around the national government: John Adams, John Quincy Adams, Charles Francis Adams, and Henry Adams. Their positions were won on the basis of merit rather than hereditary right.

14. Rehm, "Levites and Priests," 302.

15. Wildavsky, *Moses*, 183.

of the high priest Eli some two hundred years after Moses, Eli's sons were not suitable for continuation in high government office due to corruption. The new government administration under David, which took over Saul's magistracy, appointed new priests to office, Zadok and Ahimelech. (2 Sam 8:17) Only two generations after David, the northern half of the country dumped David's own "forever" kingdom in favor of one more to their liking. (1 Kgs 12) The overall picture in Israel suggests that government officials, at least at the local level, made an effort to find a Levite to serve the clan or tribe (Judg 17), but could deviate from that norm without much trouble. On the national level the office was also nominally hereditary in the sense of chosen out of a wide pool of priestly family applicants, but was actually an appointive office perquisite of the chief executive.

In the broader ancient Near East, the high priest often made the law as well as administered it, under the general supervision of the monarchy. The priest usually handed down the office to sons for many generations somewhat like what the Brahmin priestly caste did in India for so long, and just as the monarch handed the monarchy down to his sons. The office was an hereditary fief granted by the monarch's dynasty of rulers. But in Israel in the time of judges and early kings, the priests, as executive department workers, did not make the law. They administered and taught and adjudicated the law. They did what they were directed to do by the national legislative department and they and their sons could be dislodged from their positions.

In early Israel, in contrast to the political way of life in monarchic city-states, the central government building complex was stripped down to a mobile building made of linen and animal akin, not bricks and mortar. (Exod 26) Central government functions were almost non-existent. One priest, Aaron, handled the departments of justice and treasury. Moses served as his own secretary of state or allocated those duties to Aaron. There was not even a war department, unless one makes the stretch that Joshua and/or Caleb served in that role. Citizens served as their own lawyers rather than hire specialists. (Deut 6:1–9, 20–23) Priests were available to hear cases that the citizenry could not sort out among themselves. Priests at this time were ordinary citizens, with a little aptitude for service to the people, a little understanding of the law, a little training in science and health, and a literary bent.

In one sense, the government had to have educated priestly workers to help teach the people to be priests unto themselves, so the ideal of a classless society with an extremely limited national government bureaucracy was overstated even at the beginning. But it was still the goal in Israel. The Israelite governmental national "priesthood," in the first 200 years at least, was necessarily a greatly watered-down priesthood, since national government was greatly watered down. Government was administered almost exclusively on the family/clan level, as the fifth article/commandment of government suggests. Fathers and elders served as priests in their own families and clans, thus to a degree actualizing the ideal of a kingdom of priests. Alternatively, wealthy fathers hired priests if they felt inadequate for or too busy for the job.

During the period of judges, there is a story about one apparently wealthy family that hired a priest to be its own localized government services administrator. (Judg 17) One would imagine that this local priest, in addition to conducting sacrifice rituals, would have been responsible to conduct educational, health, social welfare, judicial and other domestic activities related to promoting independence and prosperity in the family or clan. This story of Micah the householder and his priest reflects the fact that most of governmental activity in human services was handled on the local rather than the national level during this period of time.

A Closer Look:
Priesthood in the Bible

ANY DISCUSSION OF THE priesthood in ancient Israel is fraught with difficulties for readers of the Bible. Those difficulties stem from the fact that the priesthood is assumed to be a fully religious position. In fact, it is usually a civic position, many of whose duties are secular in nature. There are initially two reported varieties of priesthood suggested by their separate investitures by the new government in the wilderness: the Aaronic priesthood and the Levitical priesthood. In the time of Moses, each one is associated with administration of a different department of government. Their various descriptions at later points in the Torah/Pentateuch are likely connected with various political strains and geographic priestly traditions.[1]

Both priesthoods initially had to do with attendance upon the "tabernacle," which is the mobile seat of national government in the wilderness. (Levites: Deut 9:8, 18:7; priests: Deut 18:5, 21:5) Aaron, the high priest, wore "the breastplate of judgment." This indicates that his activities had to do with the administration of government. The chief magistrate is often called "judge" in Israel, and his activities are called "judgment" because the executive department handles judicial duties as well as administrative. (Exod 28:15, 30) The priest is the assistant of the chief executive and therefore is involved in "judgment" activities as well.

While priests attended to sacrifices, Levites, such as Korah, attended to a different kind of business associated with the tabernacle. They took down and set up the tent of government, and carried the Ark of the Covenant

---

1. Some scholars suggest the Aaronic priesthood was a later accretion to the Pentateuch and associated with Bethel and Jerusalem, perhaps at a time of the split into two kingdoms. Northern Israel elaborated a priesthood based on the tradition of Moses, and other Levite genealogies. See Rehm, "Levites and Priests," 298.

which housed the two tables of laws. (Num 1:47–54) Thus, they seemed to have both the job of building maintenance/security and the job of workers in a type of Library of Congress, or repository of official government documents.

After entry into Canaan, the Levites dispersed into forty-eight limited-size Levitical "cities" throughout the realm.[2] Aside from a "city" and a small suburb, they received no land allotment. (Num 16:9–10; Josh 21) If Levite government employees had received extensive land allotments as government employees like other tribes did, Israel would be liable to criticism for mimicking the hated custom of powerful monarchs giving land grants or charters to political supporters who then could be called upon to provide ongoing support for the monarchy. The Levite land policy is thus a clear indication of democratic sensitivity to and distance from political cronyism.

What the two priesthoods in Israel had in common is that they were the most literate groupings in Israel, surely among those who could read and write. In fact, the Levite tribe in Egypt was known as the most educated of the twelve tribes. Many of them had Egyptian names, indicating the prior elevation of their families to full citizenship and perhaps even ruling circles. That literate scribe-priests were needed in government is clear from numerous indications across the ancient Near East that they were used to copy and keep official records and interact with officials from other countries. In monarchies, the literate priests most often served as propagandists for the dynasty, and kept lists of names from various censuses to be used for taxation purposes. In Israel, however, they were used for the opposite purpose, to hedge up the republic against national taxation. It was the priestly-literate population who were involved in government in classical Greco-Roman civilization and in the ancient Near East.[3] As late as the time of Jesus, the priests at Qumran were scribes of the community law kept there.[4]

As the literate ones, it is no surprise that priests emerged as guardians of the basic law, the Ten Commandment constitution. Deuteronomy sees the Levites either as adjudicators of the commandment law, or its teachers. (Deut 33:10) They promulgated regulations for specific administration of broad legislature-based policy initiatives. Their regulations were known as "torah," or teaching, instruction, or case law.[5] (Lev 10:10–11; Deut 17:8–13,

---

2. Hanoch Reviv sees this happening at the time of monarchy; see Reviv, *Elders in Ancient Israel*.

3. Horsley and Thatcher, *Renewal*, 76.

4. Ibid, 81.

5. Cody, "Priests and High Priest," 609.

21:5; Ezek 44:24) In Exodus and Numbers, priests were said to be involved with criminal procedure. (Num 5:11–31)

As national priest, Aaron served as the highest figure appointed by the elected chief executive. He was certainly akin to the "vizier" in monarchic cultures circling round about Israel. He was second in command and combined several necessary functions of the national executive branch in his office, including legal and financial,[6] military (Exod 17), and law enforcement.[7] (Exod 32) We will discuss other, less obvious functions below. The story of Aaron's ascension to this position in Moses' cabinet with such extraordinary powers is told in the story of the Golden Calf in chapter 5.

The sense moderns have that ancient priests were primarily involved in religious activities probably stems from priestly association with religious-sounding holiday festivals linked to the founding of the republic. These included ritual civic sacrifices and more mundane pilgrimage sacrifice rites. (Exod 23:14–19; Leviticus 1–7) One commentator reminds that in spite of this semi-cultic connection, in Deuteronomy there is a "dearth of cultic detail ascribed to the priests and Levites." In fact, he points out there is only one clearly cultic role mentioned for priests in the entire book of Deuteronomy.[8] (Deut 26:5)

In contrast, priests were deeply involved in secular political, economic, human services and academic/publishing activities. For example, priests administered the every seven years Hakhel, or debt release holiday, which included conducting the reading of the law before the nation gathered in assembly there. (Deut 31:9–13) The book of Deuteronomy reflects both Moses' interpretation of the law after forty years in the wilderness, and editorial editions from later dates. In Deuteronomy, it is written that the nation's newly elected chief magistrate was to write a copy of the law for the priests to keep in their care. (Deut 17:18) In such a case, priests act somewhat like a modern Federal Register staff and were early scribes, or copyists and translators. They likely served as recorders and historians in their role as scribes, like the Roman "Rex sacrorum" priesthood.[9] For example, it is said that the "lips of the priest guard knowledge." (Mal 2:1–9)

---

6. We will explain legal functions in the section on Deuteronomy below, and the financial functions in the section on the Golden Calf below.

7. In Leviticus the high priest makes atonement for all the crimes ("sins") of the people. He thus undertakes a proto-type of the modern governmental pardon function. He qualifies himself to undertake the pardon function by practicing "self-denial" and observing days of rest during which he can make time for study; see Walzer, *Jewish Political Tradition*, 171, 173–74.

8. Berman, *Created Equal*, 65–66.

9. Hooker, "Numa's Religious Reforms," 87–132.

A Closer Look: Priesthood in the Bible

In the main, it seems that priests were to act like good government employees and confer "benefits" through "justice" and to establish a reputation for "virtue."[10] (Wisdom of Ben Sira 45:26) Part of their justice function was to serve as interpreters of the law as members of the high court of law and justice, somewhat like Supreme Court justices. (Deut 17:8–13) Priests were also active in local government in adjudicating civil and criminal cases. (Deut 19:17, 21:25) Priests served in administering oaths, which comports with their traditional role in the judicial system. (Exod 22:7–10) In addition to serving as judges, priests likely took on other duties as assigned by the magistrate on the national or local level.[11] The fact that priests functioned in a largely secular services role allowed the prophets to attack them for corruption of the public sphere of government.[12] (Mal 2:1–9) For example, the prophets said they showed partiality in their judicial rulings.

In Israel, as elsewhere, priests were devoted to public health and health care work. In the Old Testament, priests monitored "leprosy" and other diseases/impurities. They were still carrying out that function as late as New Testament times.[13] (Lev 11–22; Luke 17:14) Related to their work in health was their work involving divination, which essentially was the science of making recommendations or predictions about environmental, physiological, economic, political, and military conditions affecting the nation.[14] (Judg 18:5; 1 Sam 14:3, 36–42; 22:9–10, 13, 15, 18; 23:9–12; 30:7–8) These oracles/predictions could be assisted by means of the Urim and Thummim (Judg 20:27; 1 Sam 20:27; 1 Sam 22:10; 2 Sam 5:19), or by consulting the entrails of sacrificial animals in a process called "extispicy." In essence, priests, much like prophets, with whom they often competed, functioned somewhat like modern pollsters and political advisers, answering questions about the mood of the people and whether the nation should go to war. (Exod 28:29–30) Thus, they functioned like the Roman priestly group known as "augures."

Due to the dearth of national government staff, priests likely got involved in budget matters and in infrastructure planning. They also likely were involved in diplomacy, according to the example set by Aaron at the court of Pharaoh. In this, they functioned somewhat like the Roman "fetiales" priests, who served as embassies to negotiate international treaties.[15]

10. Walzer, *Jewish Political Tradition*, 185.
11. Berman, *Created Equal*, 65.
12. Walzer, *Jewish Political Tradition*, 180.
13. Avalos, *Illness*; Elazar, *Covenant and Polity*, 183.
14. Cody, "Priests and High Priest," 609.
15. Smith, *Dictionary*.

They also surely served as political advisers to the elected leader. In strong monarchies, priests handled everything that the king's capitol city "temple" handled: central banking and budgeting, revenue collection and storage, education and public health, public records, and war department weaponry and materials quarter-mastering. We learn that David stored his shields and spears in "the temple of the Lord," a sign, as we will discuss below, that the temple served as a civic/military facility as much as a religious facility in Israel, as elsewhere. (2 Kgs 11:9)

In sum, it may be seen that priests in Israel performed public ritual/ceremonial functions (sacrifice, festival feeding), scribal functions (copying, translating, recording, storing), teaching functions (reading the law, instructing in the significance of the foundational stories and laws at the national holidays), judicial functions (interpreting the law, making decisions), public health and health care functions (assuring purity/good health, quarantining diseased persons), divination functions (political forecasting), financial functions (revenue/taxation/tithing, treasury/banking), law enforcement functions (e.g., enforcing adherence to constitutional law; see Num 25), and diplomatic activity. In these functions, the Aaronid priests had the Levites to help deal with building maintenance, ceremonial ritual support, and office help at the capitol building/temple. (2 Chron 19:11) The priests often took residence in the temple, and ministered there as physicians, public health officers, librarians, agricultural produce custodians, money-changers, and capitol police. (Matt 26:51, 57) They also played a role as civilian military enlistment overseers. (Deut 20)

4

Moses As Executor Of The Law

IN THE WILDERNESS, THE Hebrews did not say to Moses, "You have failed to provide proper sacrifice to God." Rather, when they dissented, or "murmured," they essentially said, "You have not delivered food, water, land, health and safety." These are civic kinds of concerns, rather than religious. As one of the civic founding fathers of the Israelite nation, Moses played several political roles, as we have suggested above. The role we are concerned about in this chapter is his function as administrator of the law enacted at Sinai. Moses went through four broad stages of leadership during his term as Israel's first chief executive, which stages correspond roughly with the political development of the electorate he was associated with. He first served as political organizer/office seeker, essentially running for the position of "nasi" or pan-tribal chieftan. This was during the time he spent meeting the elders after his return to Egypt to persuade the people to petition for economic and religious rights and during the time he spent meeting with Pharaoh. He next served as emergency power strongman/revolutionary leader of a fleeing people who were politically in a "state of nature."[1] The migrating tribes had not yet formalized a system of government and thus gave Moses considerable latitude to make crisis decisions. Thirdly, he served as facilitator/recorder of a constitution-making effort while Israel was camped at Sinai. Finally, he served as an elected magistrate in a system of mobile, democratic-leaning, republican government in "the wilderness." The length of his term of office, long for a democratic regime, can be explained by the fact he not only led the people through a revolution and a period of constitution-making, but also through a migration which required a considerable amount of logistical coordination due to the complication of regular military activity and large scale multi-tribal travel. The forty year

---

1. Walzer, *Exodus*, 75, reflecting Spinoza's view.

period referred to in the Bible for the time he spent leading Israel in the "wilderness," may have been an idiom for "a long time." Key to our thesis in this book is that in the end, he gave up power voluntarily before the people crossed Jordan rather than try to impose his will on a people reluctant to have him continue.[2]

The first given revelation from God to Moses related to political organization of the tribes. God said, "Go and gather the elders of Israel together . . ." (Exod 3:16) This was like saying, "Go and do democracy." When elders came together in the ancient Near East, it was for the purpose of elections, policy-making, or rendering judicial decisions. One author suggests that any political jurisdiction available to the Israelite tribes while in Egypt "under the thumb of Pharaoh" was "apparently exercised by the elders of tribes or clans."[3] Moses had to stir-up the semi-dormant civic and cultural leaders of the people with a specific policy proposal—obtaining religious worship and labor rest for Hebrews by means of a one-time holiday observance. His hidden agenda was to prepare for a longer-distance, larger-scale travel effort.

When Moses carried out his agitation activity among the elders, he acted in both the role of policy advocate and candidate for office. Success in gaining some rights for the people would result in winning their nod to have him serve them as political or administrative chieftain either during their continuing stay in Egypt, or upon their exit from Goshen. Educating the citizenry in the importance of democratic law and practice was perhaps the primary role that prophets subsequently filled for generations after Moses set the original example. His work with the citizenry qualified him to be a "prophet," seen in this book as essentially an inspired political party leader. Political organizers/prophets/judges after Moses operated freely in Israel by authority of constitutional law.[4] Their aim was always to try to defeat threats to their frail democracy or to inspire a return to the very sophisticated ongoing civic project undertaken by their ancestors. On the other hand, Moses' work as an administrator earned him the trust of the people as an actual government official. Israel first conferred official duty upon him on a temporary basis during the flight, and then on a longer-term basis after Sinai.

During the stage of office-seeking, Moses served as advocate and mediator between Israel and Pharaoh and as organizer of preparations for a pilgrimage that could be temporary or permanent. In conducting this shuttle diplomacy, Moses essentially served as a foreign affairs officer or embassy

---

2. Wildavsky, *Moses*, 175–98.
3. Ibid., 143.
4. See our interpretation of the first commandment in part III.

from the Israelite people to Pharaoh. Aaron essentially served as his mouthpiece, like a secretary of state would serve a chief magistrate. (Exod 4:10-17) The Israelites were already starting to act like an independent people.

As Israel got closer to the "go" date, Moses assumed a kind of emergency power needed to assist the elders in preparing for departure. For example, he used this power to curry favor with the Egyptian people and to enable loans from them for the pilgrimage journey. (Exod 11:1-3) The urgencies occasioned by Pharaoh—giving and then retracting permission to depart—escalated to a dire level when Pharaoh not only gave permission but ordered the Israelites to settle their affairs and depart. (Exod 12:30-36) Moses now undertook the task of provisioning the people with meat (the Passover sacrifice) to give them physical strength for their quick exit from town. He also implemented public health measures to protect Israelites against an outbreak of disease among the Egyptian population. This outbreak, remembered as "the death of the firstborn," or tenth plague, provided extra encouragement for them to leave and a type of insurance-by-distraction to prevent Pharaoh from changing his mind once again. (Exod 12:1-28) The tribes left so suddenly that they packed bread dough before it was leavened, and unleavened bread became a symbol of the liberation. (Exod 13)

The second phase of emergencies requiring his firm, though not autocratic leadership, consisted of logistical activities like executing the strategic escape at the Red Sea/Sea of Reeds (Exod 14), provision of water and bread in the desert (Exod 15-17), organization of a militia to deal with a confrontation with Amalek (Exod 17), and organization of a migratory system of government officers called "judges." (Exod 18) All of this was prior to formalizing a government at Mt. Sinai. (Exod 19-20)

At Sinai, Moses received or drafted and then brokered the ratification of ten articles of government which gave broad outline to a system of balanced and limited national government, and power-sharing with local political entities. His constitution-making activities served as a bridge between the second and fourth stages of leadership, between broad, but temporary emergency power, and term-limited and tightly restricted executive department power. In part III, we will analyze the content of the ten commandment constitution used to formulate the permanent system of government.

Soon after the constitutional law was ratified at Sinai, the national government with Moses as its administrator conducted a census, organized the tribes for travel, constructed a mobile tabernacle or town hall at which government meetings would be held, offered civic sacrifices for the well-being of the nation, and organized the national government by electing national legislators—seventy of them. (Num 11:24). The process of election is signified by the passage stating that "seventy men of the elders of the people" were "gathered" and "set . . . round about the tabernacle." The fact that they were "gathered" and "of the people" means chosen by the people, and "set . . . round about the tabernacle" suggests they were moved from other locations in the camp to the central government location of the traveling camp.

We have said that Moses wielded considerable emergency power during the Exodus. In one sense, the grant of emergency power ended with the "gathering" of the seventy national elders, or legislators, whose job became to make policy/legislation for Moses to execute. (Num 11:16–17) When Moses himself recommended laws, the council of seventy national legislating elders either enacted them or rejected them. In certain cases, "all the congregation" (all the people) gathered and exercised power to legislate. They even gathered as a whole to adjudicate important socio-political violations of the law somewhat like a grand jury would gather. (Num 11:25) This, for example, happened when one citizen violated the day of labor rest. (Num 15:32–36) The entire camp give their assent to capital punishment, and all participated in stoning the violator.[5]

Organization of the national legislature into a group of seventy created the necessary separation between the legislative and executive power expected in a democracy. But as many commanders in chief do during times of national emergency, Moses may have held on to some of his emergency powers longer than the people thought was prudent. This happened at Meribah, where Moses resisted the will of the elders and effectively impounded the resources they wished to use to find water. Later on, first Miriam and Aaron, and then Korah/Dathan/Abiram once again challenged the residuum of Moses' emergency powers, and not until then did the government in the wilderness settle into a period of stability.

The time of Moses' constitutional term of office, the fourth phase of his leadership, is characterized by working out of early details of organization and operation of the national government. These highly secular activities are often overlooked during the course of church educational activities focused on the Old Testament. Few Christians profess much interest in or understanding of the book of Numbers, wherein constitutional government is given its start in actual practice. That early practice included the taking of censuses (Num 1, 26), dealing with urgent public health and domestic law issues (Num 5, 9, 19), educational preparation of youth for civil service (Num 6), taxation policy (Num 7, 15, 18, 28–29), protocol and procedure for public assembly (Num 10), payment for high ranking and mid-level government employees (priests and Levites; Num 18), international activity

---

5. Wildavsky, *Moses*, 149–50.

like negotiations aimed at obtaining transit rights through foreign national territory (Num 20:14–21), settling the constitutional issue of female inheritance rights (Num 27), elaborating/adjudicating a law of contracts (Num 30), settling some early land allocation issues with two and a half tribes (Num 32, 24) and with Levites (Num 35), and settling a policy requiring intra-tribal marriage of heiresses. (Num 36) In addition, there were some rather earth-shaking issues related to theory and practice of the constitution: the legitimacy of Moses' election as magistrate (Num 12), law enforcement related to labor law/Sabbath breaking (Num 15), a debate about power-sharing with tribal chiefs and the limits of political dissent (Num 16), a proposal for closer integration of church and state (Num 16), and a struggle over authority for implementing internal improvement projects like well digging. (Num 20)

During the course of all these civic events, Moses emerged as a long-suffering political leader who most of the time was at the service of the people. He regularly paid deference to the legislature and to the people as a whole and thus set a precedent for the next 250 years of Israel's limited government, judge-led society. The people stood up to their constitutional responsibility to direct the republic. They voiced their policy wishes as to timing of migration, form of government, and handling of financial matters. They asserted their expectation that the administrative branch make good its promise to lead them to a land of milk and honey. They let Moses know when their expectations of him were not met, and further, even rejected his policy proposals when they ran counter to their own.

For example, one of Moses' initial proposals would have required a larger national presence in the lives of the people than the people deemed advisable. Moses' desire to enter Canaan immediately from the south and engage the Canaanite population there would have required a large standing national military bureaucracy and a dedication of considerable financial resources. The people, through their elected elder representatives, rejected that early expansion of government in favor of attention to civilian policy matters and local sovereignty in those matters. Many of those matters would play out before entry into Canaan rather than after and would leave them in a better position to establish themselves quickly in Canaan than if they had followed Moses' advice. The long course of wilderness wanderings after leaving Egypt gave Israel the opportunity to tackle and put behind them a few of the difficult political issues common to democratic start-up regimes: electoral issues like the length and contour of an emergency term of office; finding a balance between liberality and conservatism in permitting political party factionalism and proliferation (Num 11:26–30); and the development of processes for oversight of the administrative activity of the executive branch, including something like an impeachment power exercised by the legislative branch. In fact, Moses got embroiled in several no-confidence proceedings based on charges ranging from inadequate fulfillment of political promises, to corruption, to usurpation of functions of government that did not belong to him. Moses submitted to those proceedings and provided testimony in his own defense, which seemed to carry the day.

During the "wandering" period, Moses and the elders also dealt with appointment of civil servants, establishing methods for making proper appointments (Exod 17–18; Num 17:1–11) and for removal of civil servants. (Num 16) They dealt with the problem of government budget surpluses common in enthusiastic, early-stage republican government. (Exod 36:2–7) They made effort to match accountability with authority in government administration and thus took a stand against bureaucratism and selfish manipulation of government workers. (Num 18:1) These kinds of activities are all tell-tale signs of an authentic historical memory. In addition, Moses wrestled with every popular democratic leader's inevitable temptation to repress elements of the population and force allegiance to policies rather than persuade such allegiance. He was even tempted to found his own dynasty.[6] In other words, he acted like a limited chief executive of a republican nation-state typical of both ancient, medieval and modern types.

Early on, Moses succumbed to a particularly nasty temptation typical of both emergency power and settled power situations. He stumbled into the constitutionally forbidden realm of executive department law-making at the Waters of Meribah. (Num 20) He did not want to expend limited resources to obtain additional water supplies for the journey at a time when the elders and people desperately wanted to do so. He came under severe censure for resisting their policy directive to him in this matter, including disqualification for leading the Israelites across Jordan and into Canaan. One surmises that he believed he had proper constitutional prerogative under his grant of power to decide military supply issues. But the people made clear to him that even during emergency conditions, the people in the new Israel set the policy, not the administrator. The people's input and demands forced Moses to relent, change his mind, cater to their wishes. In addition to successful drilling for water, an important political precedent was set at Meribah.

6. Wildavsky, *Moses*, 105.

The Personality of Moses and the Constitutional Tradition

The practice of democratic government on the national level in ancient Israel after Moses' departure from the scene took its cues from the executive department precedents set by Moses during his leadership in the wilderness. Moses established a number of precedents which were ultimately rolled-up into an expectation that a future leader should be one "like unto Moses." His activity, despite some bumps and bruises along the way, was thought to be exemplary. In the first place, an executive magistrate in Israel ought to exercise considerable restraint as to political ambition, like Moses. Moses did so by repeatedly telling God that he didn't want the job of revolutionary leadership. Other democratic societies have similar remembrances of leaders who reluctantly responded to popular demand, worked during an emergency in the public interest, and then retired from government early in life to return to other pursuits. These include Cincinnatus in Rome and George Washington in the early American republic.

The magistrate also ought to be non-violent, like Moses. Moses demonstrated non-violence by patiently negotiating with Pharaoh rather than assassinating him or leading an uprising against him. Furthermore, the chief executive ought to take care to use wisely any emergency power he is entrusted with and return that power to the people and the rest of the government once the emergency is past, like Moses. Moses did this by declining to go into Canaan and continue his rule there. Additionally, the judge of all the people ought to submit to any impeachment process initiated by the people, their local leaders, or the national legislative body, like Moses. As we mentioned above, Moses submitted to the non-confidence/impeachment process initiated by tribal elders. Finally, the presiding elder ought to allow for legitimate political organization activities supportive of the foundational principles of the new republic, like Moses. Moses shared power and government position with Aaron, allowed dissident political party work, i.e. "prophesying," carried out by Eldad and Medad, and gave a hearing to Korah, Dathan and Abiram before ruling against their movements.

The writers and editors of the Pentateuch took care to portray Moses as demonstrating a lack of ambition for power. From the standpoint of democratic political theory, it must be said that while democrats are suspicious of ambition for power, at the same time democracy requires citizens to prepare well and participate in local government when called to do so. We discern in the Mosaic narratives a three-part ideal of good citizenship revolving around the idea of civic preparation, participation, and responsibility. In Israel, everyone must be a good citizen and must be busy about helping others locally. Everyone must be as attentive to the neighbor's needs and rights as to his own. Moses definitively answered Cain's question, "Am I my brother's keeper." His proposal that Israel should aim for being a "nation of priests" suggests that everyone is responsible for and must care deeply about what is going on not only in the family, but in the clan, the tribe, and the nation. Moses himself cared enough about his fellow citizens that he heeded a call to act in their interests even when he felt inadequate to the task. Good citizens must cultivate a positive attitude about democratic government and join in the fray when needed.

What good citizens have in common first of all is the proper temperament for participation in democratic affairs and for leadership. They must be patient, restrained, and non-violent in their daily dealings with neighbors. Foundational political figures like Abel, Jacob, and Joseph set the bar high for Moses. Early in his career, Moses was headstrong and tended to violence, but in time, he learned to hold his tongue and lower his fists. Citizens must also prepare for leadership, and in particular for rotation in and out of positions in local, and possibly higher levels of government. Moses had a head start due to his upbringing at court, but learned that that was not nearly enough preparation for the task which came to be his. He had to figuratively sit at the feet of the ancestors by rehearsing the traditions about them, but also had to sit at the feet of a democratic leader in his own time, his father-in-law Jethro.

Citizen leaders must model proper conduct while participating in government. This includes, most particularly, ethical methods of dealing with others and respecting precedents set by particularly eminent leaders. Leaders must conform to electoral standards, respect and not exceed the charge given to them for the particular job at hand, and refrain from repressing political opponents. They must submit to public scrutiny and establish patterns of accountability in their administrative work.

The third political story line and ideal of good citizenship that we look at here is the idea that administrative leaders must understand the supremacy of the legislative branch of government during the time of normal operation of the government, during crisis periods, and especially during periods of temptation to war. Moses' political skills and model conduct in office were also on display in the matter of the Golden Calf, where he carried the day by negotiating shared executive power with Aaron, by involving the elders in constitutional deliberations to save the republic, and ultimately by pleasing the majority of the people in his activities. The story of Korah, Dathan, and Abiram details how an ethical democratic republican leader should handle outright revolt against the constitution from a determined but misguided minority. (Num 16) Throughout these civilian debacles

Moses demonstrated that he understood and respected the supremacy of the legislative branch of the national government.

Moses also assured his people and his posterity that he understood the military power to be in the hands of the legislating elders of the people rather than in himself. It is clear the people understood they had the power to declare war, not Moses. They didn't consent to Moses' proposal for early engagement of the Canaanite city-state kings, and Moses relented. Both legislative and executive branches believed the war power lay with the people and their national legislative representatives, not with the executive magistrate.[7]

As with many frail new democracies, the Israelites understood they were not ready for war against established entities in the region round about them. They stayed away from strong kingdoms. One passage in Exodus reads: "And it came to pass, when Pharaoh had let the people go, that God led them not through the way of the land of the Philistines, although that was near; for God said, Lest peradventure the people repent when they see war, and they return to Egypt . . ." (Exod 13:17) What is implied here is that the legislative body of the people, the elders, agreed with Moses that such an immediate engagement of a dangerous and strong people would be unwise. The elders gave unanimous consent to an indirect approach to Canaan.[8]

Later on Moses and the elders tested whether they were ready for entry and attendant war-making by agreeing to send spies in from the south. After hearing the report of the spies, Moses wanted Israel to enter Canaan and engage armies there, but the people solidly and uniformly said no. The people and their elders were still not ready.

Moses, as chief executive, did not wield the war power as a monarch would. The representatives of each tribe, the elders, exercised the war power, as in all democratic republics. Moses, operating under a constitution that he himself drafted, knew he was without standing to force the issue and gave in to the will of the people. (Num 13:22-23; Deut 1:2) Later on, the people exercised their war power decision-making once again. This time, Moses

---

7. This is the same theory of democratic war-making that Madison outlines: "Those who are to conduct a war cannot . . . be proper or safe judges whether a war ought to be commenced . . . " Madison also remarked, "In no part of the constitution is more wisdom to be found, than in the clause which confides the question of war or peace to the legislature, and not to the executive department . . . the temptation would be too great for any one man." See Shinkoskey, *American Kings*, 26–27.

8. The same can be said of the American revolutionaries after defeating Britain. Washington, Adams and Jefferson studiously avoided war with France, Britain, and Spain, knowing the frail new republic could not survive it. Madison avoided it as well throughout his first term, until the nation believed it must engage at least in a mostly defensive war (1812) again the British. See Shinkoskey, *American Kings*.

counseled against war, but the elders wanted to go to war. Moses accepted their decision once again. Unfortunately, the migrant militia were defeated at Hormath by Amalek. In hindsight, Moses was right and the elders wrong, but the will of the people's representatives necessarily prevailed anyway. Even later after nine and a half tribes were finally ready for entry, two and a half tribes said they were not inclined to enter Canaan, and in fact would rather settle outside of Canaan. The nine and a half ultimately conceded the right of the minority tribes to go their own way, thus avoiding war with them.[9]

We learn from Moses' behavior in these critical moments that the executive department must not usurp the policy-making authority of the legislature (such as infrastructure spending and the war power), must not lose faith in the councils of elders, must fight to uphold the life of the republic and the authority of its laws against subversion and violent overthrow, and must allow tribes to have their head with regard to major decisions even if they turn out to be wrong. Moses turned his emergency policy-making power back over to the duly constituted national legislature, exercised great patience with the assembly when it went awry (accepting its decisions), maintained hope for the fulfillment of the dreams of the people, and fought for their perquisites when insurgents tried to put a quick end to the journey.

We return now to the specifics of Moses' ethics and character as qualities for participation in government leadership. Moses met the requirement to care about his fellow citizens and their major predicaments in society. He cared about securing relief from their sufferings in the labor force. He cared about their opinions and believed they had the ability to govern themselves. He cared enough about their survival that he was willing to risk his life in periodic confrontations with Pharaoh. But Moses nevertheless still had trouble with the idea of serving in a position of high-level leadership. He was certain that he was under-qualified for such an exalted position. Moses perhaps did not initially understand that his very reluctance to serve was actually a key attribute of a good democratic leader. But the editors of the Bible understood it clearly, for they depicted him making continual and strong complaints against the idea of serving in a revolutionary democratic leadership.

One author writes, Moses was "quick to admit frailty . . . hardly the usual pitch for political power."[10] In a real democracy, no citizen comes out of a hereditary line of rulers with life-long training for the job. All are mostly

---

9. Wildavsky, *Moses*, 83, 133.

10. Wildavsky, *Moses*, 28–69, especially 36. Early American presidents did not campaign for the job and would have disqualified themselves if they had.

ill-prepared for the work of top leadership. An honest person will admit this readily. Moses first protested that people would not believe his story about the reappearance of the God of their ancestors in the burning bush at Sinai. (Exod 4:1) He next complained, hoping to disqualify himself, "I am not eloquent." (Exod 4:10) He asked that God make someone else his agent to interact with the people. (Exod. 4:13) Later, he asked "Why is it that thou hast sent me?" (Exod 5:22) Even, later, feeling the responsibility of ethical, almost paternal leadership of the citizenry weighing heavily upon him, he said, "Have I conceived all this people? Have I begotten them, that thou shouldest say unto me, Carry them in thy bosom . . . unto the land which thou swarest unto their fathers?' (Num 11:12) In contrast, a typical exploitative politician would be happy to exercise control over as many people as he could get his hands upon. Moses' reluctance to serve as self-important and paternalistic father of the nation set a pattern for later political/constitutional movement leaders like Jeremiah and Isaiah who were similarly disinterested in taking on the responsibilities which seemed to be thrust upon them.

Democracies do not want people in positions of power who want to be there. They want people there who don't want to be there, as long as those people have a good constitutional education and strong personal values. True democratic republicans understand the self-less, substantially unremunerated, thankless work this entails and can think of better things to do. It is often the case that once a democratic leader has almost bled-out in his effort to serve the people, he is unceremoniously put out to pasture. But if Moses was to be a good citizen, he had to heed the call, first from God, and next from the elders of Israel. He would serve, even if he disliked the job and even if he understood many of the people would remember his failings more than his successes.[11]

Perhaps a hundred years after Moses, Gideon confronted the issue of growing ambition for high office in his day. He did that by refusing greater

---

11. In his reluctance to assume power, Moses was in good company. After the American revolutionary war, George Washington retired from public service and did not seek the office of the president, much as Cincinnatus retired after a single tour of duty in Rome. These leaders took it only when it was offered to them. In the early American republic, James Madison never made a campaign speech. William Harrison, the ninth president, was the first whose supporters actually publically and actively campaigned for the presidency through a campaign committee. Andrew Johnson, the seventeenth president, was the first to travel in obvious active pursuit of the presidency, although he did not speak directly to election issues, but just "showed himself to the people." Nearly one hundred years after Washington, presidential candidates like James Garfield and William McKinley still did not travel away from their homes during the campaign period. See Shinkoskey, *American Kings*, 24 and throughout.

executive department power in spite of his popularity. He led his people in a crisis, temporarily, because he was a capable leader. He emphatically did not believe it constitutional for him to assume permanent power, nor that his children would automatically be good leaders just because he was. He recounted the old Mosaic formula that leaders could be found at any time from out of the ranks of the ordinary people, and did not need to be trained in the house of a monarch. He reminded, "My clan is the humblest in Manasseh, and I am the youngest in my father's household." (Judg 6:1–6, 11–16)

At the time of Moses' meeting with God, it was not clear at all to Moses that he possessed the proper personality for the job of national emergency leader. He was honest, which was good. But he believed the task was far above his head. Also, perhaps, there was a legitimate question in his own mind whether he could be non-violent in temperament, given to rational communication rather than drama and temper tantrums. That sort of behavior alienated others and undermined peaceful, orderly government. Abraham, Isaac and Jacob, and perhaps Joseph, set precedents in non-violence and deference to others through negotiation. Their examples were hard to follow. The people's choice of a personality suitable for the back-breaking work and patience required of a ethical, democratic leader is an extremely difficult one.

On the other hand, Moses seemed a likely heir of the Abraham lineage's pacifist inclinations in several ways. Three times in his early career he intervened "on the side of the oppressed" and in order to pacify potentially explosive situations. He intervened in a fight between an Egyptian and a Hebrew. He intervened in a quarrel between two Hebrews. He drew water for a chieftan's young daughters threatened by shepherds at a watering hole. (Exod 2:14, 17) Later we see that the distance between Moses' political personality and Pharaoh's was immense. Moses bargained patiently and honestly with Pharaoh. Pharaoh bargained dishonestly, reneging on his agreements. Moses did not covet Pharaoh's power and did not get angry. Pharaoh got insanely jealous of Moses and had a hair trigger.[12]

Later, Moses bore-up under the grumblings and murmurings of his own people in the wilderness, avoided conflict with democratic-leaning neighbors, dealt humanely with Miriam, and stayed the plagues, perhaps providing health care treatment even for his political opponents. (Num 16:21, 46, 48) All of this points to a personality softened by experience, elevated by spiritual and political development, and educated through the diligent study of the history of nations, including Egypt, Midian, and Canaan.

---

12. Wildavsky, *Moses*, 37–38.

A democracy provides opportunities to a wide variety of concerned citizens to participate in governance processes. Opportunities usually come first on the level of local government. Moses appointed thousands of camp officials to serve the community during the long migration to Canaan, demonstrating a republic's decided commitment to citizen participation.

As emergency commander in chief, Moses was personally sitting to judge disputes among the people without assistance, in one sense a good thing from the point of view of citizen access to the national leader, but in another sense a bad thing. Ongoing micromanagement of this sort would fit into a pattern of government control endemic to dictatorial regimes, strong monarchies, and war-time democratic governments where the commander continues to rule this way after the emergency has passed. Moses understood the problem. He took the advice of his father-in-law and delegated his emergency power to temporary command leaders of groups of thousands, hundreds, fifties, and tens. (Exod 18:24-27) He accepted that the people were capable of learning how to "judge" one another, that is, administer camp activities. Such judgment need not be the exclusive prerogative of highly trained national leaders appointed by a national ruler. In addition, it is likely that these civilian administrators/militia commanders were nominated or ratified by the tribal elders themselves.

Jethro tutored Moses in the practice of democracy by encouraging the camp to bring their legal causes "unto God," which, translated, meant to the people themselves acting under the ethical influence of heaven. Jethro said, "Be thou for the people to Godward, that thou mayest bring the causes unto God and thou shalt teach them ordinances and laws, and shalt show them the way wherein they must walk, and the work that they must do." (Exod 18:13-23) Moses was in this way advised to tutor the people in the habit of democratic government. In such a system all mature citizens should plan to rotate through local governmental office, whether legislative or administrative/judicial. In sum, Moses taught the people how to judge themselves, and then stepped out of the way while they did so. Proper democratic conduct while in office is to train the people and then give away power to others who accept the training well. Once encamped at Sinai, Moses continued the pattern of giving away power, as we shall see in the example of the Golden Calf.

Moses set standards for model conduct while in office with respect to electoral issues and with respect to the term of office. Moses' behavior set the tone for constitutional an-iconism, that is, limits on power while in office, which tone held well in place through most of the first two hundred years of the republic. Moses had to deal with electoral politics and issues before precedents or laws were clearly set. The general idea was that elections were held if and when there was a lack of confidence in the leader and his party. Moses was the leader elected at Goshen for emergency duty, then elected a second time to head the new government set up at Sinai. When some people, his own brother and sister at first, and later Korah and others, questioned whether he had the confidence of the people to continue to govern in the wilderness, Moses threw the question open to the people and they reaffirmed their faith in his leadership. He submitted his personal life to the glaring light of critics, and survived the debacle.

We have suggested above that Moses refused to repress legitimate political speech criticizing his administrative rule. This is a mark of ethical democratic leadership. He patiently listened to at least ten incidences of citizen "murmuring" against his leadership. When he suffered a challenge to his position as leader by members of his own family, Miriam and Aaron, themselves likely representing various constituencies among the migrants, he acted with admirable restraint. Moses' brother and sister, Aaron and Miriam, leveled charges of foreign entanglement against him when they objected to his marriage to an Ethiopian woman, a woman of "Cush," likely referring to Zipporah. (Num 12:1; Deut 17:15 no foreigners to serve as king) But this attempt at impeachment of Moses was a weak charge, since the marriage was contracted before the constitution prohibiting such outside-the-confederation political marriages was ratified at Sinai. They likely were trying to weaken Moses and force him to deal his way out of the difficulty by entering into a triune executive leadership junta with the two of them, thus joining him as co-equal leaders. God then said, and the people apparently agreed, that Moses was the only authorized magistrate, since it was only he who was elected, and not they: "With him will I speak mouth to mouth . . ." (Num 12:6–8) In summarizing the incident, Wildavsky says, "She [Miriam] had shamed . . . (the) leader."[13] She could be punished rather harshly. However, instead Moses then shored up his democratic chops by dealing humanely with Miriam, rather than clapping her in irons.

With his forgiving manner, Moses set a precedent for other chief executives in how to deal with political opponents. The basis for choosing a chief executive in the future was that the people should try to find one "like unto Moses." Such a one must have both a scientific and a humane bent. His predictions about natural events, like the Egyptian plagues, and his predictions about political events, policy matters, foreign affairs, etc., most often should come to pass. Others must try to measure up to this standard of practical intelligence. Would-be politicians who could not match this level of sophistication were merely "dreamers of dreams." (Deut 18: 21–22)

---

13. Wildavsky, *Moses*, 152.

It was clear that there was no constitutionally-set term of office for the chief executive office in early Israel, as was the case in the early American presidency. Even the question of the term of office of leadership of the ongoing migration to Canaan was still quite open, as the activities of Aaron, Miriam, Korah, Dathan, Abiram, Eldad, and Medad made quite clear. They all took steps to bid for the power that Moses held. A series of Bible vignettes outline Moses' appropriate responses to the temptation to extend the scope or length of the emergency power he wielded as chief magistrate. Overall, he seemed to want to get the emergency phase of the venture over quickly so he could retire from office. In fact, Moses had wanted to enter Canaan immediately, and begin the settlement right away. Above, we viewed this as a policy that would enhance the size of the national government. But perhaps Moses had the view that early entry, while requiring extensive national resources at first, would then necessitate an earlier devolution of extensive emergency national government power to tribal leaders so they could administer local police power in the areas where they settled. In fact, appointing tribal captains at a number of levels as Moses did early on, could be seen as a training program for just this sort of devolution of power. But Moses' plans were scotched by the electorate. The people were not ready for settlement yet. They kept Moses on as leader in the wilderness for "forty years." When the time came that the tribes were ready to seize the land and real political power for themselves, Moses demonstrated once again that he had no desire for regularized power, and retired before entering Canaan.

5

The Molten Calf: A Gold Mine of Political Information

THE GOLDEN CALF STORY yields significant information about the formulation of the early Israelite government and its national processes. The story plays out in Exodus 32 and runs like the following. Moses left the camp at the foot of Mt. Sinai, ascended the mountain, communed with God over the composition of the foundational charter of government, and returned to camp carrying two tablets of stone with the law written on them.

While Moses was gone for what seemed like a lengthy period, the people rallied around Aaron and asked him to make a molten idol for them. Aaron asked them to donate their gold earrings for the purpose, and after the idol was cast, he built an altar and proclaimed a feast for the next day. On the morrow, the people offered sacrifices early, then devoted the rest of the day to food, drink, and "play," many apparently cavorting around in a state of nakedness.

Moses heard the noise of singing as he descended toward camp. He then saw the calf and the dancing. In anger, he broke the two tablets of law. Reaching camp, he took the calf and put it in the fire, ground it to powder, threw the powder into water and had the people drink it. At some point he had a conversation with Aaron. Aaron shifted blame to the people, saying they were "set on mischief." Moses asked for his own closest supporters in the Levite tribe to slay the worst of the mischief-makers, some 3,000 men.

It seems apparent that Moses invited his own difficulties in one sense. Instead of sticking around close to his people and encouraging them in gainful activity, he slipped away from camp to draft a constitution. Moses did not, and perhaps could not, entrust the task to another, for he was the intellectual and political leader of the entire venture. It was his job to do. While he was away, the people complained, as they do about Congresspersons

The Molten Calf: A Gold Mine of Political Information 57

leaving Washington D.C. during session today, that he was not at his desk. They spoke of him like a stranger, referring to him as "this Moses," not realizing he was working hard to help them. They said, "We wot not what is become of him." (Exod 32:1)

While Moses was in seclusion, it seems that Aaron seized an opportunity to build a political base for himself by pandering to the popular desires of a people who were not in a particularly sober frame of mind. They were apparently ready to "do" permanent government right away without adequate debate and discussion. They were feeling their oats, having eluded and defeated Pharaoh at the Red Sea and then having organized themselves into a tightly regimented camp for the march to Sinai. In their haste to do government, they clearly defaulted to a system that might be called molten monarchy. A hallmark of such a system was citizen dependence upon a substantial central government and a wealthy ruler. This was perhaps the easiest sort of government for the Israelites to set up because it was the most familiar to them.

What was really going on here? Was Aaron as innocent of fault as he purported to be? The Biblical point of view seems to be somewhat neutral toward Aaron, entertaining his story as plausible, but casting a somewhat jaundiced eye at it. In explanation of his behavior while Moses was gone, Aaron remarked, "They said unto me, Make us gods . . ." (Exod 32: 22–24) This suggests that either he or some of the elders suggested a heavy dose of taxation to support the proposed new government. The citizenry gave their valuable jewelry to him to make the idol, which then became the possession of the central government. Aaron mollified the people, humored them, stroked them, let them feast, and led them to believe that their contribution of wealth to the national government would take care of their problems. He did all of this when instead they should have been deliberating about self-government. Moses corrected this problem upon his return.

Aaron shunned the responsibility of a real democratic leader to encourage self-government and instead allowed the people to lead him astray, or, more likely, allowed them to lead him in the direction he already wanted to go. What Aaron did was something Gideon seemingly refused to do later on after settlement—lunge toward kingship. (Judg 8:22–23) We will see, however, that Gideon wasn't quite as innocent as he purported to be either.

The molten calf of the early wilderness experience is usually thought of as a religious idol, representing apostasy from the religious culture of Judaism. As such, it is theorized that it may have been an image of Yahweh, or a foreign (perhaps Egyptian) deity, in the form of a young male bovine.[1]

---

1. Spencer, "Golden Calf," 1065–69.

In fact, in the ancient Near East, the casting of a national idol of a protective deity did not mean that a particular type of creed or religious worship was to be mandated for the population. A precious metal idol represented the overall worldview and culture of the populace, including their general approach to the arts, science, economics, and government finance. Indeed, the idol represented the type of government that the tutelary god of the nation supported, usually divine kingship of some sort, characteristic of city-states. Thus, it seems reasonable merely in light of a surface examination of the events of Exodus 32, and in light of the persistent prophetic critique of centralized politics later on, that in casting the idol Israel was heading for lavish depictions of nature in art, divination science rather than prophetic-predictive science, aristocratic primogeniture and government control of the economy rather than agricultural and pastoral egalitarianism, and strong kingship. These were things Moses believed the camp of Israel were trying to leave behind, and should not be turning to again. He apparently was successful in convincing them of that because they agreed to have the calf destroyed and accepted a charter of laws in place of a leader with undefined powers.

How did Moses deal with the between-the-lines political issues involved with this crisis? What essentially happened was that Moses recognized that Aaron represented the wishes of a considerable segment of the people. He did what many campaigning chief executives are wont to do in this situation. He compromised by offering Aaron a position in his administration if Aaron would throw his support to Moses and Moses' concept of constitutional law. From Aaron's point of view, the purpose of the calf venture was to organize his supporters and position himself to bargain with the program of the revolutionary leader who had perhaps the greatest support among the people. He likely anticipated having to give political ground, but wanted to get something out of it for himself. Aaron essentially offered Moses a deal by calling him "my Lord," acknowledging Moses' superior political position. When Aaron took a position of innocence in the matter, by essentially saying the people demanded the calf-style government of him, he signaled that he was willing to compromise. (Exod 32:22)

Moses essentially took the "presidency" of Israel, and offered Aaron the priesthood, the number two position in an ancient Near East nation. The position essentially combined the duties of attorney general, state department, and oracular functions, and perhaps supervision of the treasury. That Moses succeeded in solidifying Aaron's support with the offer of a

The Molten Calf: A Gold Mine of Political Information

vizier-type position is revealed later in the matter of the Korah affair. Moses was able to call upon and receive Aaron's support against Korah.[2]

Thus, the Golden Calf affair is not really a story about simple religious idolatry—making an image of a favored god and perhaps then innocently worshipping the object rather than the god. It is, in the first place, a story about political coalition-building and cabinet selection by Moses. That in itself demonstrates a process absolutely typical of a republican style of government anywhere in the world and in any period of time. In fact, the whole scenario, in the second place, also illustrates what normally is a top priority policy debate over national taxation and banking in any democratic regime. The United States experienced exactly the same kind of national power debate during the administration of its first president as well. The American founders and early government administrators debated the size of the national government financial apparatus and the type of treasury/banking system they would need to deal with revolutionary era debts. That was the case with the Israelite founders as well, as Israel owed considerable amounts of debts to unnamed parties in Egypt. Obtaining financial capacity for the government by means of jewelry contributions was likely preparatory to paying off such debts. The calf "story" thus, for several reasons, gives the administration of Moses, indeed the very existence of Moses, Aaron, and migratory Israel, the ring of considerable historical authenticity.

As we mentioned above, priests in ancient governments customarily officiated not just in public ritual matters, but in administration of justice and in collection of "tithes," which in fact were simply national taxes to support government administration. In the early days these taxes were gathered in at the mobile tent known as the tabernacle. That was to be no different in Israel than any other place. In fact, in the period of time just before the Exodus, the Amarna Age in Egypt, resources in the form of gold, silver, animals, produce, and other property, including molten idols, were deposited and kept at the national temples, which served as state office buildings. The central government most everywhere, including Mesopotamia, Egypt, Ugarit, and Carchemish, were obligated to provide services for their people domestically out of such resources and also to meet international obligations from such treasuries, such as tribute obligations. One common use of such central bank funds was to compensate foreign merchants or families whose goods were stolen, or whose members were killed while traveling abroad.[3]

---

2. The resolution of the golden calf affair was thus much like the strategy John Quincy Adams used to end a political stalemate. He offered Henry Clay the position of secretary of state in order to secure the presidency for himself.

3. Wells and Magdalene, *Law*, 2:274–276.

Temples had treasury officials charged with carrying out inventory, storage and disbursement activities. King Solomon in Israel, for example, took in over 600 talents of gold each year and had a treasury secretary in charge of managing the central repository. (1 Kgs 4:6, 10:14) Legal issues were brought in courts throughout the ancient Near East in regards to matters relating to deposits of money and flocks.[4] (Exod 22:7-8, 10-11) Citizens gave one another grain or silver as interest-bearing loans, so banking activity was not restricted to national banks alone.[5] Certainly, setting up some sort of national treasury for the migrating tribes of Israel had to be a priority of the highest order if the community were to function on any kind of cohesive basis. The question at hand was how great an endowment should be made to the national government. Aaron wanted more, Moses wanted less. Aaron wanted government to function and be financed on the national level. Moses wanted it to function and be financed on the local level, as the second set of tablets made clear.

The casting of the Golden Calf constituted Aaron's attempt to establish solidarity with the Egyptian government and its royalist banking/finance system. It also signified Israel's willingness to repay debts owed to the Egyptian people and their financial institutions. The Federalist Party within the nascent American government, led by Alexander Hamilton, succeeded in doing what Aaron tried to do, but ultimately couldn't get away with. Hamilton's actions in setting up a national bank initially cemented financial relations with royalist Britain, at least until Andrew Jackson, playing Moses, reversed that early action. For his part, Andrew Jackson demonstrated considerable historical perspicacity when he called Federalist bank advocates "worshippers of the golden calf."[6] When Moses destroyed the calf, it not only signified a break with the Egyptian finance system and the Egyptian political system, but it dramatically repudiated the debt by evaporating any means the Israelites had to make payments on the debt in the foreseeable future. Jackson destroyed the American golden calf as well, by dismantling the national bank for a period of many decades.

For their part, the Israelites agreed with Moses' plan to repudiate the debt likely because, in part, it saved them money, and because, as a practical matter, they did not anticipate having much to do with the Egyptian economy in their subsistence farming in Canaan. For a political leader such as Moses, who was trying to nurture a former slave people in the direction of self-government, repudiating the debt was the first great hurdle to get

---

4. Levinson, "First Constitution," 1876.
5. Wells and Magdalene, *Law*, 2:38.
6. Shinkoskey, *American Kings*, 49.

THE MOLTEN CALF: A GOLD MINE OF POLITICAL INFORMATION   61

over in convincing the people they could operate as a nation on their own, without the assistance of any great king power.

When the people agreed to destroy the calf, they took the huge step of acknowledging that the gain which the Egyptian economy took from their labor power over recent years was entirely illegitimate. The huge national buildings their forced labor helped to build did not accrue any benefit to them, though it accrued some benefit for the average Egyptian who could use and admire the buildings. The Egyptian government had used them spitefully. Egyptian clans and bankers, on the other hand, saw an opportunity to cement an economic relationship with a highly motivated and hard working people. They jumped at the opportunity to finance the Hebrew holiday weekend in the desert. Some analysts have suggested that their floating of loans to Israel on the eve of their departure may have had the character of a "manumission" (freedom) gift given to slaves who have ended their service and were now striking out on their own. More likely it was a debt they expected to collect from the pilgrims once they realized their ongoing dependence upon Egyptian society.

But what did Moses propose as an alternative to Aaron's national banking system? The law written on Moses' first set of plates possibly spoke to the development of an an-iconic, or minimal national treasury system. Such a policy of conducting minimal, depository banking on the national level,[7] and of the keeping the bulk of government itself as well as its financing on the regional (tribal and clan) and local (family) levels, was shattered when Moses saw that Aaron had committed the people to a monarchic, or strong national government system of finance. From Aaron's point of view, if the people were to repay debts to Egypt, they needed to get in the habit of paying taxes to the national government, as they did in the act of giving their jewelry to be melted into the national idol, and to symbolize their solidarity with the system of strong national government financing characteristic of other nations in the ancient Near East. They did that in the formulation of the idol. The existence of the calf was likely the very collateral wealth in the national treasury that would allow them to borrow from other nations for government projects in the future and also to place payments on their Egyptian debt on an extended schedule agreeable to the Egyptians. The gold in the Hebrew "Fort Knox"—a molten calf stored in the mobile tent of meeting—could be figuratively or literally chipped off or melted down for whatever purpose the national government wanted. After Moses brokered

---

7. Independent national banking in the early American democracy meant financing programs out of domestic revenue and not foreign loans, and also use of the bank as a depository bank rather than a loaning bank. This made the bank more like a checking account than a savings account.

the destruction of the calf, it is likely that he negotiated a return most of the way back to that an-iconic, or minimal national government system, by means of the second commandment published in the second sets of plates. This law prohibited precious metal idols for use in the central government.

The second commandment directly repudiated, that is, rejected any repayment, of the debts owed to Egypt, at least by the national government. The gold was ground to dust and disposed of in a way that it could apparently never be recovered again. Although the Bible is not clear on the subject, it is likely that some of the Israelite debt was contracted well before Moses even arrived in Egypt to stir up the Hebrew people. After all, the people were working at hard labor and were likely being paid a pittance, and thus had need to borrow to survive. This borrow-or-foreclose pressure was likely part of the oppression which made the people "cry out." Individuals who appreciated their loans and perhaps had a close relationship with their creditors, conceivably could still repay their individual debts if they wanted.

The narrator of the Exodus 32 passages we are analyzing here refers to the calf as representing "your gods, O Israel, who brought you up out of Egypt." (Exod 32:4) This is perhaps a way of stating two truths: first, that the many hundreds or thousands of Egyptian personal loans seemed to have made the Exodus possible as a practical matter; but second, that the loans were not really necessary and became a vile substitute for the power each migrant had within himself/herself to survive independently of the largesse of Egyptians. They needed only one God, the heavenly "king" who championed self-government, to be their banker. Instead, however, they hedged their bets, confiding their faith in the many gods of Egypt as well. The jewelry each family had taken on loan became a political snare to them. The loans were a crutch that only a disabled people really needed. Israel was capable of being financially well and strong on its own.

In New Testament times, Steven recalled the molten calf incident by stating Israel made "gods to go before us." (Acts 7:40) By this he meant that Israel placed their trust even at the outset in economic dependency not only upon a number of foreign bankers, but upon a foreign monarchy. The phrase "before us" in Exodus and in Acts is deeply suggestive of the analysis we give the golden calf story here. When Israel left Egypt, she left as a debtor committed to repay loans at interest, and thus continue in part the economic dependency she had known in Egypt. Israel put the "god" of economic dependency in a position of prominence before (in front of) her own eyesight and failed to see she was capable of governing herself, since democratic government did not require a great deal of national financing to operate. She could easily survive a short trip into the wilderness, and could build a new government there without much money to finance it, and could probably survive even if they were certain they were not coming back.

Egyptian financiers wanted to bind the Israelites economically and thus politically during their supposed three-day pilgrimage to worship. They wanted to make it difficult for them to get clean away, taking with them all the free labor they had been providing the Egyptian polity. The new debt was essentially a method to ensure that they would return, or at least not go very far on their own. If Israel did not return physically, she would still have to return financially by paying the debt. This mistrust Egyptians had of the group leaving Goshen, as we shall see, was well-placed. Moses hoped to convince the group to become an independent state, and Pharaoh's troops pursuing them even after he had given his consent for them to leave cemented that decision for them. Thus, "spoiling" of the Egyptian people did not really occur so much when they left the Nile Delta region with the gold given them by the Egyptians, or when they successfully crossed the Red Sea and moved father eastward on a journey longer than three days, but when the decision was made to destroy the molten idol and not pay back their creditors.

In sum, when Israel chose a molten idol to "go before" the citizenry, she was essentially placing her trust in gold, in luxury, in national banking, in aristocracy. Gold and concentration of wealth would be her servants, her advisers, her means to finance the military, the thing she depended upon . . . the means to all political ends. Moses and the prophets and narrators of the Bible would rather have them place democracy, law, justice, a God of freedom and self-government in a position of reference to "go before" them. In a democratic society, these were not only necessary, but sufficient means to the desired end of happiness.

As a practical matter, Moses' appointment of Aaron as high priest acknowledged Aaron's interest in matters related to national finance. George Washington's appointment of Alexander Hamilton to deal with banking matters followed the same pattern. Hamilton had considerable ability in the financial area. In ancient times, priests, after all, looked after the treasury composed not just of gold, but of taxes given in the form of produce and kept at storage sites on national government estates. The appointment also settled the matter of the revenue system and of the banking system used to support national spending. This was likely a compromise that gave Aaron some independent budgetary authority, albeit a minimal supply of revenue agents. Even as late as the time of Jesus, the high priests of the Israelite society were collecting and overseeing taxes owed not only to the Herodian leaders of the Judean society, but also to Rome. High priests like Ananias, just like Aaron long before, employed their sons in the national banking system and the priestly bankers raked in part of the take of the taxes, making them very wealthy, just as customs officers did in the early American republic.

The seductive potential of a national bank reared its head once again soon after Israel settled down in Canaan. Gideon made the first thrust in that direction by creating a golden ephod for use in the government. Solomon later expanded the national treasury, and Jeroboam committed the northern kingdom to calf idolatry, although he divided national power into two regional banking centers rather than centralize it in one. This was like the American decentralized approach in its early Federal Reserve system when it went back to national banking.

The donated jewelry for the calf was a prototype for the "donated" jewelry Gideon asked of the people somewhat later in the period of Judges. Those later donations/taxes were used to endow a priestly patronage position for himself and "his house" (ie, sons) in perpetuity. It is likely that power-hungry national political leaders and bankers in Gideon's party convinced the people they needed to beef-up government so government could better take care of them. For Gideon, this was a sort of substitute for the offer of kingship which he could not live with and which he turned down. The prospect of a civil service sinecure for his family was one that he could live with philosophically. The narrator of Judges, however, roundly condemned him for it. (Judg 8:24–28) In like manner, the people of the Exodus, in the view of the narrator, should not have made/kept [perhaps secret] ties with Egyptian bankers and aristocrats, but should have severed economic ties once they left Egypt if they fully intended to sever political ties.

The early national government mobile "tabernacle" office building, after time, became an immobile "temple," where national and international tax and banking activities were centered. Even after the first temple's destruction, it was rebuilt and took up again its multi-faceted functions, including national banking. In the time of Jesus, the newly refurbished second temple served as the Judean national bank that not only held tax revenues but made loans to and collected a high level of interest from farmers who could not make their tax payments. The author of b. Pas. 57a recalls: "Woe to me because of the house of Hanan (Ananias) . . . Woe to me because of their fists, for they are high priests and their sons are treasurers and their sons-in-law are temple overseers." Not all Judaic parties were critical of national banking activities to be sure. Some rabbis of the Talmudic era understood that it was historically the prerogative of chief magistrates to impose tariffs on products coming into the country and to keep them in a repository for administration of the legitimate needs of the government.[8] (b. San. 20b)

One of the central events of Jesus' activities was his disruption of the activities of the central bank section of the Judean temple. All four gospels contend that Jesus expressed severe criticism of the economic arrangements then prevalent at the national temple office building and the effect those arrangements had on Israel's traditional commitment to political independence and local economy. One obvious concern was that tribute had to be paid to a foreign government (Rome) that had recently veered toward luxury, monarchy, and imperialism. (Matt 17:24–27, 22:15–22) Also, Rome required Judea's own puppet government to function like the government of the Caesars as well, with a heavy concentration of wealth in the hands of the central government and a wealthy leader. This concentration of wealth was demonstrated in all the buying and selling, money changing, and moving of goods in the temple area. (Matt 21:12; Mark 11:16.) There was too much ownership and operation of the economy on the national level . . . in essence, too much national spending and too much power concentrated in one place. Jesus objected to this.

The Gospel of John gives a helpful interpretation of Jesus' cleansing of the temple: "His disciples remembered that it was written, the zeal of thine house has eaten me up." (John 2:17; Ps 69:9) This is a reference to the opposition David endured coming from the members of the royal retinue, who were constantly plotting to overthrow and supplant him. Members of the "house" of monarchy, of well-heeled central government, often consumed/destroyed its own effectiveness due to the incentives that individual members and cliques had to take control of the resources and the patronage power of the huge apparatus of state. The same was happening in Jesus' time in the house of Herod, only Herod and his sons were not as ambivalent about the size of the central government as David had been. Jesus did not trust human beings with that much wealth and power in one place. In Herod's house they tended to shred one another and the citizenry in the process of trying to concentrate more power and wealth in their own hands.

In the cleansing of the temple episode, Jesus objected not only to Roman colonial government in Judea and its tribute requirements, its revenue agents, and its contract bankers, as well as the complicity of Judean aristocrats in the whole arrangement, but also the increasing nationalization/regulation of the once locally governed farmer economy and increasing government-based social welfare activity. For example, he criticized Pharisee support of the policy of the national government providing care for the

8. Walzer, *Jewish Political Tradition*, 143.

elderly. This overstepped its legitimate bounds. Families themselves should care for their own. (Mark 7:12) All this made the national government a "den of thieves" rather than what the original constitution intended. The Ten Commandment constitution envisioned a citizenry fully dependent only upon individual initiative and working through local government to meet its needs with little support from a central government. Such a limited national government he referred to as "a house of prayer." Prayer, representing individual initiative, together with devotion to God and written law, was much cheaper than taxation and dependence upon political celebrities.

After Jesus' death and during the Jewish War of 66–73 against Rome, the people of Judea burned the bank archives in Jerusalem to destroy records of debts, thus repudiating the debt owed by simple farmers to the high priestly administrators and their Roman patrons, just as Moses and the elders had repudiated those illegitimate debts to Egypt. The Jewish revolts of 4 BCE, 40 CE, and 66 CE were revolts against a national central bank system and a pattern of excessive spending by central government, just like Moses' tax revolt against Aaron's top-heavy government system, and like Andrew Jackson's revolt against national taxation and banking during the early American period. One historian writes, "all of these [later Jewish] protests . . . (were) rooted in Mosaic covenantal principles."[9]

---

9. Horsley and Thatcher, *Renewal*, 22–26.

6

Deuteronomy and Democracy

MANY YEARS AFTER THE Golden Calf incident, Moses delivered a farewell address that many commentators correctly observe reveals a good deal about Israelite government and politics. The political science of Deuteronomy is complicated by the challenge in dating the material in it. Scholars are divided. Some feel a core piece of Deuteronomy is from this initial period of "conquest." Others suggest that the book was written in the time of Samuel in the eleventh century BCE as a manifesto for how a constitutional king must function—that book described as Samuel's "law of the kingdom." (1 Sam 10:25) Others suggest that it was written or heavily edited in the seventh century BCE at the time of Josiah to justify his reforms centering around the centralization of sacrifice. Still others argue it comes from the time of Greek and Roman classical democracy in the fifth or fourth centuries BCE.[1] Those who argue it is from the time of Moses point to the Bible's own story about the high priest Hilkiah in the time of Josiah who discovered an old manuscript he called "the book of the law"/"book of the covenant" which apparently demonstrated by contrast with the early days how far from political principle Israel had strayed in the time of "kings." (1 Kgs 22:3-20) We are less concerned about the dating of layers of the book than we are in teasing out the vectors of democratic practice promoted by the book's final product.

Deuteronomy provides legislation which enacts the basic form of government outlined in the Ten Commandment constitution in the same way early legislation in the United States during the Washington, Adams and Jefferson terms of office set up boundaries for organization and operation of the three branches of the American federal government.[2] In three key

---

1. Elazar, *Covenant and Polity*, 194.

2. Some scholars see the many laws of Deuteronomy, rather than the Ten

chapters, the book details the powers of the judiciary, the priesthood, the chief executive, and the political parties/prophets. (Deut 16–18) Deuteronomy's legislation probably originated during all three early periods of the Bible: the wilderness, judges and first temple kings periods.

A passage pregnant with originalist constitutional theory in Deuteronomy 17 notes that strong kings tend to multiply horses (expand the military), multiply wives (i.e., get involved in political marriages to women of other nations and therefore involve Israel in military alliances), and multiply gold and silver (expand the national budget by increasing taxation). Many, accordingly, read Deuteronomy 17 as a legal restraint on the size of the military, the treasury, and the king's harem. Here the king is essentially denied the war power, the legislative power, the social welfare police power (the power to announce debt remission), as well as a foreign affairs alliance power. As regards the war power, for example, Israel's highly ritualized battle preparation policy had no mention of the magistrate/king. The laws of siege, engagement, prisoners of war, and booty are prescribed by law and thus taken out of his hands as well. The limit on the king's horses was effectively a limit on the standing army, since horses have to be stabled and maintained even in peacetime.

Indeed, the Deuteronomic section of the Torah (political instruction), limits the institutional power of national rulers in military, cult, judicial, economic, and socio-sexual matters of conduct. Checks and balances are evident by way of the broad distribution of national governmental functions between the chief executive/king, the judiciary, prophets, and priesthood. Each of these agencies of the national government functions independently from the others, with their authority coming from law and/or God rather than from the chief executive. The priesthood, for example, make a separate covenant with God and with the people to rule in their particular sphere without interference from the magistrate.[3]

In particular, the Deuteronomic magistrate is not the lawgiver as in centralized political cultures. In Deuteronomy, he administers only, since he does not even adjudicate the law. Judicial power is independent of the executive and legislative power. Levinson writes, "Deuteronomy . . . enshrines separation of powers and their systematic subordination to a public legal text—the "Torah"—that delineates their jurisdiction while also ensuring their autonomy. This legislation establishes an independent judiciary while

---

Commandments, as the government charter for ancient Israel. For an example of this point of view, see Levinson, "First Constitution."

3. Elazar, *Covenant and Polity*, 205.

bringing even the monarch under the full authority of the law."[4] The King's responsibility is to read and learn the law so he can administer it. He is admonished not to stray from the commandment law to the right or left. (Deut 5:29; 6:2; 10:12; 17:11l 27:14; 31:12) He is bound by the law, not lord over it.[5] (Deut 16–18) Levinson adds, "Although its language is legal and its metaphors are religious, Deuteronomy articulates a complex vision of political philosophy..." In New Testament times, the Judaic leader Josephus recognized Deuteronomy as "the code of those laws of ours which touch our political constitution."[6]

Priests in Deuteronomy are teachers of the law, interpreters of the law, and keepers of the law. (Deut 17; 19:17; 21:5) There is no real mention of a cultic role for priests in Deuteronomy. For example, they do not receive an oracle (essentially a plan/vision for the country), as only a prophet/judge/chief magistrate does that. (Deut 18:9–22) Therefore, they are not to serve as chief executives. They share a judicial role with judges. (Deut 19:17, 17:9, 12) Priests are elected, and must not use divination, meaning they must produce scientific, historical (i.e., wisdom-type) interpretations of law only. They are essentially government workers. Judges and priests are to publish decisions based on law, not on whim or favor. (Deut 17:8–13) They are to be fully independent, appointed by the people rather than by the ruler.[7] (Deut 16–18)

Neither the king nor the priest in Israel can monopolize science and education and put a heavy political stamp on these institutions, in contrast to cultures which fuse the political and religious function in the person of a despotic ruler or a high priest. In those other cultures the official priesthood is not only on the state payroll but exercises "a monopoly on science, astronomy, engineering, and math."[8] The king in Israel is not the only or even the best mediator of the scientific or divine realms. There are scribes, prophets, priests, judges, and ordinary family patriarchs who share this burden.

While Deuteronomy is best known for one specific section focusing on limitations on the chief magistrate's power (Deut 17:14–20), this particular section provides only a small amount of the evidences of democratic practice and distrust of kingship promoted by the book. Because the section comports well with other warnings about the power of kings in 1 Sam 8 and Mishnah Sanhedrin from the rabbinic era, most accept that the language

4. Levinson, "First Constitution," 1853.
5. Berman, *Equal Justice*, 28, 59.
6. Levinson, "First Constitution," 1859.
7. Berman, *Equal Justice*, 65–68.
8. Hazony, *Dawn*, 73.

reflects an urgency to avoid concentration of power in the hands of one man and to place it in the hands of the law and legislature instead.

Deuteronomy is clear about discouraging specific kinds of political idolatry that the second commandment prohibits in a general way. Idolatry is understood as dependence upon autocratic or aristocratic leadership to provide government services, rather than more acceptable dependence upon broad and democratic decision-making through elders. Citizens and leaders are to destroy all signs of idolatry in the culture of the land they are returning to. (Deut 7:5; 25–26) In particular, they are to engage and defeat absolutist city-state political systems in Canaan. These monarchies offer their own royal offspring for international political marriages in order to create alliances which bind the local population to the policies of outside powers, at the expense of the wishes of their own people. (Deut 7:1–4)

Sentiment against strong kingship is expressed not just in the law and practice of Deuteronomy, but in the point of view of the narrators/editors of the Pentateuch's earliest stories. This means Deuteronomy can be interpreted as a restorationist politico-legal document aimed at getting the nation back on track again. For example, in the early stories God defeats strong kings militarily (Exod 14–15); God's servants defeat kings militarily (Gen 14:14–16; Num 31:6–8); kings are made to sue for peace vis a vis the democratic faithful (Gen 21:22–34); kings can be "converted" so as to recognize democratic values (Gen 14:18–20; Gen 41:38–39); kings can be humiliated before God or his servants. (Gen 12;17–20; 20:6–18; 26:8–11; Num 22–24)

Gathering material stemming from the long sweep of its history, the Bible presents stories of both ordinary and extraordinary citizens who stand up against oppressive kingship. Pharaoh's daughter's action in adopting a Hebrew baby is an act of disobedience against monarchic rule, much like the action of the mid-wives of Exodus 1:15–21. Prophets challenge royal authority (Moses before Pharaoh; Nathan before David in 2 Sam 12:1–14). Elijah censures Ahab (1 Kgs 18), and Jeremiah opposes king Zedekiah's foreign affairs policy. (Jer 38:2; 37:13) One author writes, "Gideon's brusque refusal of a crown (Judg 8:22–23) and Jotham's biting fable (Judg 9:7–21) show the whole notion of monarchy was rejected as improper."[9]

Economic idolatry—emotional, financial, and political dependence upon aristocracy—is likewise shunned in Deuteronomy. The Bible as a whole stakes out a position in favor of economic democracy and extensive local social welfare activity by virtue of its policies relating to family land tenure, liberal lending practices, debt easement, minimized taxation, and social programs for poverty relief such as levirate marriage. The means to

---

9. Bright, *History*, 167.

assuring the continuation of these economic values is found in education of the sort mandated in Deut 6.

Deuteronomy makes clear local government and individual citizen responsibility to provide economic assistance to others: "There shall be no needy among you." (Deut 15:4) Only in the localities can the people know which individuals or families are truly needy and take steps to replenish their lives. This democratic principle is buttressed by a wealth of statements in both the entirety of the Hebrew Bible (Old Testament) and the New Testament. A principal sentiment is the idea, "God is no respecter of persons." (2 Chron 19:7; Acts 10:34; Rom 2:11) This means that the people in God's system of government are not to make class distinctions of any type. Rights are not to be diminished or enhanced by the amount of property one has. One author reminds that in Deuteronomy there is no word for "class, caste, noble, or landed gentry."[10]

Education is an important public policy support for democracy in Israel. All citizens are to become just as literate and knowledgeable as members of the priestly class in other nations. Israel committed itself to literacy by adoption of the Phoenician alphabetic script and using it to write its own history. It also published a policy of mass legal literacy and general education for the masses. (Deut 6:6–9) Constitutional law was apparently read before assemblies: "You shall read this law before all Israel . . . Assemble the people . . . so that they may hear . . ."[11] (Deut 31: 11–12; Josh 8:32–35; 2 Kgs 23:1–3; Neh 7:72—8:18) The law was not only to be read/recited every seven years at an assembly of all of the people, but was to be written in stone and exhibited for all to see on Mount Ebal. (Deut 27:1–8)

We have suggested above that perhaps the most important political principle promoted in Deuteronomy and communicated through education is that the people, either directly or through their representatives, are the policy-makers and the magistrates are merely the implementers or administrators of the people's will. The principle of mass ratification of important constitutional provisions was their practice all along the way leading to Canaan. For example, the people ratified the original constitutional law at Sinai, and they ratified the Deuteronomic amendment to the constitution on the plains of Moab before crossing Jordan. As a part of his farewell address, Moses reminded the people of this process in his farewell speech. He recalled that he originally recommended a temporary governmental system in the wilderness after consultation with a proponent of the decentralized Midianite government system, the high priest Jethro. Moses proposed policy

---

10. Berman, *Created Equal*, 19, 61, 80, 181.
11. Ibid., 11, 32–33, 46, 115.

to the tribes, the elders passed the legislation, and Moses implemented it. (Deut 1:9–18) In the wilderness, Moses acted as simple policy implementer whether he agreed or disagreed with the policy. He agreed with the idea to send spies into Canaan and made it happen. He disagreed with the idea it was too early to enter Canaan, but he deferred entry for many years rather than contradict the will of the people.[12] (Deut 1:22–40)

In Deuteronomy, the chief magistrate is made to understand that he is ultimately merely a citizen who has temporarily been put in charge of administering the laws made by the legislature and who can be removed at their pleasure. The legislature is either a representative council/assembly of elders, or an assembly of the whole citizenry of Israel. Deuteronomy requires that each new magistrate write out a complete version of the constitutional law and read it again and again so he cannot miss the law about his limited role. (Deut 17:18–19) We argue in Part III that the earliest form of the constitutional law was the Ten Commandments, and Deuteronomy includes a copy of that in its text as well. (Deut 5) The kings' reading of the law will ensure "that his heart be not be lifted up above his brethren." (Deut 17:20) Use of the word "above" is a clear reference to the notion that rulers tend to think of themselves as having more power than their subjects so that they can stray away from their constituents' wishes. It is made clear here that only the people can increase the functional power of the magistrate, or "nagid." (Deut 17:14–15)

We have touched upon the Biblical war power policy in our section on Moses' leadership in the wilderness. The war power is perhaps the most important duty to be kept out of the hands of the chief magistrate. Deuteronomy picks up on and expands the general outline given in Numbers. The law of Deuteronomy 20 specifies civilian control of the military by means of "officers." The civilian officers serve as recruitment operatives. Military officers are not picked until after the officers administer extensive draft exemptions typical of democratic regimes who wish their war efforts to have broad support and voluntary rather than mandatory participation from the citizenry. Deuteronomy stresses that family and economic development activities like marriage, home building, and vineyard planting continue in spite of, or in counter-balance to, the need for tribal security activities. The exemption for the "fearful and faint-hearted" may not indicate lack of courage, but may simply evince an informed lack of conviction about the urgency of the current military cause. (Deut 20:5–9) Additionally, there is no provision in the law to allow the annexation of friendly territory. That prospect is categorically prohibited, thus clipping the wings of an aspiring

---

12. Ibid., 10–11, 64.

expansionist ruler. (Deut 2:4–5) Also, Israel must follow humane rather than rapacious war measures causing destruction on a long-term basis. There is to be no cutting down of enemy fruit trees in order to use the wood for battering rams or siege-works. (Deut 20:19–20)

An important statement about shared sovereignty between national, regional, and local units of government is made in Deuteronomy as well. Moses recalls that each of the tribal units of government were represented in carrying out the spying operation in Canaan soon after the exit from Egypt. (Deut 1:23) This demonstrated broad support for the operation and a need for the widest possible consensus on the decision to be made after the operation concluded. The first chapter thus provides a theory justifying a grant of considerable power to parental households and clan leaders. Deuteronomy also outlines a power to give national land to private citizens, as Moses does to Caleb, without providing similar authority for land to be taken away from private citizens and nationalized instead. (Deut 1:34–36) In fact, law and tradition state that private land must be returned to its original owners even after it has been legally sold to cover debt.

At the end of the book of Deuteronomy, in a chapter pregnant with the political science of democracy, Moses gives a blessing in the form of a grant of police power to each of the tribal political sub-units of the federation based on the idea that "He (God) loved the people," (Deut 33:3) so much so that he gave them power to determine their own fate locally.[13] These blessings are an affirmation of the intent of the Ten Commandment constitutional law to position virtually all social, economic, political, military and police matters on the local level. When national effort is needed regarding defense matters of interest to the entire confederation, the council of tribal chieftans/governors ("nesiei ha-edah") often functioned in place of or in the absence of the "shofet" or "nagid," the executive department leaders during the early period. The chieftans dealt with items of national concern like negotiating a treaty with the Gibeonites or taking on special assignments of utmost concern to the entire polity.[14] (Josh 18:1–10; Num 13:3–15)

Deuteronomy makes clear that democratic organization and the practice of local self-determination are not to be diluted with the passage of time. The citizens of succeeding generations are not to "add unto the word which I command you, neither shall ye diminish aught from it . . ." (Deut 4:2) The chief magistrate is to read the original constitutional law "all the days of his life," and so with each succeeding ruler so that the magistrates

---

13. See our section on the Fifth Commandment regarding the politics of the blessing of the tribes.

14. Elazar, *Jewish Polity*, 66.

and the people "keep all the words of his law and these statutes, to do them . . ." (Deut 17:19) The constitutional law is to be read to new generations of citizens every seven years, "that their children, which have not known any thing, may hear, and learn to fear . . . as long as ye live in the land . . ." It is clear that the original construction of the law is to last as long as their residency lasts. The implication is that lack of respect of the constitution will be the reason for losing the land. (Deut 31:10–13)

At the conclusion of Moses' grand speech, all of the citizenry, including current and aspiring elders and priests, pledge allegiance to the re-established new constitution, together now with its various policies implementing the constitution for the settlement period. (Deut 29:12, 14; 31:12) The book of Deuteronomy begins with the story of Moses and after the farewell speech it also ends with an eye cast on the great republican as well. In a poignant physical demonstration of selfless citizenship, the great democratic leader not only withdraws from office, but dies and is buried in a place no person knows. This assures that no monument or memorial can be located at the site to encourage hero worship and perhaps to facilitate the raising up of his offspring or his party's supporters as kings. (Deut 34:5–6) Leaders are not to be objects of continual worship by the citizenry, but temporary servants of the policy wishes of the people. Samuel, perhaps the last of the popularly elected leaders to uphold this tradition, said "I have hearkened unto your voice in all that ye said unto me . . ." (1 Sam 12:1) Sometime later, when the court's old-timer advisers speak to Solomon's son Rehoboam about soft-shoeing his policy initiatives, they recall Samuel's practice as leader: "If thou wilt be a servant unto this people this day . . . then they will be thy servants forever." But Rehoboam is drunken with power, rejects traditional political wisdom, and demands that the people serve his interests instead. (1 Kgs 12:7)

By retiring as he does, Moses falls on the sword of Meribah, the place where there was a great rupture between he and the people. In the Biblical view, the prophet Moses was ultimately exiled into the mountains into early retirement because he did not listen to the voice of the people at Meribah and had lost the trust of the elders. In spite of Meribah, he had been needed to finish his job during the remainder of the migratory period. It was understood, however, that at the point of crossing Jordan his term would end. Israel proceeded on to settle the land admirably under Joshua, but ultimately and quite quickly after Joshua various of the tribes became absorbed with local Canaanite socio-political life and strayed from constitutional values. One such tribe, Benjamin, became a virtual enemy of the confederacy of Israel.

7

Judges Follow Precedents Set in the Wilderness

AFTER MOSES DELIVERED THE farewell address we now have today encapsulated in Deuteronomy, Joshua and the children of Israel crossed into Canaan, divided the land among the tribes, engaged those regimes not hospitable to republicanism and to their historical claim to the land, and finally settled down to local home rule. After Joshua died, however, there was apparently no charismatic (that is, highly ethical, popular, and God-spirited) teacher/leader in Israel until perhaps the time of Samuel, with the exception of the prophetess Deborah. Nevertheless, democratic activity in the period of wandering in the wilderness seems to have effectively set a pattern for confederate Israel's political behavior in Canaan well after Joshua. One author begs the question we intend to answer in this chapter. He writes, "The centuries immediately after Moses' death offer us an opportunity to observe what happened to Mosaic political ideas..."[1]

For example, it is apparent that the assembly of confederate voters, or "mo'ed," which had taken direct part in government at Sinai and at Moab before the Jordan crossing, was in operation soon after entry into Canaan, when Joshua recited the law to them at Mount Ebal. (Josh 8:35) Much later, the assembly, in fact, exercised its constitutional duty to commit the tribes to conflict in the matter of the war with Benjamin, thus following the pattern set with respect both to the "spy" story and the engagement against Amalek in the wilderness. (Judg 20) The mo'ed also exercised the constitutional power to set peace terms with Benjamin, since one passage states, "The whole congregation sent word to the children of Benjamin . . . and announced peace to them."[2] (Judge 21:10–13)

1. Wildavsky, *Moses*, 251.
2. Stockwell, *History of Democracy*, 73.

Overall, judges do not, as one observer writes, "seek, inherit, or transfer leadership." Other than with Abimelech, there is an orderly, constitutional, electoral process in evidence. However, a certain degree of constitutional decline started soon after Joshua's death. (Judg 2:11–15) Otherwise admirable judges came to be associated with wrinkles in the fabric of limited government in Israel. Gideon, recall, refused hereditary rule, thus mimicking Moses' political ethics, but went on to flirt with a stronger national government by fashioning an ephod idol and taking on some priestly functions in addition to secular duties. (Judg 8:22–27)

Demonstrably less ethical judges, like Sampson, who slept with Philistine prostitutes, and Abimelech, who flatly usurped national power without popular consent, portended even greater corruption and political profligacy to come after the period of judges. There is a poignant paen to the leadership example of Moses given in the parable of Jotham, who, like Abimelech, was one of Gideon's sons. (Judg 9:7–15) Jotham reminded the people that Moses did not seek out leadership power, but had to be convinced to take it on. Abimelech, on the other hand, was virtually overwhelmed by the desire to rule, so much so he imposed his own rule on the people. The parable makes clear that ethically better qualified leaders often refuse a job in government because they worry about the corruptive power of the position. The people themselves can govern themselves without a ruler unless there is a pressing need for a military commander in chief. Wildavsky reminds, "The righteous ruler is known by his reluctance to serve in peacetime."[3]

The Mosaic political idea of sparse, term-limited, pan-tribal leadership carried sway during the period of judges. Occasional "national" leaders during the period of judges usually led their own tribes and only a few others. Deborah had only six of the twelve tribes in her coalition. Gideon had three or four with him. The judge was usually not appointed to handle emergency duty for the confederation upon the onset of provocations, but "only after the people have suffered a period of abuse."[4] There was clearly no rush to national leadership even in times of great vexation. For example, Israel suffered seven years at the hands of Midian before Gideon took the reins of power. (Judg 6:1) After Ehud there is no mention of a new judge for another eighty years. (Judg 3:30)

But even while the elders and judges generally honored the system of limited government, corruption nevertheless seems to have crept into their ranks. Jephthah, for example, gathered "worthless men," likely mercenaries rather than patriotic citizens, to fight for him. Jephthah agreed to lead in

---

3. Wildavsky, *Moses*, 254; see also Hazony, *Hebrew Scripture*, 146–47.
4. Wildavsky, *Moses*, 253–54.

wartime, but would not do so without substantial perks for himself. He bargained for and received the power to be permanent tribal "head" in Gilead. This portended permanent national leadership, and probably reflected an anomalous situation even at the tribal level, where leadership likely rotated regularly to prevent corruption. Finally, Jephthah sacrificed his daughter as a burnt offering in the manner of the Canaanites to give thanks to God, forgetting the ethical advance achieved by the ancestor Abraham, who learned that God desired a sacrifice of democratic political effort, not human flesh.[5] (Judg 10–12)

Some believe the Bible tries to make the point that the decline of unity, civic virtue, and moral strength during the time of Judges is evidence of the inadequacy of a confederate government which kept substantial sovereignty on the tribal and local levels, and that allowed every man to judge for himself. (Judg 2:16–19, 21:25) In effect, a weak national government was the problem, not the solution. It seems demonstrably true there eventually was real degradation of moral and ethical behavior and much political in-fighting among the tribes well before the time of the ethical leader Samuel. For example, Manasseh and Gad opposed each other, and Gad would not even give bread to Gideon's troops. (Judge 6:15) Also, the civil war between the sexually restrained northern tribes and the sexually debauched southern tribe of Benjamin has parallels with the destruction of Sodom in the time of the ancestors. Both Sodom and Benjamin reverted to a level of sexual promiscuity beyond common acceptability.

However, the point of view of the authors of the Bible is not that centralization of government will help improve moral fiber and political stability. It is rather that there was a lack of ethical, charismatic, God-spirited leaders available to teach the people like a loving father or mother instructs a child in how to govern itself. When the politically ethical and strict constructionist judges like Joshua, Deborah, and Samuel leave the scene, the political slide gains momentum toward a far-too-liberal construction of the Ten Commandment constitution. The tribes turn to a semblance of localized "anarchy" because they do not practice the communitarian ethics portion of the local sovereignty law their immediate ancestors committed to. Before he is gone, however, Samuel is forced to negotiate the enactment of either a constitutional amendment or specific statutes authorizing a permanent national executive magistrate, called a "king." Samuel put the new policy into a book of law. (1 Sam 10:25) Use of the word "king" is a misnomer in one sense because leadership did not become hereditary in the

---

5. For a helpful summary of the activities of Jephthah, see Hazony, *Hebrew Scripture*, 146; also, Wildavsky, *Moses*, 255.

south for several generations, and not in the north for a much longer time. The people's revised constitutional law presumably continued the historical antipathy to a luxurious court laden with taxes, government employees, and a large standing army.[6] (1 Sam 8:10–18) The new office was a kingship only in the sense of constituting a regularized and ongoing national executive position in government, rather than an occasional term of emergency power.

---

6. Hazony judges that Samuel's description of expanded executive power does not describe something that is "especially evil," but just less desirable than present limited government. Hazony, *Hebrew Scripture*, 145.

8

People and Elders in Government

IN THE PREVIOUS CHAPTERS, we have touched upon the politics of Genesis, the events of the Exodus and government formation at Sinai, the patterns of democratic leadership evident in the book of Numbers, the developing system of separation of powers in Deuteronomy, and confederation activities and politics in Judges. In this section we will dissect the political institutions of Israel in early settlement mode evidenced in the books of Joshua, Judges, and Samuel, with a glance forward to the book of Kings. This will include some attention to the Israelite concept of sovereignty of the people.

Summing up the era of Judges, one Biblical author gave a heavily libertarian assessment with the statement, "Every man did what was right in his own eyes." (Judg 17:6) The citizenry at that time were so bound up in local affairs that even as late as the time of Saul, many people seemed not even to be aware who the current leader of the confederacy was. He was only really noticeable, apparently, to the older population (the elder leaders of all the clans and tribes) (1 Sam 3:20), and perhaps only to those few youth who participated in clan and tribe governance or in military activity.

Our story about local government by assemblies and elders begins with a young Saul trying to carry out the difficult task given to him by his father of finding some lost "asses." (1 Sam 9:3) Saul's servant told him there was a seer, or "man of God" ("ro'eh") in the vicinity of their present search. (1 Sam 9:6) The seer was in fact the current limited-power, national prophet leader of the last days of Judges. (1 Sam 3:1) He was essentially a man of the law—the one who typically "judged" cross-tribal cases and headed the political party devoted to faithful continuance of the ten articles of confederation. (1 Sam 7:15) Saul was ready to return home empty-handed when his servant told him, "There is in this city a man of God, and he is an honorable man; all that he saith cometh surely to pass." (1 Sam 9:6) Here is the very definition of a good government employee ... one who can be trusted to do as he says he will do in conducting the people's business. Such a responsible government administrator apparently either knew about lost or stolen animals or knew whom to consult. The seer was old and had been judging in Israel most of his adult life, and while Saul did not know of him (Samuel was not regularly basking in the sun of political glory apparently), the older servant of the household did know of him.[1]

This entire story looms large in explaining the pattern of limited national government in early Israel. The "conquest" of Canaan required a certain level of unified attention from the tribes, at least in the beginning. During the time of the conquest and early settlement, there was some foreign relations work to be done that required the assent of all the people. For example, Israel made friendship treaties with cities having governments with an oligarchic or democratic flavor similar to theirs, like Gibeon and Shechem. They fought against those with strong monarchies like Heshbon, Taanach, and Jerusalem, where the local kings did not favor free-thinking Israelite masses settling near them and interacting economically and socially with their own cowed citizenries. Aside from minimal foreign relations work, public governmental activity even at the tribal and clan levels was minimal. Families and clans quickly got down to the business of governing themselves on the lands they were working without interference from chiefs, judges, or even more localized elders.

Each family was almost a nation unto itself in such a frontier environment. The real political authorities in Israel were the family, or house of the father ("bet ab"), the clan ("mispaha"), and rarely, the tribe ("sebet," or "matteh").[2] (Josh 7:14–18) The father, and the parents together, had authority to deal with civil and criminal matters within the extended family household, which encompassed household servants and field workers as well as children. The clan was active mainly in matters like Levirate marriage, involving remarriage within the husband's family for young widows when there was not a male descendant. (Gen 3:8, Deut 25:5–10; Ruth 1–4) They also handled serious criminal matters like blood revenge (2 Sam 14:7), and policing the citizen obligation to correct economic difficulties, like the obligation to save a relative from impoverishment. (Jer 32:6, Ruth 4; Lev 25:25, 47) Otherwise, it could be said "The development of authority

---

1. This becomes not a story about animals, but about Samuel finding a fit citizen for expanded national executive responsibility during the time of the Philistine crisis.

2. Bright, *History*, 478.

outside the household is remarkably weak," or, in other words, "The permanent political institutions end at the local or at most at the tribal level."[3]

However, we do find various mentions of usually temporary dignitaries called prince(s) ("nasi," "nesiim"). We also find heads, known as rulers or nobles, called "ro's" or "rashei," who lead larger groupings than families.[4] (Exod 6:14; Num 36:1; Judg 11:9, 11; see also the genealogies in 1 Chron 5, 7, 8, 19, 23) There are also local leaders during crisis called captain, or "qasin."[5] (Judg 11: 6, 11; Num 1:16; Josh 9:15, 18–19) Princes, heads and captains may have functioned as presiding elders over a "a clan or two."[6] There was little or no governorship at the tribal level, much like African, Etruscan, Hittite, Greek, Mesopotamian and Midianite confederate tribal societies.[7]

Tribe-wide action seems only to have taken place in the larger tribes of Ephraim, Benjamin and Judah. (Judg 8:1; 15:10) One historian of the period explains, "The tribe is a political coalition of the clans of a region . . . clans could sometimes count themselves as being in one tribe and sometimes as being in another." (1 Chron 7:37; see also 1 Sam 9:4) Tribes could divide (e.g., east and west Manasseh) or merge (Simeon into Judah). Tribes thus were not so much ethnic groupings as political units and even served as regional geographic location names, reflecting clear and marked geographical dividing lines, like Ephraim, Benjamin, Judah, and Napthali.[8]

The tribal chief, called "nasi," may have represented the tribe at the annual covenant renewal meetings, which served as the glue that held the tribes and clans somewhat together. (Exod 22:28) Membership in the overall league fluctuated.[9] The larger pan-tribal confederate compact enacted upon entry into Canaan came into play only in serious crises, such as the time of the Philistine threat.[10] These kind of intergovernmental arrangements may not have been much different than the tribal confederation compacts of the nearby Aramean, Ishmaelite, Edomite, Keturah, and Horite peoples.[11] In fact, the nature of the constitutional compact itself, the Ten Commandments, required that the social, economic, political, and police

---

3. Albertz, *Israelite Religion*, 72–74.
4. Elazar, *Jewish Polity*, 69.
5. Albertz, *Israelite Religion*, 74.
6. Ibid.
7. Gottwald, *Politics*, 38; Bright, *History*, 162, 166.
8. Albertz, *Israelite Religion*, 73.
9. Bright, *History*, 166.
10. Albertz, *Israelite Religion*, 74.
11. Bright, *History*, 167.

business of the nation's people be conducted almost exclusively at the local level, as we will see in part III.

In summary, Bright reminds, "The tribal system was . . . exceedingly loose. Early Israel had none of the apparatus of state: neither central government, nor capital city, nor administrative machinery, nor bureaucracy." Also, "The league had its focal point at the shrine which housed the Ark of the Covenant, at least by the end of the period located at Shiloh. There the tribesmen would gather on stated occasions to seek the presence of Yahweh and renew their allegiance to him, and also to adjust matters of controversy and mutual interest among the tribes. Each tribe was presumably represented by its head, very probably the chief magistrate ("nasi"), who by virtue of this position, stood under especial divine protection."[12] (Exod 22:28; Exod 34:31)

Multi-tribe or confederation-wide judges and assemblies functioned only occasionally until later in the period of Judges. Those "minor" judges who did not perform during times of military crisis, may have administered domestic law and settled controversies between tribes. In the meanwhile, tribes acted like independent nations and squabbled frequently. (Judg 8:1–3; 12:1–7; 19) There was no standing army in the tribe, let alone the tribal confederacy. When tribes were threatened, they had to "call out the clans."[13] When the entire confederacy, or a large chunk of it, was threatened, the people of the affected area and their elders and other leaders decided who would serve as military judge.[14] (Judg 8:22; 1:18) The authority of the confederate judge "was neither absolute, nor permanent, nor in any case hereditary."[15] This is the overall picture of Israel's heavily decentralized governmental system, which lasted for nearly 300 years after settlement in Canaan.

The reason government was so decentralized in Israel was that the people themselves retained the ultimate power, or sovereignty, in the land of Israel. At Sinai, the people ("am") organized themselves into a mass political organization called the congregation ("edah"). Gordis reminds, "It seems clear that 'edah' is the authentic term for the 'public assembly' in ancient Israel."[16] (Num 15:33)

---

12. Bright, *History*, 166; Elazar, *Jewish Polity*, 69.
13. Bright, *History*, 167.
14. Weinfeld, *Kinship and Consent*, 152.
15. Bright, *History*, 167.
16. Wolf, "Traces of Primitive Democracy," 108; Gordis, "Primitive Democracy," 51.

Non-democratic nations had organizational compacts where a certain class, or a certain ruling family, made a compact with God for their group to govern exclusively, with some leftover power for other dependent groups. But in Israel at Sinai, God made a compact with the entire migrating community, each one of them entering into an agreement to play a part in governing according to the constitutional law. (Exod 19:8) The text even goes so far to say that children participated in the decision-making with the men and women.

The people at Sinai wanted maximum power in their own hands locally and minimum power in the hands of regional and national government. On the local level they could, and did, handle everything necessary for the good and free life—those social, political, economic, educational, and even military activities usually summarized by the term police power. This they did within their own extended family groupings. There were a variety of occasions for assembling together with other families, however. Importantly, as we mentioned above, they assembled as a whole people, the "edah," for purposes of constitution-making and amending, and from time to time for national elections and for confidence votes challenging the term of office of the existing judge. Sub-groups of the whole citizenry functioned in behalf of the whole people. One sub-group known as land-owning adult "men" made basic legislative policy including war policy. Groups of elected clan and tribal officers assembled for special tribal tasks and decisions. Finally, representative bodies of "elders" assembled for more day-to-day government activities on the local level.[17]

In a given area, the citizenry as a whole—"the people," or "ha am"—formed the assembly or congregation, known either as "edah" or "moedh." It is instructive to note that the term "congregation" was understood as a political, not a religious term.[18] The goal of the people/"edah" was to live as a community of equals ("kahal") under the rule of law ("hukah," or "hok"). The law would apply to every citizen ("ezrah"), and every citizen would be responsible to his neighbor ("rea") by a mutual obligation of respect, kindness, and assistance ("hesed").[19] The national "edah" was most often an ad hoc, national political body comprised of elders (representatives), or "men" (the whole adult male citizenry) representing tribes across the entire confederation. One author asserts that the term "congregation" defined "the ultimate source of political authority."[20] As we have said, smaller groupings

---

17. Elazar, *People and Polity*, 29.
18. Wolf, "Traces of Primitive Democracy, " 105.
19. Elazar, *Jewish Polity*, 7.
20. Wolf, "Traces of Primitive Democracy," 105.

of the citizenry existed and functioned to represent the whole people of an area. These were called "men of Israel," (Josh 24:1, 2, 19, 21), "men of a city" ("anse hair"), or "men of a region" ("anse gilad"). They were the free adult males who were economically independent and arms bearing. Such assemblies decided whether to call an army for defense (Judg 11:1; Josh 22:12; Judg 20:1-2, 9), send military support for others (1 Sam 11:10), accept strangers into the community (Judg. 19:22), punish tribes not carrying out the decisions of the "edah" (Judg 21:1, 18), punish elements of the people who did not participate in the war of the "edah" (Judg 21:10), call for peace (Judg 21:13), and make treaties with foreigners. (Josh 9:18–21)[21]

The basis of the power of the assembly of all the people was the land they held in private, inheritable possession forever. As long as the land was theirs, political power was theirs as well. The full citizens who owned land also served in the militia. A particularly distinguished fighting individual among their group was called "a mighty man of valor/wealth/power" or "gibbor hayil." (Judg 6:12, 11:1; 1 Sam 9:1; Ruth 2:1) These "legally free, economically independent and therefore arms-bearing men" had responsibility to vote on policy in the popular assembly and to serve in the militia.[22] Proposals such as the policy to treat aliens and citizens equally, proposed treaties, and division of spoils between warriors and the rest of the people, were made by the kahal/assembly. (Numb 27:16, 15:15; 31:27; Josh 9:15)

The edah/citizenry in the earlier time of Moses was somewhat altered, since it was an emergency government, but it still set the pattern for later times. Moses' "edah" was governed at the national level by the legislative/judicial council of seventy "elders," a term equivalent to "senator" in democratic Rome, and "geron" in democratic Greece.[23] The administrator of the policy set by the seventy elders was Moses, God's prime minister ("eved adonai"), who was responsible to both the legislative/judicial branch and the people as a whole. When they "murmured," (expressed their will), he listened and did what they directed.

The early government under Moses was, then a bi-partite form of government on the national level. It consisted of presiding elder/commander in chief (along with the somewhat subservient high priest and the priest's corp of employees) along with the seventy-person legislative/judicial body). Later, this developed into a tri-partite form of government on the national level: the king (together with the priestly corps of government officials), the

---

21. Weinfeld, *Kinship and Consent*, 152.
22. Albertz, *Religion of Israel*, 73-74.
23. "Elder," 578.

national legislative body/Sanhedrin, and the independent national judiciary of judges/elders described in Deuteronomy.

The "gate" of the city was the gathering place of both local elder councils of government, and the local assembly of the people. (Deut 22:15; Ps 69:12; Prov 24:7; Amos 5:10) This seems to have continued the pattern set by Moses and Joshua when all the people in migration met at the "tent" where secular matters like migration policy, rights of inheritance, the administration of justice such as capital murder, and distribution of land were dealt with. (Exod 18:21–25; Lev 4:13–14; Num 8:9, 11:16, 19:4, 27:1–6, 35:24–25; Josh 19:51) Wolf suggests, "The assembly had almost unlimited functions, both in the early days and in later times when it was perforce representative . . . Its functions were judicial, legislative, and executive . . . It was judicial in hearing the pleas concerning inheritance, for revenge against rape, and for refuge to a slayer. It was legislative in the decision to wage war or to make peace. It was executive in the punishment of murders, wild tribes, and unacceptable or irresponsible leaders or rebels."[24]

The assembly, or mass legislative body, was still an important factor well into the time of "kings." The assembly consented to important events in the history of the weak monarchy instituted in the time of David and even in the return of exiles to Palestine after their exile in Babylon. The assembly consented to the restoration of the Davidic dynasty in the person of Jehoash after the assassination of Ahtaliah. (2 Chron 2:33) It gave its approval to the constitutional reformation of Hezekiah. (2 Chron 29:28; 30:2) It ratified the post-exile policy decision to separate from foreign wives and to restore fields and vineyards taken on pledge. (Neh 5:13; Ezek 10:12, 14) Gordis judges, "The collective assembly of ancient Israel was never formally abolished. New conditions led to the diminution of its functions so that ultimately it was convened only in hours of critical importance."[25]

A critical detail which needs further study is whether the people registered consent for the large decisions of the confederate government by tribal voting or by individual voting. There is much to recommend the idea that the tribe was the sovereign decision-making unit in the confederacy rather than the aggregated vote of the whole people. On the confederate level, the tribes likely registered essentially one vote per tribe. But the tribe looked to the clans, families, and individual citizens for their votes first. It seems clear, for example, that voting took place in the tribe to decide whether to accept or reject a proposed confederate initiative like defense of one or two tribes against outside threats. Tribes could not be compelled, but rather could

---

24. Wolf, "Traces of Primitive Democracy," 108.
25. Gordis, "Primitive Democracy," 56–57.

nullify or refuse to participate in actions that neighboring tribes took up in advancement of the confederation's interests.

The whole congregation heard serious inter-tribal issues like the threat to the constitution of the confederacy posed by the tribe of Benjamin. Since the issue posed the question of war, and the war power resided in the whole people, a national democratic plebiscite was called. (Judg. 20:7–11) In such situations, citizens may have physically lined up behind spokespersons of one side of the issue or another as in other ancient assemblies. Alternatively some sort of standing up may have constituted the act of individual voting as suggested by the statement "All the people arose as one man." (Judg 20:8) At any rate, a certain level of positive reaction to a proposal constituted acclamation, or sufficient motivation to proceed. Those families, clans, or tribes who opposed the measure were apparently then free to nullify their own participation in the policy decision, as when several tribes declined to participate in Deborah's campaign against Sisera. (Judg 5:14–18) Clans and tribes could not be compelled to respond to crises, but certainly had moral encouragement to do so.[26]

In fact, the legislature of the whole could trump the policy proposals of the presiding elder. For example, Joshua and Caleb proposed a policy of direct entry to Canaan from the south, "and all the children of Israel murmured against Moses and against Aaron," the two who had engineered the policy position. The level of indignation was such that many wanted to stone Joshua and Caleb. (Num. 14:10) This is as much to say that Joshua and Caleb came close to treason against the constitution. The term "murmuring" thus essentially described a negative vote on the proposal of the presiding elder. Moses complained that the people turned down his legislative proposals, ie. "murmured," ten times in the wilderness. His reputation as one who had been inspired of God was not enough to trump the will of the people. The people communed with God at Sinai as well and thus had substantial spiritual credentials too. As late as Josiah, the king in Judah "could not make a [international] covenant binding upon his country" without the consent of the people. He could also not pass a constitutional reform without the people who "stood" in support of it. (2 Kgs 23:1–3)

Presiding judges like Samuel could be caught up in impeachment proceedings requiring them to give account of their stewardship as presiding elder of the land. One such proceeding was convened to decide whether the corruption of Samuel's sons, apparently serving as his assistants (as sons of early American presidents did), had actually reached to him. This would be much like the legislature determining whether cabinet-level bureaucratic

---

26. Wolf, "Traces of Primitive Democracy," 102; Vaux, *Ancient Israel*, 167.

corruption in U.S. Grant's administration or Richard Nixon's administration had reached to the president himself. Samuel asked the impeachment proceeding to answer "Whom have I defrauded, whom have I oppressed?"[27] (1 Sam 12:1–5)

Deuteronomy suggests that the individual citizen had a responsibility to participate in such assemblies and contribute to the decision-making, as the guilt-laden, finger-pointing term "you" makes clear (for example, "you shall not wrest judgment").[28] (Deuteronomy 16:18–19) There was to be no political innocence in Israel and no shirking of citizenship responsibility to vote. Strictly local matters of government, as dealt with by the town assembly (ha'ir) are the subject of a number of passages in the Bible corpus. (Deut 21:1–9; Ruth 3)

People undertook vows or acts of citizenship in order to officially be a part of the "edah." Initially, the "edah"/citizenry took political oaths requiring them to distance themselves from the ways of slavish political royalists like the Egyptian and Canaanite people. (Lev 18) They committed to not intermarry with distant cousins whose tribal systems had already gone over to heavier centralized government, like the Ammonites and Moabites. (Deut 23:14) They committed to celebrate their citizenship by participating in the annual national "passover" political holiday. (Exod 12:43–45) They committed to undergo a surgical procedure (circumcision) to show not only their commitment to membership in the community and curbing the kind of excessive sexual appetite demonstrated by Canaanites, but likely their public commitment to prevent the spread of disease as well. (Josh 5:2–9)

We have said it was not possible or desirable for the assembly of all the people in an area to handle all government matters of the area. Local matters of government were delegated from the beginning to local bodies of citizens known as elders. Elders decided matters in groups consisting of individual family estates, farm neighborhoods or small villages of ten or so families, and larger clans of several villages/towns. In time, when the tribes built small walled cities, these bodies of citizen elders met in the "gates" of the city.

The day-to-day government of early Israel at the local level, where virtually all of government happened, was done by elders. An individual elder ("zaken") was head of an individual family.[29] During the time of Moses, elders functioned in a temporary hierarchical system of judges to govern groups of ten, fifty, one hundred, and 1,000. (Exod 3:16–18, 18:19–25; Deut

27. Wolf, "Traces of Primitive Democracy," 102, 104.
28. Berman, *Created Equal*, 69.
29. Vaux, *Ancient Israel*, 8.

1:15) Clan and tribal groupings of elders were called "zakenim." In early times, these fathers representing local groupings of the clan or tribe handled administration of the domestic law and also settled conflicts among the clans on an ad hoc basis. Elders served as "chiefs of the fathers," and as "heads of the children (of Israel)."[30] There were elders of families or clans in a particular small area (1 Sam 11:13), elders of a region like Gilead (Judg 11:5), and elders of a tribe. (1 Sam 30:26) The "ir," or ha'ir, was the township or city. It had an assembly of elders called the "sha'ar" or "ziknai ha'ir."[31]

Elder is a functional term for a representative of the people. Such an elder could inherit the title, be appointed to the title, or be elected to the title. Individual elders had executive, legislative, and judicial powers, much as an assembly of elders had. The assembly convened only for especially important decisions. On the local/town level elders had primarily social/domestic, criminal justice, and civil law powers. These included remarriage of a widow (Deut 25:9; Ruth 4:2), dealing with a rebellious son (Deut 21:19), delivering the killer into the hands of the victim's family for blood vengeance (Deut 19:12), placating the effects of murder by an unknown culprit in the vicinity (Deut 21:3, 6), and defamation of a virgin's reputation.[32] (Deut 22:15)

Elders, together with priests, arranged the legal events of the seven year release of debts required by the law.[33] They continued to function in aspects of local administration of the law during the period of monarchy as well.[34] Elders functioning in governmental councils acted as civilian officers of government, apparently playing little direct role in institutional military activities. They apparently deferred to the presiding elder "judge" in civil matters affecting larger groupings of the people.[35]

There were an abundance of early constitutional issues requiring elders to put their heads together and make decisions on. As we mentioned in the chapter on wilderness government, the elders had to deal with issues of sharing of national power/impeachment in the Miriam and Aaron versus Moses affair, the attempt by Korah, Dathan and Abiram to overthrow the constitution by usurping power and enacting a new radical democratic regime, the authorization of legitimate political parties in the matter of Eldad and Medad who were independently organizing some of the people, and the

30. Walzer, *In God's Shadow*, 185–98.
31. Elazar, *People and Polity*, 26.
32. Encyclopedia Judaica, "Elder," 578; Albertz, *Israelite Religion*, 74; Walzer, *In God's Shadow*, 189.
33. Berman, *Created Equal*, 80.
34. Ibid., 77.
35. Walzer, *In God's Shadow*, 189; Berman, *Created Equal*, 77, 80.

issue of the degree of regional autonomy that could be granted the two and a half tribes settling east of Jordan.

As we mentioned above, the regime under Moses also had to deal with establishing national holidays (Exod 12:43–45), requirements for citizenship such as circumcision, laws against intermarriage outside the polity, establishing and further refining a national separation of powers, including establishing the national legislature (Num 11;16–18) and the judiciary system (Exod 18:13–27), setting up a system of cities of refuge (Deut 19, Josh 20), setting up mechanisms for obtaining leadership and succession in leadership (Num 27:18; Exod 29:7), handling jurisdictional maters (Deut 16:18), and setting up mechanisms of national law enforcement. (Deut 17:8–13)

In time, there were constitutional issues and crises relating to appeals by judges for pan-tribal responses to external threats (Judg 3–7), the offer of kingship to Gideon (Judg 8), dealing with usurpers such as Abimelech (Judg 9) and later the popular desire for a king (1 Sam 9–10), getting through Samson's sexual relationships with Philistines and dabbling with foreign marriage (Judg 14–16), allocation of land for unsatisfied tribes such as Dan (Judg 18), and issues surrounding civil war between the tribes, including preservation of the twelve-tribe system. (Judg 19–21; Judg 20:16) In fact, the rule of Judges is basically a history of constitutional issues decided by Israelite elders over a 250 year period.

As Israel got further along in its history, the press of the elders' work extended to a variety of other matters, often having their source or precedent in wilderness times. On the national level elders/legislators, after listening to the people, nominated and/or selected the national executive magistrate[36] (1 Sam 8:4; 2 Sam 17:1–4; Judg 11:5–11), proclaimed war (Josh 8:10; 2 Sam 17:4–15; cf. 1 Kgs 20:7), represented the settlement to outsiders, and conducted international negotiations and conclude agreements. (Exod 3:16, 18; 4:29; Num 16:25; 1 Sam 11:10, 16:4; 2 Sam 3:17, 5:3) They also performed public ritual ceremonies (Exod 12:21; 18:12; Lev 9:1; 1 Sam 4:3; 1 Kgs 1:1,3; 1 Chr 16:25) and acted in times of national crisis.[37] (Exod 17:5–6; Josh 7:6; 1 Sam 4:3) Elders legislated on the national level to deal with Syria's tribute demand of King Ahab in the north. (1 Kgs 20:8) The elder assemblies on the

---

36. This is like the parliamentary system of government in the British commonwealth where the national leader is chosen by parliament, and like Madison's Virginia Plan for selection of the American president by Congress, which was modified into the electoral college approach.

37. Encyclopedia Judaica, "Elder," 579.

national level thus carried forward the democratic separation of functions between legislative and executive into the period of monarchy.[38]

Elders worked together with the people as a whole and its princes as far as prosecuting crimes against the state like political idolatry. Idolatry, a capital offense, consisted in promoting a government system other than the democratic/consensual system established at Sinai and at Shechem. Such a person essentially proposed, "Let us go after other gods." (Deut 13: 2–29; 17:2–7; 18:20–22; 25:1–3; Josh 24) Thus it is significant that elders were on display in the delegation to Samuel requesting a stronger executive department of government. Apparently sufficient numbers of elders no longer had a problem with creeping monarchy, or taking just a little peek at "other gods." Isaiah, for example, wrote, "The Lord will enter into judgment with the ancients of his people, and the princes thereof [elders in the king's cabinet] . . . the spoil of the poor is in your house."[39] The seventy national elders also participated in the trial of Jeremiah, adding to their resumes as backsliding representatives of the people. Indeed, seventy of them (possibly the entire national assembly) were judged to have been engaged in just such political syncretism in Solomon's temple. (Ezekiel 8:11). In time, conscientious elders apparently were shunted aside in favor of appointed court "prophets" who usurped their functions. For example, elders were no where in sight at the time of Hezekiah's rejection of the Assyrian demand for surrender and Zedekiah's rebellion against Babylonian overlordship. Only close political advisers were consulted.[40]

Overall, in the early days at least, elders served in most ways like elected representatives of the people in republican systems of government. They were law-makers. Legislative duties had to be in the hands of the most highly representative branch of government so as to ensure the widest possible diversity of views and ensure that such powers would not default into the hands of individual, power-hungry rulers. The term "elders" could also refer to the male citizenry in general or a representative grouping of the adult male citizenry sitting in assembly. (Deut 33:5) It seems likely that women could also be elders, since Deborah served as chief elder/judge of all Israel.[41] Elders also could function as assistants, like cabinet members, to presiding elders/judges like Moses. (Exod 18:13; Num 11:16) These

---

38. Wolf, "Traces of Primitive Democracy," 98–108; Gordis, "Primitive Democracy," 45–60; Gottwald, *Politics*, 36; Albertz, *Israelite Religion*, 73; Berman, *Created Equal*, 69; Walzer, *In God's Shadow*, 191–92.

39. Walzer, *In God's Shadow*, 193.

40. Ibid., 193–94.

41. Wolf, "Traces of Primitive Democracy," 100.

presiding officers could also be called "princes," but not in the sense of heirs to a hereditary throne. They might also be called ministers, or "sar, sarim."[42]

How did elders get their positions? Elders at times inherited their functions from their fathers, as Isaac and Jacob did, but could also serve as appointed officials (Deut 16:19), earning their positions through special study and experience. For example, they earned their reputations by settling disputes and interpreting the law if it could not be settled in other ways.[43] (Deut 19:17–18; 25:1–3; 17:8) Judges as well as later "kings" had to stand for election. There are a variety of English (Kings James version) terms used to translate Hebrew vocabulary related to election. During judges, when a situation presented that required a multi-tribal leader, the people would "cry unto the Lord for a deliver." This is a way of saying they sought out a war lord by an electoral process. One source outlining the history of elders in Israel states, "This very 'cry' is not merely a religious lament of repentance but an official prayer (request) of the body politic. The assembly was seeking leaders to be over them." For example, they said to Gideon, "Rule over us," seeking out and asking him, like early Americans sought out and asked the retired George Washington to stand for election. An assembly of elders also went political head-hunting and carried on negotiations with Jephthah to draft him into political leadership. (Judg 18:18, 11:5) Jephthah wanted to avoid charge of usurpation and demanded election even in the current case of a pressing crisis, thus demonstrating some sensitivity to the constitutional law.[44] An assembly of elders also negotiated with Gideon. The final presentation of Saul was to the whole people, and not just to representative elders. (1 Sam 10:17–25)

David was elected first by the "men of Judah" in the south, and next by a gathering of the men of the north at Hebron. (2 Sam 2:4, 7; 5:1–3) David was not sired for kingship, but "adopted" as king by the citizenry to serve their purposes.[45] (Ps 2) When Rehoboam stood for election before the people of the north at Shechem, they rejected him. He did not listen to their concerns about taxation: "All Israel saw that the king hearkened not unto them . . . [they said] what portion have we in [the house of] David?" They then elected Jeroboam instead, and seceded from the union of tribal states: "All Israel . . . made him [Jeroboam] king over all Israel." Wolf notes that "official investiture of a king" was by consent of "the people's assembly."

---

42. Elazar, *Jewish Polity*, 69.
43. Encyclopedia Judaica, "Elder," 578.
44. Gordis, "Primitive Democracy," 9.
45. For the use of "adoption" as a term of election, see Halpern, "Kingship and Monarchy," 415.

(1 Kgs 12:20) Further, "Inheritance of the crown in Israel was seldom by right or by blood but by acclamation of the congregation."[46]

Various terms are used in the Bible to describe the electoral process. The term "stand" is used as a way to mention political commitment, either to basic law, or to specific policy, or to elect a candidate. An example is, "Ye stand this day all of you . . ." (Deut 29:10) Its basic meaning is consent to or commit to as in "stand to the covenant." (2 Chron 34:32) This is essentially a loose method of determining the overall level of commitment among the populace. But the electorate could also stand up from a sitting position to show support for a particular candidate or issue. This is suggested by the phrase "They all arose as one man." (Judg 20:8) The term "shout" is used in the sense of a voice vote, as when Samuel asked for a vote on his nominee for king: "All the people shouted, and said, God save the king." (1 Sam 10:24)

The term for selection of a leader by a legislative body for presentation to the people for their vote is "anoint," as when the "men of Judah" anointed David as king to administer a broad area of pan-tribal land. (2 Sam 2:4, 5:3) Another term used is "certify," apparently meaning to elicit a vote of confidence among the men, the elders, and the people, for continuation of a term of office. This type of election was used to re-enthrone David after his abdication. (2 Sam 15:28) The word "heart" signified popular support for a leader during the time of David as well. It was said that the "hearts of the men of Israel are after Absalom." (2 Sam 15:13) But later the political winds changed and it was said "the heart of all the men of Judah . . . (is for David's) return." (2 Sam 19:14) Finally, the term "murmur" seems to indicate negative popular opinion with respect to current government policy. We mentioned above the term "cry" as a sort of candidate-seeking process or nomination process prior to actual election.

The judicial function in Israel was a shared activity involving village elders and also priests called on to settle hard cases by oracle or ordeal because of their superior knowledge of the law. Levites instructed the people in the constitutional law so they could know their political and economic rights. (Num 5:11–31; Deut 17:8–11; Judg 10:1–5, 12:7–15) The judicial system in later times imposed a hierarchical system of judges upon the traditional local court of elders held in the city gates. Deuteronomy, which reflects both the earlier system mixed with a later reform during the time of kings, mentions no mid-level of tribal courts, only judges in the city gates and at the central court. (Deut 21:5, 18–21; Deut 22:21) At some point, adjudication by tribal elders in the middle level of government seems to have been

---

46. Wolf, "Traces of Primitive Democracy," 105–08; Walzer, *In God's Shadow*, 189, 196; Gordis, "Primitive Democracy," 49.

usurped and replaced by adjudication at the national court level. The people as a whole, that is, "you," nevertheless still chose elders/judges and administrative officers in the localities. For example, Deuteronomy (reflecting law from both the early and later periods) says, "You shall appoint judges and officers . . . in all the settlements . . . (given) to your tribes." This may have reflected an original division of local labor or may have reflected the fact that in the later times seen by the editor of Deuteronomy, judges handled only judicial matters, and officials now handled administrative matters.[47] (Deut 16:18)

---

47. Levinson, *Legal Revision*, 124–27; Berman, *Created Equal*, 74, 194.

A Closer Look: Three Crowns of Jewish Government

DURING THE TALMUDIC ERA, the rabbis determined that their early history supported the idea that there were three separate spheres/branches of authority in the national government, called keters or "crowns." These were "keter torah," "keter melekh," and "keter kehunah." The rabbis believed that "keter torah" was the realm of the prophets, "keter melekh" the realm of the chief executive, and "keter kenunah" the realm of the priests. In our interpretation of the politics of ancient Israel in this book, we accept this basic division but define it more politically rather than religiously, and also find some overlap in the realms.

The realm of the prophets was fundamentally a political responsibility. The literary prophets, for example, were rarely if ever found in church or performing religious ritual. Their job was to study and interpret the original constitution on a non-partisan, public-interest basis, analyze current events in light of foundational principles, organize a constitutional party of political followers, agitate/educate for cultural and political reform, and leave a written testament as to their convictions to help stimulate a continuing democratic movement after they were gone. As party leaders, it was their job to affiliate with or nominate the best available political candidates for national office, as Samuel and Nathan did, for example. Samuel nominated Saul and later David, and Nathan threw his support to David. In the early days, national/tribal governmental leaders themselves were prophets (Abraham, Isaac, Jacob, Moses, Joshua, Samuel), but in time, as the nation embraced kingship, prophets had to operate on the outside of government. The closest they got to court politics was to act as advisers to reformist kings like Hezekiah and Josiah. The Bible speaks of two categories of prophets, the mundane class of political pundits who gathered around the national court

A Closer Look: Three Crowns of Jewish Government

and tried to get jobs as obsequious advisers, and authentic prophets, who were inspired by a higher power to be selfless teachers and servants of the people and not interested in political fame or government position.

The realm of "keter malkhut" was inhabited by elected presiding officers given different titles at various times. Abraham, Isaac, and Jacob were remembered as "patriarchs." Moses and Joshua were remembered as God's prime ministers "eved adonai." Later yet presiding officers were called judges ("shofet," "shofetim") like Deborah and Samuel. Still later on in the period of transition to stronger central government, presiding elders were called captain/commander-in-chief or "nagid" as in the case of Saul. Later yet such leaders were called king or "melek" like David, Solomon and the rest. Also included in this group were tribal chiefs or "nasi," and the council of tribal governors or "nesiei ha-edah" (Num 7:2–11; Josh 9:15), who functioned perhaps similar to our modern national council of governors. Government civilian employees in the executive branch were known as "shoter"/"shoterim." (Deut 20:5–9) The rabbinic tradition came to look for the return of a charismatic, God-spirited political leader like Moses, Joshua or Deborah, or someone from the lineage of David called deliverer/savior, or "moshiah" (messiah).[1]

The rabbis correctly see the realm of "keter kehunah" as the sphere of priests, but attach too much importance to the religious duties of the priests. As we have shown above, the priests did perform public ritual activities such as a non-partisan benediction on important events (Num 6:22–26) and civic sacrifice. (Leviticus) They also acted as military chaplains (Num 10:35–36; Deut 20:2–4; 1 Sam 4), and sought oracles or advice from God. However, sacrifice was in large part a secular tax activity swathed in religious wrapping, as was "tithing." Military religious work was ancillary to the tactical task at hand, and obtaining oracles was often more a function of political wisdom or crude scientific determination, such as examining the entrails of animals, rather than direct heavenly revelation. Priests, as the educated class, were involved as inter-tribal arbitrators. (Josh 22:13–14) The current priest witnessed political and economic transactions like a sort of national recorder. (Josh 19:51) Priests also served as public health officers (Lev 11–15), public finance/revenue officers, and officers of a type of department of state in international affairs. Levites were subsidiary government employees who served as civil servants in all of the above activities, including caring for the tabernacle and temple (Judg 18:5; Deut 17:8–13; Deut 21:1–9) and judicial activities. (Deut 18:9)

---

1. Elazar, *Jewish Polity*, 65.

The branches of national government were often called upon to interact with each other to fulfill their constitutional responsibilities to solve a particular issue. One such issue occurred at the end of the period of limited national government in Israel. Samuel as constitutional party leader and prime minister (serving as authority in both "keter torah" and "keter malkhut"), was asked by the elders, or national legislature, to broker a stronger central government system in order to handle the Philistine threat. The people wanted a permanent official to stand apart from the essentially volunteer (or minimally paid) prime minister/prophet position and to serve in government with a permanent civilian staff and a small standing army. (1 Sam 9–10)

Samuel essentially gave up his executive branch "keter malkhut" position to the king, but continued to serve in the "keter torah" position. In fact, he designed the new constitution for kingship and obtained consensus for limits in its ability to concentrate power. As political party leader, he tapped a potentially capable leader on the shoulder (figuratively), and talked to him about maintaining democratic values. Samuel told an initially reluctant Saul that the new leader did not have to come from a prominent family. The candidate just had to hook up with Samuel's party and obtain the spirit of servant leadership by aligning with the "sons of the prophet."

Saul passed this test and started prophesying, i.e., acting as a political pundit setting goals, making popular promises/speeches, and predicting victory against the aggressors. Samuel finally called the congregation together to present his candidate to them and ask for their vote of confidence in him. (1 Sam 10:24) In fact, in Israel there is evidence that national and local political parties, called divisions ("pelagot"), existed to develop candidates for office both in the fully secular magistrate realm and the mostly secular priestly realms. (Exod 8:23; Judg 5:15; 1 Chr 24:1)

Part II

9

Civic Concerns and Secular Focus of the Bible

An interpretation of the Bible that focuses so heavily on the political, the civic, and the secular, needs to justify this focus in terms of the overall content of the book. The respected Oxford Companion to the Bible takes note of the wide variety of worldly interests the Bible addresses by stating, "The Bible is consistently rooted in the concrete realities of human life in this world."[1] The Anchor Bible Dictionary describes this focus in terms of "persistent issues in human life, such as tragedy, injustice, self-control, personal relationships, and the nature and destiny of life in this world."[2]

A large number of characters in the pages of the Bible are principally defined by their non-religious interests in society. Among the military and political types there are military commanders, militiamen, regular soldiers, mercenaries, judges, elders, princes, kings, advisers to kings, and ambassadors. Among those with economic interests there are wealthy aristocrats—so called "great men" or nobles—and also lenders, artisans, tradesmen. Also, there are landholders, servants, lodgers, herdsmen, orchardists, vintners, manual laborers, brick-makers, miners. There are physicians, patients, pharmacologists, midwives. There are students, educators, philosophers, scribes/academicians, and wise-men/scientists. There are religion-oriented

---

1. Ryken, "Bible as Literature," 461.
2. Knight, "Tradition History," 637.

personnel like priests, Nazarites, necromancers, sorcerers and diviners and psalmic worshippers as well, but their stories pale in number and in breadth and depth of description compared to the others. Legitimate priests, as opposed to illegitimate popular religious practitioners, are most often involved in secular, rather than religious activities, as we have seen in the section on *A Closer Look at the Priesthood*.

There is very little in the Bible about private altar/shrine/cult/church organizational structure, meetings, creeds and practices. The patriarchs and others established shrines, but the civic and legal nature of these activities is often made to take a back seat to their religious content. The usual mention of the topic is by the prophets who say there is too much popular and speculative focus on religion and not enough on civic ethics and public citizenship. Moderns look at everything in the Bible as being about religion, because a long period of tradition has presented it that way. Skeptics, agnostics, atheists, political scientists, sociologists, economists, and secular historians would do well to reclaim the large swath of biblical territory that is rightfully theirs and study anew this fascinating early account of democracy and socio-economic life in Israel.

An example of the civic and secular focus of the Bible is the work and writing of the supposedly hide-bound religion-oriented prophets themselves, both "action" prophets like Elijah, and literary prophets like Isaiah. The problem with the interpretation of prophets as religious figures is that they are virtually never to be found in church. Their work is almost always the public work of criticizing the government or lobbying to change it. Privately, they seem frequently to be about the charitable business of delivering health services to a depressed, debilitated, and overtaxed people.

Even the heavily devotional prayers found in the Bible's psalms are often public ones, such as might be uttered today at the time of a U.S. presidential swearing-in ceremony, an inaugural address, a Congressional session prayer, or a battlefield lamentation. Such a public event in ancient Israel was Solomon's prayer at the dedication of his administration's national office building, the office complex known as the "temple." These kinds of public cultural events reveal little about private devotional or denominational life. The rich variety of such private life has been unearthed by archeologists of the eastern Mediterranean, but that information is rarely spoken of in denominational church educational programs.

When church educational programs stray from a blanket religious interpretation of the Bible's pages, it is usually to notice social concerns too obvious to overlook, like accounts of conception and birthing, infancy, puberty, friendship, courtship, engagement, marriage, divorce, infidelity, sexual relations, family government, aging, death, burial, and remembrance and veneration of ancestors. Economic concerns that often attend these social events include gainful occupation, possession of land, buying and selling, and also travel, crime and punishment, and charitable activity.

Beyond individual social and economic concerns, a persistent and outstanding focus of the Bible is its worry about community-wide issues. The major socio-political goals of the characters in the Bible in its obvious communitarian context seem to be long life, possession of the land, attentiveness to the law, maintenance of good reputation, achievement of financial security, production of numerous offspring, solidarity of family, protection of herd animals, rest and good health, clan and tribal identification, rescue from economic and military predicament, descent from important ancestors, inheritance, decent burial and positive remembrance by offspring. Good government is necessary to assist individuals and families achieve these goals. Self-styled secularists in twenty-first century America would be proud to claim many of these as their own interests. A trip through the pages of any Bible dictionary will convince one of the merit of our main assertion in this section—the Bible is a book about everything under the sun that an ancient people had to deal with on planet earth at that particular time, including, from time to time, religion.

Biblical community-wide issues can be grouped roughly into three categories: economic, philosophic/scientific, and political/governmental. Bible economic issues are similar to those of the ancient Near East as a whole and include occupational issues like growing and harvesting crops, digging wells, tending flocks, breeding animals, dealing with hired, indentured, slave and mercenary labor, labor-management relations, runaway slaves, and provision of food to large crowds during travel or at holiday gatherings. Another set of economic problems deal with ethical or legal issues: accumulation/hoarding of wealth (coveting), luxurious endowment of the royal residence, international trade and money-changing, taxation, gleaning of crops, tribute payment after conquest, inheritance/birthright distribution, loaning of money at usury, taking of pledges, honoring of sales contracts, return of land to original owners, level of hospitality displayed to neighbors, prostitution, cost of health care treatment, funeral economics, forgiveness of debt, distribution of property in divorce, and exploitative manipulation of widows, orphans, and resident aliens. A related problem area is that of economic crime, such as movement of boundary markers, failure to return of lost/straying animals, malicious treatment of workers, theft, kidnapping for sale into labor, imperial plundering of mines, forests and fields, bribery, imposition of military corvee (mandatory draft of soldiers), false measuring of grain, temple robbing, and labor on the Sabbath day.[3]

Philosophic-scientific issues in the Bible include disease causation, purity and pollution, the nature of man and of God, attribution of natural events to God, divination and extispicy (use of animal entrails to predict events), prophecy, special election versus universal experience, temporality vs. eternality, memory, measurement, numerology and mathematics, genetics, concealment, adversity, signs and portents, strangeness, corruption, sanctification, unity in nature and social life, sacrifice as a means to operate/manipulate the natural world, judgment, and classification/generalization/particularization.[4]

Political issues include local clan and tribal home rule, election campaigns for elders, judges, and national magistrates, cross-tribal and international relations, palace politics, no-confidence campaigns directed at rulers, dynastic succession and court intrigue, regicide and retribution, criminal justice, religious oppression and labor oppression (as in Egypt), religious and political factional conflict, political centralism, ethics in government (i.e., the problem of bribery), sedition and treason, equal justice, degradation of the poor, economic and military imperialism, political organizing and revolutionary activity, voluntary political migration and involuntary political exile.[5] Government policy debate takes up issues like elections, political party formation and operation (prophets and "sons of prophets" organizations), organization of government at different levels, jurisdiction issues, compulsory education, public health and private health care (cleanliness/purity, treatments/cure), social welfare ("redeeming" the poor), and international relations, including international trade, transit rights, and treaties.[6] Constitutional law issues include supremacy of the legislature over the executive, limits on the legislative power of the national magistrate, empowerment of local economies and economic agencies, judiciary formation and operation, regulation of the potential exploitation of labor and over-exuberant profit-making, distribution, expropriation and securing of land, national/local relations and distribution of powers, degree of separation of shrine and state (palace and priest), prohibition of foreign entanglement, citizen rights and responsibilities, and the war power.[7]

---

3. Moore, *WealthWatch*, 85, 91, 99, 116, 124, 129, 211, 212–15, 219.
4. See Trigano, *Philosophy of the Law*.
5. See, for example, Barr, "Politics and the Bible," 599–601.
6. Bryce, *Letters*, 42–55; Gottwald, *Kingdoms*, 349–387.
7. Kent, *Israel's Laws*; Gottwald, *Kingdoms*; Levinson, "First Constitution," 27:4.

The Bible is about a particular civic faith, that is, devotion to a political ideal of free speech, free religion, free labor, and free and almost obligatory participation in government. Those ideals are swathed in religious packaging at times. But the ancient habit of wrapping up all things political and civic in God-talk melts away completely at times and places in the Bible, and then and there the Bible's civic bent is given a naked secular hue. For example, there are entire books of the Bible so obviously secular in content that there is nary a mention of the word God. Such a book is Esther. Esther is not concerned about religious ethics such as endogamy or special dietary matters and does not pray. However, this book is one of the Judaic "Five Scrolls," and is read at the festival of Purim. The book promotes secular themes touched upon throughout the Bible: the high necessity for religious liberty to be accorded to ethical peoples; the dangers of official persecution of religion; the need to have highly ethical leaders and counselors in government; and the need for personal courage and conviction to stand up and blow the whistle on government inequity and iniquity.[8]

---

8. Coogan, *Old Testament*, 529; see also Hazony, *Dawn*.

10

Bible Literature as Propaganda for People's Government

WITH SUCH DIVERSITY IN subjects matter, characters, and periods of time, one would expect to find a wide diversity of literary vehicles used to convey the material. There are five basic types of literature in the Bible: narrative, law, prophecy, lyrical poetry, and wisdom/proverb. Literary analysts find additional or sub-types of material including letters, infant narratives (such as "exposure" and rescue stories), military contest narratives, and ancestral narratives and genealogies.[1] Bible commentators also find prophetic law suit, epic story, tragedy, parable, satire, oratory, wedding or love poem, funeral elegy, psalm of praise, and lament. A capable political analyst of the Bible can also recognize royal proclamation, inaugural political address, farewell address, coronation account, succession narrative, king list, and diplomatic correspondence. Health science professionals and medical anthropologists detect scientific or quasi-scientific theory and practice in the health field like descriptions of virginity and paternity tests, meat slaughtering techniques, and epidemiologic/plague functions/statistics. Modern government and public land officials might take an interest in boundary marker monuments and inscriptions, public records of irrigation and well digging, and state road and other topographic descriptions. Economists pay attention to sales contracts, creditor-debtor policies, and land transactions detailed in the Bible.

With such a wide variety of interests and literary vehicles to express them, it goes without saying that these compositions comes from an equally wide variety of sources, written over a wide period of chronological time. That time frame encompasses roughly some 2,500 years from the imputed or estimated period of time when the first somewhat detailed story of Abraham

1. Knight, "Tradition History," 634; Ryken, "Bible as Literature," 460–63.

was told or written, to the final editing of the New Testament some couple hundred years after Christ. In the first place, it is generally conceded that the initial set of books of the Bible, the five books of Torah (Jewish term) or Pentateuch (Christian term), which are traditionally attributed to one author, Moses, have been extensively edited. Editors of the Oxford Companion to the Bible summarize, "The Bible is the final product of a series of stages, including orally transmitted traditions, shorter and longer written units, collections edited and in some cases translated in ancient times, and final selection by various religious communities as canonical scriptures."[2]

Many hands touched and formed the final version of Moses' original records and memoirs that we have now. Evidence of those many hands touching the five books of Moses is seen in the book of Deuteronomy in a passage which describes Moses' death and burial. Moses obviously did not write the passage. (Deut 34:5–12) The first book, Genesis, dealing with the creation and claiming Moses as its author, speaks of the time of Israelite kings, which happened long after the time of Abraham and after Moses as well: "And these are the kings that reigned in the land of Edom, before there reigned any king over the children of Israel."[3] (Gen 36:31) In other words, the book of Genesis was the product of a number of much later evaluations of early events and editorial points of view about those accounts.

Interestingly, the general reader will find two different accounts of the history of the Israelite monarchy, the books of Kings and Chronicles. One reasonable hypothesis for these two basic accounts of the early history is that once Israel split into two separate countries and two separate national cathedrals, the early writings also got two different sets of editors, each giving their own flavor to the early material. We know that Jeroboam and the northern elders not only established a separate nation in the north, but also broke off association with the Jerusalem national chapel in the south, and established two separate temples in the north to replace Jerusalem, one at Dan, and one at Shechem. The Israelite north and south, like the American north and south, had every reason to see a different color or flavor in their respective early national histories. Most historians of the Bible believe that the northern-based history of Israel was used by the final editors as a supplemental, and somewhat fragmented, add-on to the dominant southern history, much in the same way as southern Confederate history is often used as a supplemental, and somewhat fragmented, add-on to the dominant northern history of the United States.[4]

2. Metzger and Coogan, *Oxford Companion*, vii.
3. Coogan, *Old Testament*, 22.
4. Coogan, *Old Testament*, 21–22, 28.

In fact, if north and south can have different opinions and tellings about history, east and west might just as easily as well. Indeed there also might be cultural or political differences within the same geographic section of a country, whether north or south, east or west. One might easily expect to find sub-stories, or sub-views within each major geographic tradition. In the early 1800s, Julius Wellhausen advanced the "documentary hypothesis" about the composition of the Torah/Pentateuch. He provided evidence of four different major sources woven together to make the final document. He called the sources J, E, D, and P, using letters to represent his terms for the sources: jahwist, elohist, deuteronomist, and priestly. Later students of Bible literary sources have postulated the existence of dozens of additional sub-sources either feeding into or separate from these basic four.[5]

What modern Bible scientists have learned is that important national writings pass through a changing political and cultural tradition in a given area. Some of the original material is passed along untouched, while other parts of the original material are touched up, essentially photo-shopped, to fit changes in the culture and changes in the political scene. Some of the earliest source material turns out to be an enigma to all who hear or view it, likely including the early editors. Modern analysis of the original as well as intermediate sources or documents used to make the final product is called "literary criticism," or "source analysis." Study of smaller units within each source is called "form criticism." The photo-shopping touch up and coloring is called "redaction criticism." Redaction deals with how the final editors combined the sources. A type of analysis called "tradition history" incorporates both form criticism and redaction criticism. A focus on the final, overarching reading of both the first five books and indeed the entire Bible with its dozens of books, is a type of analysis called "canonical criticism."

This last type of analysis sees the entire Bible canon as a complete text with its own inner unity or "spin" imposed by the final scribes, working on behalf of the then current political and cultural leaders of society. One way Bible publishers produce this spin for their particular audiences is to edit the speeches made by important figures to emphasize particular themes important to the existing powers that be. The way to dissect and expose this spin is to work on understanding how the historical experiences of an author or editor affected the presentation of his material. This is called the "socio-historical" method. For example, Ezekiel's view of history and of the future is influenced by the fact his country had been brutally conquered and dragged into slavery/captivity in Babylon. John of Patmos, who wrote the book of Revelation in the New Testament, had things to say about his

---

5. Ibid., 25–27.

own people and the Roman conquerors that is colored by the experience of brutal colonial occupation and his own experience of exile from his homeland. This is all a nice way of saying that the Bible is a political document, subservient to "powerflows" within ancient Israelite society at the time of editing. In the same way, histories of neighboring nations are colored by the flattering spin of their own powerful leaders and unflattering points of view of underground critics. Southern kings in Israel hated northern kings and their civic and economic view of the world, their national shrines and high priestly dogmas, and slam them pretty hard in the Bible, just as northern presidents and their court historians in America hate Confederate generals, presidents, and culture and slam them up-side-the-head in their official histories.[6]

In addition to this mention of all the characters, literary forms, sources, and compilations in the Bible, our part II presentation here intends to tease out for the reader some major literary themes presented by the overall book, or canon. These following six are from the author's own personal impressions, which have been formed without much partisan attachment to one religious, academic, or political tradition or another. These themes together reflect a fairly transparent argument for periodic restoration of the democratic republicanism found in the Ten Commandment law document. They also form the basis for the Bible's sense of the universal applicability and reception of the local government idea in tribal/political groups across the globe.

The first of our six under-reported themes is the idea of the pervasiveness of political and religious conflict in the ancient world, and the perniciousness of their consequences to individuals and families. The Bible is interested in domestic tranquility and international peace and worries constantly about the best available socio-economic system to actualize this. Virtually every book and every period of time is laced with incidents and commentary about this problem and its solution. If political, military, and religious territorial conflict is the pre-eminent problem of human civilization, such conflict germinates in the soil of the doctrines of political and religious superiority, xenophobic nativism and exclusion of peoples and tribes from belonging. When God speaks through legitimate prophets, he asks for peace, religious tolerance, democratic-oriented local government based on land distribution for all, and cooperation between local governments. In time, God's politics and economics get perverted by government and religious leaders who lead people away from original democratic principles.

---

6. Ehrman, *New Testament*, 132, 154; Coogan, *Old Testament*, 23, 28.

In the view of the biblical civic faith story, there is a cyclical process. First, a great reformer representing the one-minded (egalitarian) God of heaven institutes democracy in religion, politics, economics and social life. Later on, this reformed culture becomes stale, institutionalized, and oppressive. For example, the southern kingdom of Judah embraced a new or at least revamped civic religious tradition, likely based on the ancient political inclination of Aaron, which brought with it a more expansive government of the sort that Aaron had earlier advocated. They situated this new national government headquarters in Jerusalem and in the person of the military strategist David. Within two generations, however, the northern section of David's unified kingdom declared that they would focus their own civic life on the limited-government tradition of the national founder they most admired, Moses. To better represent local interests in the north, they set up two national government office complexes rather than one. A series of wars then flared up between the two kingdoms based largely on these sociopolitical differences and the cultural-religious outcroppings of those civic values.

The Bible is generous in its suggestion of solutions to the problem of culturo-political violence, whether stemming from forces external or internal to the nation. These policies range in breadth from allocation of land among the people, decentralization of government, eschewing alliances with other nations, and limitation of the scope and objectives of war. For example, Israel should not sign international political treaty documents because that leads to participation in unnecessary international conflict.

Our second theme suggests that individual human beings are endowed by their creator with a liberal capacity to determine their own fate and happiness by governing themselves and also by stepping into leadership positions to administer the law when called upon. From Adam and Eve to Noah and his wife, from Abraham and Hagar to Moses and Miriam, from Deborah and Joshua to Hannah and Samuel, from Isaiah and his prophetess wife to Daniel and Esther, and from Jesus and Mary through Priscilla and John of Patmos, all eras of biblical time testify that any man or woman may become a judge or "prophet," that is, a charismatic political tutor/organizer/elected leader, and lead the people in the direction of a humane civic lifestyle. Thus we see in the Genesis stories about the beginning of human life that democratic-oriented, progressive humankind is frequently thrust into an environment where it is exposed to philosophies of governance and cultural expression that encourage abandonment of sensible social values. God leaves humankind free to choose, but must "send" prophets to represent heavenly views to mankind. God is vitally interested in the process of human government. In fact, there is a well developed political science in the Bible which eschews kingship, unless it is the "messianic" version. That version allows for leadership by a relatively permanent chief magistrate who at the end of his term passes the torch to the ablest of his offspring. The "house" of the rulers, nevertheless, are exposed to the full glare of public scrutiny as to personal proclivities and administration of public policy. If they don't support the constitution, they are out on their ears.

Our third theme suggests that free intellectual expression is the core of the ability for self-determination, the solution to the problem of political and religious conflict, and indispensible to the work of reformationist prophets. Religious liberty and political pluralism are essential for maintaining possession of the land, long life, peace and happiness. Israel's "religious" liberty describes both spiritual and intellectual-scientific freedom and provides for ancestral remembrance traditions that focus on both religious shrine and secular school traditions that guide people's thinking in the present day. Freedom of activity derives from freedom of intellectual expression. Also important for the achievement of these goals is faithful listening to the prophetic voices that arise out of the milieu of free expression and family independence. A commandment to establish conformity with the requirements of the high God Yahweh must first ensure that the people have access to that God, based on the best interpretive theology and the best political history available among many pretenders to such authority.

Our fourth theme presents the idea that separation of semi-religious state agencies and private worship institutions from secular state agencies is the surest support of both religious and political free exercise. In the Bible history, there is virtually no mention of governmental meddling in local cult matters unless those cult practices are of a thoroughly discredited type of activity that impedes realization of the goals of the society, such as sorcery or Baalism (monarchy-oriented nature religion). The grand personalities of the Bible take care to teach and to demonstrate support for this principle and their antipathy for fusion of cult and castle stems from Israel's experience in captivity to the divine political ruler of Egypt. It also results from the precedent set by Moses in turning over priestly policy duties to Aaron while Israel was still in the wilderness, and keeping for himself secular and military affairs. Upon this model we see a succession of paired authorities after Moses and Aaron, princes and priests, who maintain a reasonable distance from each other's spheres and duties. Examples include Samuel and Eli, Solomon and Abiathar, and many others.

Our fifth theme speaks to the need for constitutional boundaries that hedge in/support legitimate social, political and religious expression and hedge out unethical forms of such expression. Legitimate and necessary constitutional activity starts with consent of the people to the laws enacted for their benefit and includes respect paid to Israelite articles of government protecting basic human rights and mandating fulfillment of basic responsibilities such as education and citizen participation. This is what several of the commandments do in Israel. But, on the other hand, citizens must periodically reassert boundaries between legitimate and illegitimate human activity, between common sense and from primitive frivolity and dissoluteness. On one side of the line stands social, physical and ethical science, and on the other side magic, rain dance and intimidation. Citizens of Israel are to study the world about them and make informed judgments, policies and decisions based on the most effective knowledge available to them. They are to hedge out discredited and unscientific practices such as divination, necromancy, and the like. Citizens, inspired by the work of wisdom prophets (academicians/scribes) and civic prophets (active party organizers and elected politicians), must stand up for justice and righteousness and recover lost political, economic and social ground. Several of the commandments dictate that there be no backsliding to oppressive government and superstitious religious systems and provide authority for citizen movements to recover democratic political practices.

The sixth theme teaches that individuals and nations outside Israel are as capable of acting out the democratic spirit found deeply nested in each human breast as anyone in Israel is. They can raise prophets and democracies, and evidence that they have, do, and will yet again do so are evident in the Bible text. All nations and peoples have equal access to the One God and the spirit of the laws to the extent they recognize in themselves the capacity to shake free of biased preconceptions about the world and learn from one another. Captivity to despotism is an experience familiar more or less to all communities of the world. Discerning the lessons of ancient as well as recent history is a calling open to all according to their own initiative. This is as much to say that a legitimate prophet may arise in any locale or clime, and at any time. Unfortunately, few there are who rise to such stature. There is generally a continuum line between the lesser lights who poorly understand human history and generally could care less about the peoples of the earth, and the brighter ones whose views and prognostications and activities are remembered because they are more conscientious and learned and humane than those of the lesser.

The civic salvation we have said is obtainable by means of the commandments is notable for a deeply spiritual connection, without which, apparently, the freedoms accorded by it cannot very easily come to light or be sustained. This is a deep irony. We have said it is God's goal, God's political science, to enact freedom for each individual to decide and promote his own beliefs. In order for each person's strength and destiny to be protected in the visible mortal world, there is a necessity for a supernal leadership, a connection to the netherworld of the spirit, at which place God is said to dwell. A society firmly devoted to this world and its amenities must be rooted in another.

11

Early Science and the Gods: Putting Political Content Back into Bible Vocabulary

It is interesting that what is taught today in religious and even academic circles as ancient Near East and Israelite religion is not very close at all to what we accept as religion today. Ancient cultural traditions about one god or another were not really systems of worship that consciously avoided natural processes, focusing instead on the speculative and the supernatural. Rather, they were an early form of science, and, in particular, social science. Stories about the gods, and "worship" practices related to those gods were actually earnest and honest attempts to explain human and natural phenomenon rather than sidestep such explanations. As we have explained, priests of various "religions" were the most educated members of society, on a par with prophets.

The gods ranged from sky to sea to land gods, and from war gods to love gods, from healing and trade gods to wisdom and writing gods, from royal and aristocrat gods to middle class, labor and slave gods.[1] One god presided over each area of obvious interest and concern to the ancients. Ancient religious ritual was really the early rationalist science of trying to make an impact on the god and the natural realm guarded by the god. The ancients studied hard to understand how the god worked, and made sacrifices/gifts to try to elicit information or manipulate the part of the cosmos under its stewardship. It was also important to know the history of a god's work in its own realm in order to properly predict or influence it in a particular direction.

In fundamental form, religion was primitive natural science and ultimately political science. As such, it was often co-opted to justify the capricious state of socio-political affairs under the reigns of great kings. Kings

1. Pritchard, *Atlas*, 68.

Early Science and the Gods 111

and their court priesthoods published stories that conditioned the people to believe the activities of the throne-holders were at the center of concern and importance in society and in heaven.

Israel, as progressive as it was, still attributed much of its public and private activity and success to the founding "god" or spirit of the republic, much as other ancient Near East governments did to their own national gods. Thus, Israel attributed (tipped its hat) to God in civic matters such as organization and operation of government as if God actually organized and operated the government for them, matters of war and peace as if God actually led the charge into battle for them, and international affairs as if God rather than great kings controlled empires. It posited a role for God in acute and chronic disease as if God visited disease upon malcontents and criminals, and presided over treatments and cures as if God guided the course of the medicines or the knife of the surgeon.

However, it was becoming increasingly clear to humankind at the time of ancient Israel that they themselves were the real agents of control of at least the earthly portion of the cosmos. Much of what was happening on earth was due to human effort. Humans could herd animals, grow crops, build canals, and make water storage vessels rather than have to hunt and gather and pray for rain. Humans, if they worked together and unleashed their potential, were true shakers and movers. They could put their stamp on most events. If God created the natural world initially, human beings actually took over and ruled in God's place, with only occasional heavenly guidance. This was the sum and substance of Israel's earliest teaching—humankind was made to have dominion over the world, rather than the God who created the earth. (Gen 1:26) The creator God merely asked that human beings use the rule of humane law to govern themselves rather than the capricious rule of mighty men. (Gen 2:16–17) By enfranchising, encouraging, and educating all human beings, humans could tame both themselves and the globe.

As science advanced over the 2,000 year history of Judaic civilization before the great Jewish diaspora that took place shortly after the death of Christ, and many mysterious things became knowable and controllable, it was not necessary to attribute so much of life to an unseen, unknown, and mysterious physical force in the heaven. Creation was unfolding before the eyes, hands, hearts, and brains of a humankind acting on its own democratic and libertarian power. The founding god of Israel had been right. Human beings were made in his image, and had his powers of creating, building, learning, healing and nurturing. They did not need to rely on self-important kings to make the crops grow, direct the animals to pasturage, watch the city so it could be safe, and make women and children to be happy. They could make these things happen themselves, as the nomadic ancestors had demonstrated in oral and written accounts handed down through their families. Increasingly, it was not necessary to attribute God's instant and individual hand to such things as disease and disability and to teach that individuals got sick because they had offended God or mankind. Nature itself, following its own sometimes capricious law independent of human worthiness, could be responsible for disease, as the Biblical prophet-scientist Job argued. Citizenries could defend themselves in their hill country abodes, and repel imperial adventurists from their lands. They could build roads, and carve out a niche in international trade. They could form their own families, and pass lands and possessions down to them without confiscation and distribution from the king's palace and storehouse. They could pass down detailed histories of the struggles of founders of the nation.

Today we think of the Bible as a strictly, or mainly, religious text, in part because, like most ancient cultural writing, the Bible wraps up its scientific, civic, and secular content with religious packaging in the form of a great deal of God-talk. In the Christian era, churches of all kinds, including Judaic denominations, have exploited that Biblical religious packaging to their advantage, and that has involved marginalizing the length, breadth, and depth of Bible commentary on topics quite un-religious in nature. Concepts such as holiness, purity, sin, sacrifice, circumcision, temples, tithing, sabbath, priesthood, congregation, pilgrimage, and commandment, seem obviously religious in nature. But, in fact, these terms are in actuality quite better understood as civic, secular, and political activities related to mundane and non-denominational health, welfare, and finance activity based in the public sphere. They are vocabulary used to describe the entire diverse citizenry and their civic duties and laws irrespective of their actual religious beliefs.

Confucius, the famous Chinese political philosopher and historian, reminds his readers in the Analects that the first thing to inquire about in the writing of history is what a few western translators have lamely dubbed "the rectification of names." By this, Confucius meant what in modern English terms we would better call "definition of terms." We will attempt such a brief definition of the actual semantic meaning of the ancient terms used by the Bible in this section. For example, did the Hebrew term translated "holy" actually mean to the ancient Hebrews what the modern Christian term means today? Were the terms "purity" and "cleanness," and "impurity" and "uncleanness," originally related to religious or sexual morality as we think today, or were they related to something else entirely to the ancient Hebrews?

A key term needing rectification or definition is that of the Hebrew word translated as "temple." Temples of the ancient world today are most often thought of as places of denominational religious sacrifice to the gods. In fact, temples inside and outside of ancient Israel were multi-purpose public buildings accessible by all sectors of society, including a variety of academic, economic and political interests and irrespective of religious denominational affiliation. Temples inside and outside of Israel served as national treasuries, military armories, universities, health care facilities, agricultural storehouses, national libraries, law research and law enforcement agencies, gathering places for national political activities such as election events, holiday remembrance venues and coronations, seats of supreme judicial decision-making, places where oaths/agreements such as treaties were heard and recorded, and, finally, non-denominational national chapels for public sacrifice events.[2] In short, temples served as the principle public office building complex supplementing the royal palace. Their staffs served essentially as early secretaries of health, education, and welfare, secretaries of the treasury, attorneys general and public marshals, chiefs of military staff, public revenue agents, and copyists and librarians of public records.

Temples were places where public health "purity" laws were enforced, administered, and supported, particularly by the priestly staff there. Purity/impurity and cleanness/uncleanness are best understood in terms of health status. If people were sick, they could not participate fully in the life of the community, in part, because they might infect others with their illnesses. It was the job of the priest to define the point of onset of communicable disease, keep track of the incidence and spread of such disease, and to clear individuals for re-entry into full community activity. Leviticus states, regarding incidents of plague, "The priest shall look on him and pronounce him unclean." (Lev 13:3) As late as New Testament times, when Jesus healed a patient of "leprosy," he told his patient to go and report his return to health to the priest serving as the local public health officer. (Matt 8:4; Mark 1:44; Luke 5:14)

Priests specialized not so much in leading private religious worship and instruction, as in instructing the citizenry in history, law, literacy, and science, and providing scribal and adjudicative services to public governmental entities. They officiated at public and private festivities involving food preparation, distribution, and consumption, and thus essentially served as

2. Wolf, "Traces of Primitive Democracy," 101; Avalos, *Illness*; Ward, "Temples and Sanctuaries – Egypt," 369–72; Robertson, "Temples and Sanctuaries – Mesopotamia," 372–76; Dever, "Temples and Sanctuaries – Syria-Palestine," 376–80; Cole, "Temples and Sanctuaries – Greco-Roman," 380–82; LaSor, "Temples," 731–34; Wells and Magdalene, *Law*, 279.

sanitary butchers, public health sanitary officials and public restaurant operators. Priests also served essentially as private school head masters, government policy specialists, and judges with jurisdiction over certain parts of the law relevant to their competencies.

And yes, priests also conducted public ritual sacrifices. Public ritual is often mistaken as private religious sacrament. Public ritual concerned only that part of religion that impinged on public affairs. This included political punditry (prophecy), sacred holiday ceremonies recalling early political events in the nation, and chaplaincy services provided to national leaders at the national cathedral/temple.[3] Throughout the ancient world, whether the Near East or the Far East, particular protocol/format/ritual was prescribed for each form of public activity. Those activities included elections, appointments, coronations, calling of law-makers to session, signing of laws/decrees, opening of public meetings, and calling out the militia. Sometimes the tradition required that a trumpet be blown to initiate the activity. (Exod 19:16; Lev 23:24; Num 10:2) Other times, the tradition required that "sacrifices" be made. There were several kinds of sacrifices, whose purpose was usually to deliver some kind of needed resource to the government.

The first of these was the burnt offering. This is the sacrifice of an animal for God only. The meat was completely burned and was not to be consumed by government employees or the people. This kind of sacrifice reflected citizen and government working together to bend the God's favor in the direction of the community. The "first fruits" offerings, whether it was the meat offering or the cereal offering, was not really a voluntary contribution to the government. It was required of all, but couched as a joyous opportunity to support the limited functions of the national government. The first fruits were given to the priestly officials of government as compensation for their services to the citizenry, like a salary or a fee.

Much of what passes for religious denominational "tithing" in the Bible is actually better understood as public taxation. Such revenues, whether delivered to the government in the form of the first fruits of crop production or of herds, or in the form of precious metal coinage, would be used for a variety of secular programs, including roads, wells and irrigation canals, military activity, and for the support of government personnel. (2 Chron 26) The fact that tithing was actually the payment of public tax for the service of

---

3. Americans have a national cathedral/temple in Washington D.C. just as Israel had one in Jerusalem. This is an Episcopal chapel that served the interests of early Episcopal politicians in Washington, and later ones, such as George W. Bush. But this American "temple" plays very little role in the actual private religious activity of the nation, just as Israel's temple placed little direct role in the day-to-day religious activities of the ancient Jewish people.

government administration is underscored by the well established fact that there was no strictly established and enforced national church in Israel.[4]

There were also thanksgiving or well-being sacrifices/offerings which were given to the government after the successful fulfillment of a citizen concern, prayer or wish. This is akin to our modern "giving-back" to the community after one has been blessed with prosperity or some other success. The well-being sacrifice was somewhat close to the sacrificial offering made to the government upon the return of good health, called the "purification" offering. When one transgressed the moral law, became diseased, or committed an offense against the law unknowingly, one had a mandatory obligation to essentially pay a fine to the government in the form of an animal or portion of a crop. When a serious crime had been committed, the victim rather than the government was generally compensated, except for crimes against the government. Priests by law took delivery of such public sacrifice receipts and, after consuming some of them for themselves and their families and employees, also provided distribution of some of the tax wealth to the needy among the citizenry. Priests also burned incense at the altar, perhaps a more overtly cultic or religious activity. (2 Chron 26:16) Fully secular political leaders like judges and kings were forbidden from carrying out the incense burning and the sacrifice rituals.[5] (1 Sam 13:9–14)

Ancient pilgrimage travel and holy day celebrations were not so much like modern religious pilgrimage events to places of the birth or death of religious founders, but more like our own citizenship travel activities on national holidays centered around thanksgiving, labor and veterans concerns, harvest celebrations, tax season collection events, and other important political events. Pilgrimages were undertaken for purposes of gathering the population together for electoral assemblies, participation in educational workshops, facilitating health consultation and hospitalization stints at hospitals, delivering children to educational institutions for special training, delivering animal donations to religious shrine altars of choice, participating in regional or national holidays, and participation in law-making and law-adjudication activities. When citizens were condemned for "sin," they were not found to be violating private religious laws, but were committing felonies against the criminal laws of the land and thus had to be tried in the gates of the cities or at regional government judicial sites. Many psalms were written and delivered to lend a quasi-religious tone or element to such public assembly or government activity events.

4. Shinkoskey, *Prophets*, 81–117.
5. Milgrom, *Leviticus*, 17–67.

Israel made pilgrimages to government sites to renew the covenant made by their ancestors to uphold the Ten Commandments, just as we make pilgrimages to Philadelphia to see the Liberty Bell at Freedom Hall, or to Washington to see the Washington Monument or to the Library of Congress to see the Declaration of Independence, or to the Supreme Court to see the Ten Commandments emblazoned in stone all around the building. (Deut 14:23) When ancient Israelites carried out these travel and re-enactment traditions, they followed the pointed Biblical examples set by Joshua, Josiah, and Ezra. There were also such political renewal events promoted by Hosea and by Jeremiah.[6]

The term "congregation" is invariably associated in modern times as a gathering of religious worshipers. In fact, a congregation in ancient Israel was not religious gathering but a political assembly for the purpose of conducting the activities of democracy. Those activities included presenting oneself and one's family for census enumeration, the delivery of taxes, voting for public officials, making laws and constitutional amendments, giving assent to war, and educational activities and memorial observances. The whole "congregation" of Israel was the entire citizenry, and included those who worshipped an array of different denominations of the main deity, and a variety of other deities as well. Those citizens worshipped in a vast array of different settings, administered through local religious specialists and not national government priests. The term "commandment" has been pirated by modern church establishments to mean religious law. In fact, a commandment was a broad constitutional policy statement enacted by the democratic processes of a government representing all manner of citizens belonging to a wide variety of churches, and thus was not partisan religious law at all.

The Bible concern for voluntary redistribution of wealth from the well-do-do to the poor, disenfranchised and marginalized, reflects a concern for good citizenship, most of which was rendered outside the agency of government and even outside of the ecclesiastic area. Citizens working on their own were obligated to care for the physical needs of orphans, widows, and strangers. Individual citizens like Job believed they must act in place of God, who promoted financial compassion and rescue of the oppressed. In Israel, the powerful were encouraged by tradition and law to protect the powerless, as exemplified later by the code of knightly chivalry in medieval England.[7] (Job 29:12; 31:16–23; Ps 68:5; Isa 1:17) In fact, "holiness" in the Israelite context is best translated as devotion to citizenship rights and responsibilities. To be holy is to be free, independent, healthy and responsible.

---

6. Anderson, *Old Testament*, 131–33, 292–93, 349, 493–95, 639.
7. Coogan, *Old Testament*, 532.

Political holiness leads naturally to moral and ethical holiness, since it is based on responsibility to provide stability and prosperity for others.

Israel had a civic religion like any other nation did in ancient and modern times. In other words, Israel was a political entity tinged at the edges with a religious tradition associated with its founding. This is another way of saying that people who founded the nation had religious beliefs and made room for exercising those beliefs in their political and legal institutions. Israel's "civic religion" was based on the necessity to stand up against tyranny and imperialism, to assert and maintain small-group kinship customs and ancestral legal institutions, and to construct a democratic governing structure for society that assured humane and individualistic social, economic, religious, and political activity. Therefore, Israel's civic religion constantly made reference to and promoted civic remembrance of the activities of the founders of the nation, much as citizens in the United States do today. It also constructed "bright line" barriers against despoliation of this legal heritage and the humane policies it enacted for the people, sometimes expressed as worshipping "other gods." The gods established nations, and a particular democratic god established the Israelite nation. The politics of this God must be adhered to, at the peril of dissolution of the nation and destruction of its peoples and lands.

PART III

12

Ten Oppressions in Egypt, Ten Solutions in Israel

Israel's ratification at Sinai of a set of laws to guide later legislation was heavily weighted by her experience under Pharaoh's oppressions in Egypt. The absence of religious and political freedom under Pharaoh Ramses II made an article of government firmly establishing such freedoms for citizens and non-citizens alike the first order of business, or first commandment (no other gods), at Sinai. Just as important, Israel wanted a say in everything the government proposed to do. Thus, they needed a document that would provide for official consent of the people to the policies of government that would be proposed by its political leaders in the future. This they achieved by bestowing sovereignty, or supremacy, on their tribal councils of elders. The elders would make the laws, not any tribal prince or head.

The second "commandment" of government (no graven images) had as its objective to deal with Egypt's "worship-style" religious and political leadership system. That system invited the citizenry to believe in the divine ruling right of Pharaohs and the necessity for a culture of luxury surrounding the court. Such a system was known among democratic-oriented cultures of the day as "idolatry," or a system of images—a political system where the ruler extended his political life and power by making sure his image was available everywhere for people to admire. With such worship of the political leader, it was easy for the ruler to become the religious leader of the nation too, especially if he also claimed to be related to one of the gods

TEN OPPRESSIONS IN EGYPT, TEN SOLUTIONS IN ISRAEL   119

himself. Israel replaced this form of government, which fused church and state and encouraged worship of a single ruler and the ruler's favored god, with a "wisdom-style" system of government which mandated mass literacy, study of history, common sense, separation of priest and palace, and freedom of worship of ethical gods. This system favored a culture of plain-living that allowed for accumulation of wealth, but set in place mechanisms to retard or reverse such accumulation.

Overabundance of the government economy and under abundance of the private economy in Pharaoh's Egypt lead directly to the third commandment which empowered private contractual agreements in economic, as well as all other local, private affairs of the new Israelite culture. Parties in the private sector swore to uphold these agreements and not undertake them lightly (don't take the name in vain). The Israelites wanted free enterprise so they could work at trades of their own choosing, not trades chosen by the government for them. They certainly did not want the national government to take the economy hostage to its own political interests, as Egypt had done. They wanted a law limiting the concentration of wealth in the government and keeping it invested instead among the citizenry, because it was the fantastic accumulation of resources in the houses of Seti and Ramses and their aristocratic courtiers, and the fearsome need of an insecure autocrat to hold on to all those resources, that caused them so much trouble in the first place.

The part of the Egyptian command economy most offensive to Israelites was the one dealing with national direction of labor which enslaved minority populations such as their own. Israel dealt with this by promulgating the fourth commandment allowing individualized direction of labor, subject only to a legal requirement for a long work week to inspire productivity. This work week was to be followed by a national holiday on the seventh day, which allowed for rest, recuperation, and a cooling off of the economy. The rest day (remember the Sabbath day) was intended to be a personal emancipation and personal freedom day to allow individuals to study, worship, plan, travel, and participate in citizenship activities.

Pharaoh's socio-political culture was based on a virulent variety of national social patriarchy that likely denied many rights to women. Recall that Pharaoh did not want women to participate with men even in worship activities, for example. Pharaoh also confined male inheritance to a "firstborn" system of economic primogeniture which effectively tied the political hands of most free men in the society and limited the powers of local government. Israel dealt with this by means of its fifth commandment law empowering family government, and empowering women within families to be honored equally with men (honor father and mother). This led quickly to the promulgation of female inheritance rights and to the rising of women to places of the highest political prominence in Israel's new society.

The second table of laws dealt with equally egregious conditions and touched upon raw memories for the migrating people gathered at Sinai. Pharaoh typically expended lives not only in his forced labor projects, but by means of his military conscription programs to support imperial adventures abroad. While the first five commandments dealt with humanitarian rights related to intellectual freedom, protection of private property transactions, personal labor freedom and family autonomy, the sixth one (no killing) placed a hold on the ability of the new Israelite government to kill political opponents, enter into military protection alliances, and conscript the citizenry into unnecessary wars abroad. The new democratic culture was to be devoted to physical non-violence, as well as economic and intellectual non-violence.

Egypt was notorious for a system of royal court sexual relations which not only allowed, but at times almost required, a prince to marry a close blood relative in order to continue a good blood-line for his dynasty. Producing an heir was of the utmost importance, so not only did he marry a cousin or a sister, but often consorted with multiple partners to produce one. The heir could then inherit a huge amount of property as well as rule in his own right. Israelite families wanted heirs to inherit the family farm and flocks as well, but did not want to encourage royal-style adultery, since that reeked of special privileges for the rich. Israel's seventh commandment (no adultery) limited polygamy and adultery for chief magistrates and regular citizens alike. The Bible's seventh commandment restriction of adultery and incest made it hard to assert a political caste system in Israel. But legislation it inspired allowed heirs to be produced in childless families at least in the case where the husband died at an early age. The widow was encouraged to remarry into the same clan by becoming the second wife of the brother of the deceased. Then the child could inherit its father's property and carry on his name.

During long periods of its history, Egypt's kings owned much or most of the land along the Upper and Lower Nile. Private ownership of land was never very secure in Egypt, and apparently was not a privilege given to Hebrew families under Ramses II. For example, there is no account of Israelites having to sell land before participating in the exodus. Because they lacked land in Egypt (and could not farm it easily even if they had some land), Israel enacted the eighth commandment (no stealing). The third commandment, as a law promoting the private sector, suggested a broad right to own land, and the eighth commandment prohibited the government from stealing it.

Such a law was vitally important because ownership of land was the basis for all other political and economic freedoms.

Moses fled Egypt because he stood up for a fellow Hebrew who was under assault. (Exod 2:11–15) He ran to a haven in Midian because there was no reasonable expectation of justice under Pharaoh's highly politicized judicial system. Moses' fair treatment in Midian may have inspired an idea in him for cities of refuge as a part of criminal procedure process in the new judicial system of Israel. Such a system tempered the oft-times wild system of blood revenge common in the ancient world, in which offended parties chased after the presumed guilty party and obtained vigilante justice. Obviously, many other persons other than Moses suffered injustice in Egypt under unstable royalist government conditions, as the ancient Egyptian story of Sinuhe demonstrates. Pharaoh could not only enact personal blood revenge when he was assaulted, but he could do so even when merely insulted, or when he sensed the slightest threat to his leadership. In fact, he attempted to wipe out the entire population of Hebrews at the Red Sea even after he had given them permission to leave. His father (or possibly grandfather) attempted to wipe out Hebrew newborn babies. The ninth commandment law requiring honest testimony (no false witness) also put the brakes on emotion-fueled justice and helped to hedge up the sixth commandment prohibition of politically unwarranted killing. It set the stage for a real justice system in Israel. It also complemented the second commandment's implied commitment to education by instilling a culture of scientific inquiry and study—a search for truth— in the new nation.

Egypt, as clearly remembered in the case of the ten plagues that befell the nation before the exodus, was a place of frequent environmental threats to health, and vulnerability to contagious disease due to dense population groupings in urban areas along the Nile River. Certainly slave camps like Pithom, where the Hebrews labored for Pharoah, were places where disease spread particularly fast. Migratory desert life minimized such threats to a degree, since many of Egypt's notorious diseases were river water-borne. Dispersed hill country life in Canaan would help even more. However, it was clear to Moses and the elders that Israel needed quarantine practices related to communicable and infectious disease (impurity) that would minimize the spread of such plagues. The tenth commandment was intended primarily as a provision for individuals to promote and protect their neighbor's political and economic and social interests (no coveting). But one of the most important civic interests was maintaining good health among the people. A legal provision requiring neighbors to maintain a reasonable physical and social distance from neighboring families, their members and their clothing and properties, gave authority to the public health purity laws of the nation.

A Closer Look: Separation of Cult and Crown in Ancient Israel

ISRAEL CLEARLY SAW SOME kind of separation of state cult and regular state administrative function as necessary for limiting national power and securing religious freedom. In the literature on the subject, there is as yet no simple accepted terminology in ancient texts like the Bible for what in modern terms we call "separation" of cult and secular activity. Those magistrates who later encroach upon the priestly office on the national level, however, were said to have set up "a snare" to their own government administration, or to have "trespassed" or done what "appertaineth not unto thee." (Judg 8:27; 2 Chron 26:18) Perhaps "coveting" is an appropriate Biblical legal term for desiring what cannot belong to one or what is illegal or unconstitutional. Judges/chief magistrates/military commanders covet priestly power, and priests covet secular power, both illegitimately in Israel.

We have already briefly reviewed the separation of ritual and secular spheres that Moses, Aaron, and the elders negotiated at Sinai. Here we will argue that there are both earlier and later evidences of this separation. The earlier is the great debate on cult and state between Moses and Pharaoh, and the later is the Levite policy established in the wilderness. The actions of Moses and the elders in the wilderness served as additional precedents to define the characteristics of executive department political leadership under the first commandment frame of government. In order for subsequent leaders to be "like Moses" they had to keep their hands off the ecclesiastic offices of the confederation members.

At Pharaoh's court, Moses, in behalf of the people and in behalf of good government, argued in favor of separating decision-making relative to priestly matters and decision-making relative to secular matters. He continuously and passionately argued for cult decision-making to be in the hands of the Hebrew community of worshippers rather than in the hands of the national ruler, and for civic ritual to be separated from secular administration. First, Pharaoh denied the Hebrew request for a holiday religious observance altogether, thus asserting the government's right to dictate religious matters. Then, after he and the elders won the right to a holiday, Moses wanted women to be a part of the three day religious pilgrimage. But Pharaoh would only allow men. Moses and the elders also asserted the right to decide for themselves which animals would be used for sacrifice. Pharaoh wanted to deny them that privilege. Because national political officials wanted to control the specific parameters of civic and perhaps even private ritual practice for Moses' people, the Israelites had a strong interest in separating the secular and sacred functions of society from each other once they were free to set up their own system of government.

After the flight from Egypt, Moses negotiated his way out of having the new nation use a molten idol to symbolize and finance the new administration. He persuaded Israel to remember their travails under Egyptian strong kingship with its system of unity of religious power and state power. They accepted a law (the second commandment) to nullify any notion of molten political idolatry in their new government system. The first commandment's emphasis on religious freedom and the second commandment's emphasis on limiting executive power together necessitated separation of priestly and secular functions. However, it remained for Israel to hammer out a specific policy that would build the sort of "wall of separation" (to use a modern term) which would effectuate this constitutional provision. Moses subsequently proposed, and the elders accepted (it could not be law if they did not accept it), an executive department organization plan that split the one Egyptian line of government authority into two lines of authority in the Israelite national administrative organization chart. In Exodus 28–29 (compare Leviticus 8–9), we see that the state invested Aaron with priestly governmental duties, leaving Moses with secular duties. These secular duties, called "judgment" in the King James Version, related to national defense and general government administration, including judicial duties.

Moses also proposed, and the people accepted, the Levite policy, which set the separation policy even more firmly into statutory law. Only members of the Levite tribe could become priests. Thus, politicians from any of the other eleven tribes who became chief magistrates could not usurp the priestly function.[1] On the other hand, Levites presumably could become politicians. However, there were two checks on this possibility. In the first

---

1. Gideon did a sterling job of not usurping priestly function while in political office, but incurred the wrath of the historian for dabbling in priestly matters after apparently retiring from full-time political office. (Judg 8:22–27)

place, Levites lacked political credentials to lead Israel. Lacking land, Levites did not have the economic basis to be politicians, and having military exemption, they lacked military experience to become crisis commanders. In the second place, if somehow a Levite overcame those severe disqualifications for office, he likely would have to shun any pretentions to priestly function once installed in secular office. This separation of shrine and state, cult and commander, priesthood and judgeship, became a check and balance on political power throughout the next several hundred year period until Saul and Solomon did harm to it, and others after them like Ahab in the north, and Manasseh in the South did yet further harm to it. The Hasmonean Jews, a hundred and fifty years before Christ, finally destroyed the Israelite version of the "wall" altogether when their high priest became a king wearing purple and sporting gold. Moses' Levite policy, however, had preempted that eventuality for a thousand years by making Israel essentially into a two-kingdom culture. It made a division of labor in the form of a horizontal balance of power between semi-religious priestly officials, and fully secular political officials. It also made a division in local society between the sacral and the secular powers. Sacred matters were left to be regulated by clan and family leaders or local priests officiating in Yahwistic denominational matters of their own choosing,[2] while civic government affairs were committed to elders and heads.

To some extent the waxing and waning of the separation of priestly vs. military/general administrative power in the national government is one of the main themes of the Bible. For example, the two great political revolutionary upheavals in the book's history, Jeroboam's revolution and Jehu's revolt, resulted in part from infractions in the separation policy. An important related theme in the Bible is the freedom of the non-governmental sphere to conduct its private sacral business without interference from the government. Initially, the nation tolerated a wide variety of political and religious viewpoints in the intellectual realm. Prophets and concerned priests spoke out when the nation defaulted either to overly broad or overly restrictive enforcement of the laws and construction of the constitution. Their right to speak was protected by the first commandment, as we will see below. The first and second commandments together gave authority for horizontal separation of administration power in the executive branch. The second commandment ensured the national government would not be beefy enough to threaten local belief or sacral activity of almost any kind.[3]

---

2. Archeological remains demonstrate that some believed Yahweh had a wife, for example, while many seemingly did not.

3. See Shinkoskey, *Prophets*, for an in-depth analysis of the human rights content of the first commandment.

Separation of cultic function from civic administration was associated with decentralized government in the ancient world. Israel helped establish this pattern, and the pattern may have been evident long before Israel in Mesopotamia. A well documented example is the case of Rome. Rome passed through three great phases: kingdom, republic, and empire. In earliest Roman society, those two functions were largely fused in the person of the strong king. During the republican period following the early kings, separation was common. Finally, when Augustus became emperor at the end of the republican period, he re-instituted control over the various priesthoods.[4] In America, the British crown exercised control over Anglican religious matters during the colonial period. Following the Roman experience, close association of church and state on the national level was prohibited by constitutional law during the early republican period, and in time the states enacted similar provisions.

Israel lived for a lengthy period as Rome did, under consolidated rule over both spheres while she was in Egypt. But once she obtained freedom and turned to republicanism, she separated those powers in order to free each administration from the control of the other. Frankfort reminds, "The Hebrew king normally functioned in the profane sphere, not in the sacred sphere . . . He was emphatically not the leader in the cult . . . The king created the conditions which made a given form of worship possible . . . But the king played little part in the cult. He did not, as a rule, sacrifice, that was the task of the priests. He did not interpret the divine will; that, again, was the task of the priests, who cast lots for an oracle." In sum, "The relation between the Hebrew monarch and his people was as nearly secular as is possible in a society wherein religion is a living force. The unparalleled feature in this situation is the independence, the almost complete separation, of the bonds which existed between Yahweh and the Hebrew people, on the one hand, and between Yahweh and the House of David, on the other."[5]

It must be said that the nations of the ancient Near East presented two basic varieties of chief magistracy with respect to sacral matters: limited connectivity, and strong connectivity. Many kings had a limited role in the cult, and the issue was apparently hotly debated when they intruded any further, if the court experience of the Mesopotamian king Urukagina (2750 BCE) is representative.[6] In early Canaan, Abraham entered into a

---

4. Jayne, *Healing Gods*, 379–80, 391–92.
5. Frankfort, *Kingship and the Gods*, 341.
6. Urukagina shifted the level of administrative involvement in priestly matters one way or the other, according to which scholarly school one reads, but arguably made political waves in doing what he did. See Mieroop, *Ancient Near East*, and Nissen, *Early History*, for example.

tribal alliance with the righteous high priest/king Melchizedek, who apparently represented a mild version of secular capture of cult matters. Possibly Melchizedek and Abraham together exemplified a type of tolerant confederacy within which small constituent units could capture or favor specific religious practice on their own, as long as they respected rights to different types of worship in the other constituent tribes. After all, Abraham, like Melchizedek, likely led his own clan in religious matters, since he was known as an oracular prophet.

A similar confederate tolerance apparently characterized Israel in the later "wandering" period. The story is told in Joshua about the nine and a half tribes who were concerned about the somewhat dissident civic-religious views held by the two and a half tribes who settled east of Jordan. It was there that they built their own regional altar, suggesting a certain degree of independence in political and religious matters. The nine and a half tribes ended up reconciling themselves to the religious and political autonomy of the minority, and that seemed to set the tone for tribal independence during the settlement period. This happened in the early American republic as well, when constituent states in the early national confederation that governed immediately after the revolution maintained separate and distinct established churches.

Moses, on the other hand, was determined to get Pharaoh out of the business of prescribing religious practice for the Hebrews. If it could not be done, he was determined to lead Israel in a mass migration out of Egypt. Israel initially patterned church-state relations, during the "state-of-nature" period before the constitution was written, on the Midianite confederation model, where the priest did the sacrifice rites, not the prince. Moses invited the priest Jethro to officiate over Israel's first national sacrifice rite, thus declining to do so himself. (Exod 18:10–12) Such an early national posture encouraged Israelites that they would be free in cultic matters to worship as they pleased, within constitutional boundaries.[7] This early practice translated into constitutional law at Sinai. The first commandment removed any doubt about the new nation's posture concerning state religion by enacting freedom of religion for all citizens, and in particular, for dissident prophetic viewpoints.[8] The prophets often deviated from the self-ingratiating na-

---

7. Americans were similarly free to worship as they pleased, subject to constitutional boundaries. When some Americans crossed those boundaries, they were prosecuted. This happened in early America when the Mormons practiced polygamy, and in early Israel when Israel experimented with the cultic prostitution practice of the people of Baal-Peor; see Num 25.

8. See Shinkoskey, *Prophets*, especially "Freedom Laws of Ancient Israel," 104–110.

tional priestly point of view about politics and religion ("big" politics and "big" religion) and instead pointed Israel back to its original constitutional understanding about limited national government and small religion.[9] The second commandment prohibition on molten idolatry prevented sacral kingship from developing in Israel. No national leadership party or individual should become so strong as to usurp sacral public ritual or usurp the prerogatives of local legislative bodies of elders either. Moses set the early standard by not only negotiating away from Aaron's push for sacred kingship before the government was finally settled, but also tolerating the religion-tinged political party organizational activities of Eldad and Medad who were "prophesying" independent of priestly activity after the government was in operation.

Upon settlement in Canaan, the wilderness policy of tolerance and separation was enshrined in permanent policy by a statute establishing a permanent civil service priesthood from the Levite tribe, and a tradition of allowing secular/military leadership of time-limited "judges" to derive from any tribe in the confederacy. This latter tradition assured that no family dynasty from one tribe could dominate national politics. During settlement, in addition, the temporary political capitol supporting the current judge's activities was separated from the sacral center where the national priestly bureaucracy and foundational government documents were housed. For example, Samuel "judged" the people at Mizpeh, while Eli supervised priestly staff at Shiloh. However, some 250 years after crossing Jordan, David overturned the practice of separate cities for the two branches of executive administration of government. He housed both houses in Jerusalem. Within two short generations after he did so, pro-constitution rebels in the north seceded from the union and set up two cities for ongoing seats of priestly financial administration of government and separate, mobile venues for secular/military administration. This practice continued in the north until Ahab, like David, merged the state capitol with the priestly capitol by building a temple for Baal in his capitol city of Samaria. Ahab's transgression was a double no-no. Ahab had not only appointed priestly cronies to government rather than using the civil service, but he subverted the law against foreign alliances by strongly affiliating with the molten idolatry kingdom of Tyre. Jehu then led a revolt against the dynasty and removed the temple from the capitol city (he did so by actually destroying it). In the southern

---

9. This early freedom could be carried to an extreme. It later resulted, for example, in Jeroboam's revolt against Solomon's royalist practice of expanding government and making international alliances with nations whose political and civic religious views offended Israel's own. On top of this, Solomon granted place for the building of local embassies in Jerusalem to support his political alliances.

kingdom, Josiah's constitutional reform returned the national priesthood to civil service status (Levites only), undoing the political crony system of appointments initiated by David and Solomon.

Bible histories in Kings and Chronicles make clear that there existed in both northern and southern kingdoms what might be called prince/priest pairs involved in government administration, mimicking in many ways the two consuls of early Roman democratic national administration, one devoted to military and the other to civilian/financial/sacral affairs.[10] At times, the priestly administrator seemed to be selected as an internal prerogative of the priestly enclave, at times was subject to popular selection, and at other times was appointed by the prince/king, as in the time of David and Solomon. David undermined the second commandment by moving secular power from local hands to the national magistrate's hands by means of his military victories and expansion of the boundaries of the nation, which brought tribute income to the national coffers. His popularity, personal spirituality, and interest in national history, allowed him the latitude to direct national sacral administrative activity by appointing the nation's high priests.

During David's kingship the nation moved not only to stronger military government, but to a type of divine kingship political philosophy, accompanied by enthronement psalms, rhetoric about the king as savior of the people, and additional priestly credentials accorded the king. As party leader as well as king, David introduces another element of strong kingship by picking his son to be his successor. At first, Solomon ruled as an ethical and educated public servant should do, and so was acceptable as a constitutional monarch. Did people understand that this was the beginning of a hereditary monarchy? Solomon later got extremely liberal socially and constitutionally and co-opted elders from tribal and local government into his federal bureaucracy. That move set the population on edge. Solomon's son Rehoboam could not sustain a hereditary approach to political leadership, especially in the north. But it was not just the hereditary aspect that bothered northerners. He co-opted too much priestly power. Priests from the time of Moses dealt with revenue/taxation matters, for example. But Rehoboam listened to those of his advisers who counseled that he could take the budget/appropriations function away from the priests. When he

---

10. The sacral official in Rome was called the Pontifex Maximus, or the king/official over sacred matters. The priestly aspect of national government in Israel might be likened to the modern pastorate of our American National Chapel (Episcopal Church-based) coupled perhaps with an Interior Department, Treasury Department or White House Office of Religious Affairs.

announced a heavy, new, and perhaps discriminatory, taxation burden on the north, the people of the north decided to revolt and secede.

In fact, it was likely laxity in priestly administration of its own affairs during the time of Samuel that threw political support to a faction seeking greater centralization of administration of government. The elders thought that perhaps an ethical king could supervise priestly affairs more effectively than the priests themselves. David appeared to fit the bill of a charismatic leader with huge respect for both God and country. Accordingly, David appointed a new priestly house headed by Zadok, after first thinking about appointing his sons as priests. The unseating of the house of Levi by David lasted until Josiah was made aware of an ancient document specifying a strong and independent Levitical priesthood as a stanchion of limited national government during the time of Moses. This text, the Book of Deuteronomy, enhanced and developed by political operatives close to the Josiah administration, aligned the Josiah reform with the edited contents of Deuteronomy. It placed clear limits on the magistrate's involvement in Levite affairs and judicial affairs, making clear that the judiciary was to operate independently of the executive department. In the deal giving local Levites power in the national government, Josiah got a stronger and more disciplined central government to help him deal with foreign military hegemony pressing hard upon the Israelite state in the south.

The views of the groups and individuals in both north and south who wanted a greater sacral role for the king persisted but did not completely prevail. Throughout the time of kings in the north and south, kings ventured into sacral affairs and were rebuked but not necessarily overturned by constitutional specialist prophets and historians. Such "royal trespass in the sanctuary," as styled by one historian, is first committed during Judges by Gideon, who wanted to exercise the priestly oracular function in behalf of the government. (Judg 8:24–27) Gideon's son Abimelech not only wanted to implement hereditary kingship, but also a twisted variety of sacral kingship. He flat-out stole money from the priestly treasury and hired his own low-life priests to run his short-lived government. During the monarchies, royal trespass in the sanctuary was committed notably by Saul (1 Sam 13–15) and Uzziah. (2 Chr 26:16–21)

During the Second Temple period after return from Babylonian captivity, the Jewish Hasmonean rulers tried to emulate either the prophetic patriarchal period of sacral princes like Abraham and Mechizedek, or the spirit-infused judges of the early settlement, but ended up taking on more the aspect of ancient Near East divine kingship. They both administered high priestly affairs and also wore the purple and gold of strong hereditary kingship. This perhaps was meant to please their Greek overlords or to entertain their constituents with the idea they were modern day Solomons. Later on, Rome overran Palestine and clearly wanted a puppet government in Judea run like the government of the divine Caesars at home. Jesus and the New Testament took a position dead set against the puppet ruler Herod and his descendants for that reason. Jesus shunned violent revolution (following Moses' approach in Egypt), instead teaching in his sermons and parables that there was much education that needed to be done among the people concerning real democratic constitutional government before Israel could become an independent nation of locally governing citizen-priests again. In fact, movement missionaries would have to serve as ambassadors of local, fair, people-oriented, prophetic government throughout the Roman world before enough political muscle could be built to nudge Roman leadership off its present pedestal of citizen emperor worship.

In sum, Moses did not try to implement divine dynastic succession. He went only so far as to establish a tradition of the magistrate appointing the priestly administrator of the government. Perhaps, even, he himself did not pick Aaron as much as the Levites did. David, however, put his toes into the waters of dynastic succession, but based apparently, on the ability of his offspring to respect constitutional values. In his view, and the party of Nathan who supported him, both the governing secular and priestly administrators of the nation, subject to the legislating body of elders, could be hereditary houses just like the priestly Aaronites were initially set up to be in the beginning. In addition, if the priests could not keep their house in order, the new hereditary monarchy perhaps could do that by exercising an appointment power over the upper echelons of their members.[11] But both the priestly house and the Davidic monarchic house had to retain the support of the people, or their sinecure (family civil service rights) could be ended. The Davidites from Judah could not sustain popularity against the long tradition of Mosaic limited government and anti-kingship which had taken root particularly strongly in the north, particularly when they eroded constitutional government so quickly and so arrogantly. It was as if Rehoboam brought shame on the House of David, just as Pharaoh Ramses II had brought shame on the dynastic house of Seti.

---

11. This struggle was like the back-and-forth struggle in early American history over control of the federal bureaucracy. Some, like the northern party in Israel, wanted a strong and extensive civil service, protected from political manipulation. Some, like the southern party in Israel, wanted political control of a larger part of the bureaucracy.

13

The First Two Commandments: Organizing Government

The First Commandment

"Thou shalt have no other gods before me." (Exod 20:3)

THE MOST OUTSTANDING CHARACTERISTIC of the God of the Hebrews was his willingness to respond to the wishes of an oppressed people. This concern for common people was the only heavenly identity that was really revealed to Moses at first, except for the fact Yahweh also guided the ancestors in their quest for freedom and land as well. It is important to note that it was the Hebrew people in Egypt who started the whole ball rolling by "crying" out to heaven. They took the initiative. Their new God initially responded by sending them a capable and selfless political organizer to help them develop their potential for self-government. God said to Moses, "Go and gather the elders of Israel together." (Exod 3:16) God seemed to be saying that the answer to autocratic government was a demonstration of the good sense and effectiveness of representative government.

Republican government was known within the ancient Near East as a type of government utilizing bodies of legislating elders. Thus it was not simply a stab in the dark that the first political act prescribed by God and implemented by Moses was the organization of such a body. That first political act served not only as a reminder of the very ancient and storied way of democracy but as a way of establishing the preeminence of elder government at the very beginning of the activities of the budding nation. Israel's commitment to the God of Sinai meant she was committed to the government processes that had their birth in the cries of the people and in the government system devised at the mountain. Later on, the first commandment institutionalized the organization and empowerment of the legislative branch of the national government. Israel was to always embrace the humane political system they wanted in the beginning of their story as a nation. That political system was based on participation of the people in the lawmaking of the tribes individually and the lawmaking of the confederated tribes collectively. Staunchly maintaining a system of legislature-based republican government is the real meaning and purpose of having "no other gods" ahead of the God of Sinai.

When the people cried out, they were looking not only for a long term way out of their predicament, but also for administrative help to ease their immediate burdens. God, who was listening, but did not act bodily in the world, found a solid person to deliver the emergency assistance the elders needed. He sent Moses, who had prior experience at Pharaoh's court, to the elders of the people and they accepted him as their crisis administrator and negotiator with Pharaoh. The gathering together of legislating elders and the acceptance of Moses as administrator were the very first electoral processes in the soon-to-be Israelite nation. These two steps set the pattern for the many later acts of political re-constitution undertaken by Israel in times of trouble or of special need. It was the intent of the people and their God that forevermore the people should voice their concerns, be relieved of their current distresses by electoral processes, and thus be continually empowered to decide their own fates.

It is this mentality, this God, that the first commandment permanently enjoined upon the people once they were free of Egypt. No other civic organizing or operating principles were to be used to displace the heavenly spirit who saw unwarranted repression and encouraged a people to extricate and then govern themselves. This same government electoral process was used to select a national magistrate for the next 250 years in Israel, and a modification of it for the next 400 years after that. Constitutional party leaders like Moses stood as intermediaries for God and advocates for God's system of elder representative government. As an intermediary, a judge or prophet could either serve as the national magistrate as Moses and Joshua did, or find and nominate a prospective national leader as Samuel did. In this latter case, the party leader submitted the nominee to either the legislating elders or to the people as a whole, who then voted. National leaders were not always successful in getting elected as easily as Moses, but politicians forevermore led in republican Israel only by consent of the people.[1] Overall, "good"

---

1. It is not always clear who voters are in various electoral events. In most cases it seems able-bodied men do the voting. In other cases, women, and even children, seem to get involved. We discussed electoral terminology in the section on people and elders.

prophets distinguished themselves by promoting legislative supremacy in government. When they arrived on the scene, they asked for a return to a God who listened to the people's wishes and for a return to the original law that put the legislative prerogative in the hands of the tribal elders. Bad prophets, which were plentiful in Israel after settlement, supported parties looking to centralize government and thus distance it from the minds and hands of the people.

There is no indication in the early chapters of Exodus that the people in Egypt had a working system of elder representatives prior to the arrival of Moses. The only Hebrew leaders were "officers," those who assisted Pharaoh's task masters get more and more work out of the people. The word "officers" in Biblical terms has a clear meaning. Officers were paid employees in the national government administration. In this case, they were go-fers for Pharaoh, and not for the people. When Moses arrived on the scene, it is likely he encouraged the people to choose their own representative officials, or elders, or at least to re-activate them or prepare them for expanded duty.

Organizing the elders was essentially both a process of organizing local government and providing a vehicle for families and clans to influence tribal and national politics by sending local elders to councils of government at the tribal level. The Exodus from Egypt was purposefully organized by the elders into bodies of tribes. Later on, the distribution of land in Canaan was also allocated by tribes. These two actions made a strong political statement about the location of sovereignty, or final say-so in the confederacy of tribes. The first organizing act of Moses and the first law given at Sinai respected those statements about sovereignty and thus set the tone for limits on the national government with respect to tribal powers. The first commandment empowered a confederate (weak) form of national government by making each tribe an autonomous governmental unit within the loose confederation. Going out of Egypt in disciplined political tribal units established a precedent for tribal rights. Obtaining specific tribal land for their own people gave them the power to effectuate their political claims due to the economic power their inalienable land gave them.

The first commandment allowed, and almost required, families, clans, and tribes to put their particular political stamp on their representatives to the national government when it came to voting on national policies. The law also strongly encouraged the people to participate in the smaller entities that made up the government on tribal, clan, and household levels. The national government, as the second commandment made clear, had extremely limited access to the private lives of the citizens, particularly their religious (i.e., "cultic") needs and practices. The national government was to be empowered only so far as to protect the separate and distinct economic, social, political, and religious interests of the twelve sovereign tribes who "signed" the covenant pact. The law existed to ensure for all of the tribes what they did not have under Pharaoh, but otherwise the national government had to stay out of the way of direct supervision of the people until a time of crisis. In fact, the reason that the national government was limited and temporary—only for crises—was because citizens on the local level were busy doing the great bulk of the real burden of government.

Accordingly, the national elders did not legislate to solve every problem of Israel. During the wilderness and judge periods they were not seen legislating on matters of health, education, and welfare. Their activities were restricted to national elections, making war and peace, intertribal relations, and perhaps inter-confederate roads and national holiday festivals and political gatherings with attendant sacrifices. In sum, the limitation of the national power with respect to the tribal power was a natural outgrowth of first commandment law. But there were other constitutional articles limiting the national government's power. The second commandment directly limited the functions of the national administrator. The third commandment limited national power over the private economic sector. The fifth commandment asserted family government rights of parents.

It is telling that God's first commandment to Moses, "Go and gather the elders of Israel together," (Exod 3:16) later inspired the first commandment given to the entire nation at Sinai. The priority and content of the first constitutional article was to define and empower a legislative body to rule in Israel. The God of Israel was the organizer and protector of the national legislature. That is how he identified himself and how he wanted to be remembered. That act being accomplished, God essentially receded into the background and let the people do the work of "salvation," essentially civic policy-making. They were to truly be the agents of their own civic salvation from day to day. God was not seen or heard again by Moses or the elders until the moment at Sinai where he assisted Moses and the elders with the writing and ratification of the entire slate of ten laws. Thereafter he was only present in the rumblings of volcanoes, in a cloud overhanging the box which housed the Decalogue, and perhaps in private counsel with Moses concerning important constitutional issues.

An encouragement from God to Moses to "Go and gather" the elders of Israel essentially meant, "Go and make sure the voices of the people in every tribe, clan, and family are heard." The first direction given to Moses effectively became the first direction given to all of Israel at Sinai and the first imperative of the society throughout all of its subsequent history. God demonstrated the necessity and supremacy of the will of the people acting collectively by being the first to listen to their cries, listen to their voices. God himself thus obeyed his own first commandment by answering the freedom "cries" of the people.[2] He respected the basic policy wishes of the people. He sided with the people's legitimate aspirations. They wanted rest from labor and the right to worship as they pleased. These two top priority items he made sure they got, after a lot of wear and tear on their national administrator Moses. The first commandment to the people at Sinai must be interpreted the same way as the first commandment given to Moses at Sinai, as an inducement for ordinary people to organize politically and petition for redress of grievances so they could save themselves from a horrible demise and create a better life. After Sinai, all of the people were enjoined to establish freedom the same way Moses established it and the same way that God did. They would do that by organizing themselves into governing bodies in the tribes and deciding policy for themselves.

We are not saying here, however, that the first commandment's only function was to authorize an election procedure for the national elders and the national magistrate, and to establish priority in authority between the two. We will see there were other issues the law defined and resolved as well. We are also not saying that because God was involved in the process, the first commandment was some kind of theological statement about religious worship. It was, in truth, a constitutional statement of the political values/ethics of ancient Israel. Israel was, from the beginning of her confederate, and later, national existence, a democracy in the broad sense of the word. The tribes housed under one roof a tremendous variety of religious and political views and this law gave them a way to express those views and mediate between them. In a more technical sense, Israel was a democratic confederation, a polity that used locally elected representatives to make the laws for a people who then agreed to live by them. The first commandment made not just elections but local power to the people actually happen. First commandment law thus clearly had a government function, not a religious function.

To pursue this point a bit further, we are implying that it is incorrect to say that the most outstanding interest of the God of the Hebrews was theological,[3] or social, or economic, or philosophic, or emotional, or intellectual. In fact, it was starkly and confessedly *political*, that is, relating to the distribution and use of power. God's interest was political in the broadest

---

2. Later on, God respects the wishes of the people even when he would rather they make different choices.

3. However, one might say he is an immanent (close) God, or an oracular (speaking/revelatory) God, or a merciful God, or some such other kind of description of his basic goodness and godness.

sense. It was that kind of politics that people set in motion when they drew up democratic charters or constitutions of government. Those charters didn't specify the policies of the government, but rather only who would be deciding the policies.

In a very important sense, this God was a civic God. People did not have a civic life in Egypt. The first commandment gave this to them. But the first commandment did not give the people a king like the people of Egypt had. God, Moses, and the elders did not want them to have that kind of civic life. The first commandment gave them a representative legislature and gave that legislature supremacy over the chief magistrate. In fact, there was a curious admonition given to Moses even before he agreed to the task of organizing the elders. That statement was, "Draw not nigh hither." (Exod 3:5) This obscure verse may reasonably be interpreted as a warning to popular politicians to stay away from the legislative prerogative of the people, their representatives, and their protective God. God and the people now stood together in an impregnable policy-making alliance, and even a very talented administrator and policy wonk must stay out of their way. God sided with the people and trusted the wisdom of their collective legislative effort over the limited eyesight of all individual pretenders to power.

In fact, in the imagination of ancient Israel, this God was the only individual leader who had sufficient ethical fiber to fit the bill as a ruler or "king" over Israel. He himself, by means of his sacred commandments and the legislative body he protects, presides as an invisible magistrate himself over all arenas of life. No human king can watch effectively over the interests of the people, but a divine king can. The divine king inspires both legislators, administrators, judges, prophets, priests, and ordinary citizens, to do their best in limited roles. That is why the Bible refers so frequently to the kingship of God. The law of this God embraces the legitimate aspirations of all the people all of the time, no matter whether "liberal" or "conservative,"[4] and no matter what their specific religious beliefs. An individual judge or prophet often represents a specific faction and set of interests. That is not so with God. Should an earthly magistrate, and God-forbid, the peoples' legislature default on their responsibilities and make bad decisions, this God and this God's law, when interpreted correctly, kicks into action again to make good things happen politically. The law makes good things happen by allowing ordinary but highly ethical citizens to study history and constitutional law and to respond to a call from on high to help the nation get back on its feet again. The way God and the law does this is by giving all of the people the civil right to speak and be heard, and all of the people the

---

4. There are biblical stories of these kinds of factions at work in Israel.

right to believe as they wish and act reasonably upon their beliefs.[5] In this environment of freedom of expression, one like Moses appears again and again in Israelite history to badger the people back into responsible citizenship and self-government.

This God is similar to other national gods in the ancient Near East in that he represents and reflects a particular people, history, and culture. But this God is different than others at the same time. This God wants to empower all the people, and not limit them as they were limited in Egypt. The only person he would set clear limits on is the national magistrate, because the magistrate potentially has his hands on so much power that he could easily be corrupted if not for legal restraints.

The first commandment organizes and empowers the legislative branch in Israel by the same method that the United States constitution organizes and empowers the legislative branch in the American democratic republic. Both the Israelite and American constitutions place information in their first articles to ensure that the people can and will act through their representatives in the legislature to maintain supremacy over all other sources of power. The articles on the legislative power of the people are placed in the first position in those constitutions for a reason.

It is apparent from "second" articles in both constitutions that the respective founders intended that the executive branches of their governments be very limited in power.[6] Chief magistrates finish in second place with respect to the people, and their secondary priority is meant to be a lasting way of political life in both nations. Israel's second article indicates that the nation is not to move toward a monarchic system of government, a golden calf system of molten image government based on economic and political ties to favored neighboring nations. Such a government often makes the laws without input or consent of the people. Both Israel's and America's second article of constitutional government specifically takes away functions from the magistrate that kings in other cultures often exercise. The two commandments/articles are intimately related. The first commandment says how the government must operate, and the second commandment says how it must not operate. Both articles are needed not only to organize the government but to make things absolutely clear to subsequent generations what the founding generation stood for in terms of priorities.

---

5. During the periods of wilderness wanderings, Judges, and early in Kings, we learn that the nation embraces many theological and political party beliefs, but still holds to only one constitution, the Ten Commandments. That constitution unfortunately, say the prophets, is later neglected even while still revered as the law of the land.

6. For a somewhat contrary view, see Eric Nelson's book, *The Royalist Revolution*. This book details how some wanted a king from the beginning in America.

There were several high priority issues needing the attention not only of the elders, but likely all of the people assembled together in Israel. The first commandment empowered legislative decision-making with respect to these issues. One of the most important issues requiring democratic say-so from the people was the issue of war and peace. Still another issue was giving consent to the length of office of the administrative office holder. We saw that in the wilderness more than once when the people forced a vote of confidence regarding the prospect of Moses' continuing leadership.[7]

We have suggested above that one broad purpose of the commandments in general and of the first commandment in particular was to enact civil rights for the people. Without these rights a legislature elected by the people would be a sham, reflecting the policies promoted by the only leader and party able to express an opinion and make policy. As we mentioned in the introduction to this chapter, the purpose of all ten of the foundational laws was to get for Israel what they didn't have in Egypt, a say-so in the conditions of their daily lives. Therefore the first law not only provided a national electoral process and a prioritization of official activity in the national government, but a bill of civil rights to help them retain political freedom throughout their time in Canaan. The first commandment surely protected religious and political rights of speech and activity, and other commandments enacted other rights as we shall see.

The first commandment, for example, provided authority for various laws related to religious freedom, including the freedom given to priests and local tribal cultures to set up altars and lead shrine worshipers at various "high places." (Exod. 20:25; Deut 18:6–8; Josh 22; 1 Sam 9:6) Bible prophets felt that some of the people went too far in the direction of liberalism while exercising their freedom to worship at the high place of their choice. Clearly, however, some high place altars, like the one where Samuel worshipped, was within legal bounds. If religious freedom was given to average citizens to worship as they wished, political freedom was also given to legitimate prophets/political organizers to do their work of upholding the original construction of the constitution through criticism of the current politics and ethics of the people. (Deut 13) Samuel took advantage of both kinds of freedom and his life was meant by Bible writers to be an example to all Israelite people.

The rights of expression activated by the first commandment came about because Israelites were not allowed free speech in Egypt. When they spoke up, Pharaoh responded by doubling their brick production quota.

---

7. Such events included the complaints expressed by Miriam and Aaron, Korah with Dathan and Abiram, and the great unhappiness of the people at the Waters of Meribah.

The First Two Commandments 139

The first commandment would now allow them to be heard and their views taken seriously and not treated with repression. The first commandment thus enacted the same kinds of rights much later embodied in the Bill of Rights appended to the American constitution. We will see that the sixth through tenth commandments round out the Israelite bill of civil rights very capably, and have parallels in the U.S. Constitution.[8]

A foundational law to promote veneration of a God of political freedom ("have no other gods before me") has little meaning without a government policy that actively protects historical memory of such a god and actively protects daily practice of a full slate of freedom laws. The first commandment enacts freedom of political and religious speech so that future citizens, prophets, historians, political scientists, can research, speak out write, organize, change the law, and get back to the state of political freedom and power that their ancestors had at Sinai, in the wilderness, and in the early days of their democratic republic in Canaan.[9] Democracy is always threatened by ambitious elected officials who push for concentration of power in the national government and in themselves, and thus become tyrants like Ramses II, or like Abimelech during Judges, or Rehoboam during Kings. The law counteracted this tendency by providing freedom for citizens to organize into political parties, and elect reformist leaders to get the nation back on track again. This would be done by returning power to local government and to legislative bodies, taking it away from tyrants who stole it from the people in the first place. When Rehoboam centralized government decision-making in the united kingdom of Israel, Jeroboam and the northern elders fomented a revolution. In the new northern government, they eased taxation, distributed government offices closer to the people, and likely brought tribal elders back into legislative prominence.

Since Israel had two independent lines of executive department authority, general managerial and financial/priestly, democracy could also be derailed by government priests who acted in self interest rather than the public interest. Under the Ten Commandment constitution and its first commandment freedom of religion, however, one priest or priestly party could not easily marginalize other priests or groupings of priests. Those priests could set up rival claims to authority and contend for both government and private cultic power. Under the constitution, freedom was given to all priests in Israel to provide health and education services, and to provide ritual services to governments and to private shrines to help the people

---

8. See Appendix I.

9. See Shinkoskey, *Prophets*, especially "Freedom Laws of Ancient Israel," 104–110.

get benefit and support from the heavenly God as they interpreted the deity. Keeping their eyes focused on the first commandment assured the people they were entitled to free speech, free assembly, free press (scribal activity), free priesthood, free prophet activity, and free elections, and Israel demonstrated its extensive use of all of these throughout every period of its history. Remembering the liberation story of Exodus and upholding the liberation laws gave people a sense that they could leave Egypt again in the future if they needed to.

Above, we mentioned that early constitutional practices in the wilderness provide a window to the legislative intent of the Sinai law. What people and politicians do right after ratifying a constitutional law provides a clear indication of what the constitution authorized them to do in terms of government operations. The prologue to the first commandment also provides a good dose of legislative intent regarding the commandment law. We mentioned above that the Jewish first commandment is the sentence taken as the "prologue" by most Christians: "I am the Lord thy God, which have brought thee out of the land of Egypt, out of the house of bondage." (Exod 20:2; Deut 5:6) Protestant Christians use the next sentence as the first commandment: "Thou shalt have no other gods before me." (Exod 20:3; Deut 5:7) Together these two verses make a strong case for the interpretation we advance here. The prologue verse suggests that Yahweh is best defined by his ability to make freedom and consensual government possible for a people. The people, however, must take the political initiative to help themselves. They must do this by implementing the second sentence/verse. The second verse asks that Israelites venerate no other god besides the God who promotes political independence for the nation and protects the widely varying interests of all the individual citizens. All this is to be accomplished by exercise of the people's own abilities to set policy for themselves. They must zealously uphold the principle of power to the people. The comfort such a God brings to the people once independence and republican representation are fashioned is really acceptable to all regardless of specific religious creed, geographic location, or ethnic identification. Many urban Egyptians and desert nomadic pastoralists of non-Israelite stock joined the Israelites in the Exodus venture. Self-determination was a universal longing in the ancient world as it is today.

The prologue sentence can be thought of as a law-as-testament or law-as-political-witness statement. Knowledge of the original political conditions and founder beliefs inevitably grows fuzzy over time, as concerned proponents of democracy everywhere know. The founders wanted their system to last. They did not want their descendants to get mixed up in despotism like what happened to them in Egypt, so they put a historical note in their law indicating the reason for the extensive democratic liberties found in their government system. That "note" is the prologue. In a similar fashion, the United States left a note as a prologue to their constitution for future generations to read and consider as well—the Declaration of Independence. The first commandment's prologue is essentially its declaration of independence from Egypt and the Egyptian political system. The note in the case of both nations essentially says, "Oppression activates an understanding of and true appreciation for the details of freedom." The note essentially provides a warning. The warning goes something like the following: "If you (Israel) ignore this testament, this historical memory, this pointed declaration, you will be oppressed again and again, and perhaps finally you will re-enthrone people's government along with a full slate of people's freedoms once again." It also essentially says, "Only the people can establish lasting peace, prosperity and freedom. Your society must continually be constructed from the ground up."

It must also be said that the prologue serves a very pedestrian and mundane purpose in addition to its high and lofty political purpose. In the ancient world, an invocation in the name of a god is not made as a religious benediction or requirement, but a legal one. Naming the god satisfies the legal requirement of naming the actual nation appearing in the matter at hand or at the international table.[10] The first commandment prologue is not trying to force religious belief, but merely to identify a particular historical situation and people.

Having "no other gods before me" means to have no other political system than the one used to free Israel from Egypt—elected representatives and ethical political leadership. Having "no other gods" means relying on Israel's own collective historical experience and all the present political maturity it can muster to govern itself rather than be governed in all ways by an overlord. Having "no other gods" means continuing to use elders as the nation's governing authorities just as they were used to organize for the Exodus. In fact, that is just what Israel did in the wilderness after Sinai. She elected seventy elders to serve as her legislative representatives. (Num 11:16-17, 24) That act is a clear indication that a specific provision of her constitution authorized such an action.

The first commandment is the first of two articles of the constitution which directly anticipate the potential for constitutional revisionism and which take a bold stand to try to prevent excessive constitutional liberalism. The first commandment provides forceful authority for an ongoing and strict interpretation of the foundational law. The idea the people are to

---

10. Wells and Magdalene, *Law,* 2:277.

"have" no other God is really straightforward, once the usual religious interpretation of the first commandment is broadened to give prominent place to the civic. Israel is to accept no other political system than the one outlining legislative supremacy over the executive department on the national level, and local sovereignty over national sovereignty in most areas of government function. Historically, these are the two most pervasive types of wandering away from democratic principle and thus the two kinds of conditions first commandment language is designed to prevent.

The idea of expected political backsliding after Moses and Joshua is discussed early on after Sinai in the book of Exodus. Enlightened prophet party leaders, citizens, and elders who detect this happening were evidently legally empowered throughout Israel's history to re-establish the government along normative constitutional lines. This, for example, Moses and the Levite party did when Korah tried to overthrow the government in the wilderness. This, Gideon and his sons did in Canaan when the people first wanted a king. In fact, a passage in Exodus 24 suggests that a new seat of temporary national government is to be established/organized in a new place convenient for the newly chosen confederate administrator whenever the people "remember my name." The name in the ancient Near East says who the god is, what he represents—in this case political self-determination and national independence from foreign entanglement. This passage in Exodus 24 essentially authorizes a confidence vote regarding the executive administration like that in a parliamentary system of government today. It also authorizes the formation of a new government—hopefully a more representative government than the immediately preceding one presently being called into question. This constitutional process happened every time a new "judge" arose in Israel, and essentially every time a new "king" was elected later on.

The book of Deuteronomy contains a number of clear admonitions to strict construction of the constitution in support of first commandment legislative power to the people and in support of the other nine commandment directives as well. It provides memorable catch-phrases like "Observe to do all the words of this law . . . as long as you live in the land." (Deut 31:9–13) A king must "turn not aside from the commandment, to the right hand, or to the left." (Deut 17:19–20) For the benefit of scribes, historians, and prophets, it is written, "Ye shall not add unto the word . . . neither shall ye diminish aught from it." (Deut 4:2) These statements together essentially seem to say, "Figure out what the commandments say and mean, and do exactly that and nothing else."

One of the most important implications of the first commandment is that it covers foreign policy as well as domestic policy. If Israel's own citizens can come up with a variety of other "gods" to tempt themselves domestically, foreign governments have the power to tempt Israel in spades. The first commandment requires that the tribal confederacy when directed by a temporary judge, and the tribal confederacy when directed by a longer-term "king," maintain homeland sovereignty over its own policy-making process. For Israel to "have no other gods" requires her to avoid treaty alliances with nations who worship others gods, that is, have different systems of government. Another way of stating the first commandment is the Bible dictum, "You must not set a foreigner over you." The God of the founders of the nation is a jealous God. He wants to maintain the sovereign independence of his own recently christened nation. He wants an exclusive political relationship with his people—one where the people are involved in major decisions on the national level, and all decisions on the local level—not one where the people are required to honor policy decisions made in foreign capitols, applied to their own soil, and implemented in the name of another nation's gods.

Accordingly, the first commandment sets the tone for international affairs as well as domestic politics, and those international guidelines are elaborated in the second, sixth, and seventh commandments. A law limiting political obedience/worship/fealty to one God (i.e., one humane political system) effectively prohibits military protection alliances, often called "leagues" (Judg 2:2) or "worship of other gods" in the King James Bible. Israel is to hold fast to her own political laws and her own governmental processes rather than trust in the laws and processes of other nations. She is certainly not to trust in other nation's chariots to help her defend herself. Isaiah argues for original construction using such a reference: "The Egyptians are men . . . their horses flesh, and not spirit . . . he that helpeth shall fall, and he that is helped shall fall down, and they all shall fail together." (Isa 31:3)

Protection treaties ultimately lead to the payment of tribute to other nations. Tribute payouts occurred late in the Israelite monarchy when Israel was fearful of Assyria, once again after Israel's return to Palestine from Babylon when she feared the Seleucid Greeks, and yet once again at the time of Jesus, when she lived in fear of Rome. Each of those periods of time were political disasters for Israel. Israel originally was committed to the spirit of humane law, the independence-encouraging spirit of the heavenly God. A proverb of wisdom in Israel relates, "The hand of the diligent shall bear rule: but the slothful shall be under tribute." (Prov 12:24) Israel's constitution required her to diligently attend to her own laws and to her citizenship responsibilities. If she did so, she would maintain her independence and keep her tax offerings working on her own soil.

One interpreter of the first commandment writes, "Israel bans the worship of foreign gods."[11] This begs the interpretation we give here. As a practical matter, the quickest way for a people to worship foreign gods is to begin to intermarry with citizens of foreign monarchist lands. This leads in time to parity or vassal treaties with foreign monarchs. This exact sequence of events happened in the time of King Ahab. Foreign monarchs who enter into treaties with lesser nations then exercise influence over decisions related to national finance, international war, and even domestic policy legislation. That is why the Bible inveighs against foreign inter-marriage and why the seventh commandment is so important to the life of the republic. To repeat once again, God wants the people to be independent and to determine their own fates. (Exod 20:5) They are not to dilute their national politics with political syncretism. Their God wishes to maintain his independence from other gods. This is the reason why Israel took strong measures to end the socio-sexual dalliances with the women of Peor early in her history. (Num 25)

In sum, the first commandment provides for the organization and operation of the national government, as any formational compact must do. In particular it asserts a huge and ongoing role for the elders of the tribes in making legislation. It also enacts the kinds of civil rights for all of the people that are needed to support their legislative right. It provides legislative intent language to assist future generations to interpret the "no other gods" language. That intent language points to the political oppressions in Egypt, the democratic processes and balanced functions (legislative and administrative) used to extricate the tribes from oppression there, and the character of national executive department leadership required to head such a venture. The intent language of Exodus 24 makes clear the intent of the founders to allow for periodic renewals of strict constitutional government so as to prevent the nation from putting other gods before Yahweh. The history of Israel provides prominent instances of citizen fidelity to this legislative intent and to the first commandment. The commandment also necessarily sets the tone for international relations and specifically prohibits alliances that would dilute the authority and power of Israel's own people.

One final word must be said about the legislative power of the people and their chosen elders. The first commandment points not just to the supremacy of the legislative body in confederation-wide matters, but also to the supremacy of local legislative councils of elders and broad assemblies of families, clans, and tribes who help the elders hammer out policies locally. The first commandment thus not only guarantees legislative supremacy on the national level, but guarantees it on local levels as well. Having "no

---

11. Collins, "Ten Commandments," 385.

other gods" means there should be no other supreme power in the land but the spirit of the humane God that inspired the people to act household by household in Egypt. Each of those households not only took political action to assert human rights by electing elders, but also made financial arrangements for their own departure and journey to Canaan. Finally, against great odds, they voted with their feet to get out of the furnace of oppression. By their individualized and highly effective actions, these people earned the right to govern themselves in the future.

Much later on, an able constitutionalist of the Mosaic law, Jesus of Nazareth, referred to the humane guiding light of heaven when he stated, "God is a Spirit." (John 4:24) God's spirit and desire in both the Israel of Moses' time and the Israel of Jesus' time was for the people to govern themselves in their social, economic, political, and spiritual affairs in local groupings as small as even a single-family household. Jesus, as well, pointed to the political nature of fundamental Israelite values when he spoke of the "weightier matters of the law" as being "judgment, mercy and faith." (Math 23:23; Luke 11:42) These summary concepts basically translate, in Mosaic terms, as democratic government (judgment), economic redemption/re-equilibration (mercy), and good faith between freely contracting parties (faith)—three substantial legs of constitutional government, as we shall see, and, in addition, the essence of the first three commandments.

The Second Commandment

> "Thou shalt not make unto thee any graven image, or any likeness of any thing that is in heaven above, or that is in the earth beneath, or that is the water under the earth: thou shalt not bow down thyself to them, nor serve them: for I the Lord thy God am a jealous God, visiting the iniquity of the fathers upon the children unto the third and fourth generation of them that hate me; and showing mercy unto thousand of them that love me, and keep my commandments. (Exod 20:4-6)

Rulers in the ancient Near East often placed their names, personal emblems/effects, inscriptions indicating a special relationship to a god, and even their facial/bodily profiles, on coins minted from gold and silver.[12] By this means, the people's own wealth was taken in taxes and turned into propaganda to support an ongoing raid on the meager results of their life's labors. The prophet Isaiah summarized the Biblical view about the negative value of autocratic power and wealth in actually advancing the people's

---

12. Shinkoskey, *Biblical Captivity*, 142.

interests: "Behold, they are all vanity; their works are nothing: their molten images are wind and confusion." (Isa 41:29) Republicans in Greece were worried about political idolatry with a fervor like that of the Hebrew republican prophets who complained about idols made by Aaron, Jeroboam, and Micah the householder. They railed against the molten bull cast by the tyrant Phalaris of Acragas. Alexander of Pherae rose to temporary tyrannical power in republican Greece like Abimelech did in Israel. He demonstrated the sexual promiscuity, domestic oppression, and imperial adventurism that Samuel warned was characteristic of systems of autocratic rule. (1 Sam 8) "He expropriated the production of the precious metal mines for himself, minted coins to pay his mercenaries, gave gifts to foreign dignitaries, and paid bribes to stay in power."[13]

When a strong king or a temporary tyrant placed a symbol of his own preferred god on a coin, he thus either directly or indirectly claimed to be the favored one, or son of, the god. This had tremendous political consequences as it made him not only the political ruler, but the religious ruler. The Greek dictator Antiochus Epiphanes IV put an image of his own head on the front of his coin, and one of Zeus on the back of it.[14] In Rome, the emperor Caligula was extolled in a sculpture image as "Gaius Julius . . . High Priest and Absolute Ruler . . . the shared Savior of human life."[15] In 2012, a cache of 159 Roman gold coins known as the St. Albans Hoard, was uncovered in Britain. The coins had names and facial or bodily images of the five different emperors who issued them: Gratian, Valentinian, Theodosius, Arcadius, and Honorius.[16] In smaller, self-governing societies, the people avoided such political and religious idolatry. In early Rome, for example, gods and governors were not represented by pictures or statues.[17] During the period of the Empire, however, the emperors made their images available to the masses in order to popularize their rule. The United States, following the historical pattern, did not allow the ruler's image on coins until 1909, some 120 years after the start of the American republic.

While placing the ruler's image on a coin is perhaps the clearest reflection of second commandment transgression, placing of an image on a statue or sculpture or monument to the ruler, like the statue of Caligula and the Sphinx pyramid in Egypt, is another. A strong magistracy is understood in the view of the ancients as a monarchic court which displays in its precincts

---

13. Ibid.
14. Coogan, *Old Testament*, 506.
15. Ehrman, *New Testament*, 25.
16. MSN News, April 15, 2015.
17. Jayne, *Healing Gods*, 378.

a precious metal molten "idol" or image of some strong animal from nature like a bull or an image of the ruler himself. Great kings of Mesopotamia erected sculptures of themselves which indicated that the power of the nation was sourced in the arm of the king rather than in the people themselves. They often associated their reigns with a particular favored god. In addition, kings promoted this kind of political "science" of idolatry in the propaganda, or hagiography, published by their administrations.

The second commandment as an article of political faith was not conditioned merely by general tribal experience with autocratic city-states in the Near East, but by Israel's particular experience in Egypt. There they were forced to make bricks for Pharoah's monstrously luxurious national building program, which, in addition to rock temples in Nubia and cult buildings at Thebes, also included his new capitol cities in the eastern Nile Delta region at both Piramesse/Pithom and Rameses.[18] (Exod 1:11) Idolatry in the Israelite scheme of things was subsequently defined as concentration of fabulous wealth in the hands of the monarch and then popular adoration of the monarch and continuing support of such a political way of life at the same time the bulk of the population suffered in abject poverty.

The national budget of a Near East strongman was monumental, as were his forced labor construction projects. His buildings were wonders to behold, things of material grandeur, virtually sculptures, images, physical reflections of his own "greatness." Typically, each new Egyptian monarch built not only his own palace, special commemorative monuments, and a luxurious burial tomb, but often an entire city or two. He did this by heavily taxing the people's paychecks. Aside from the need for cash for his personal building program, Pharaoh typically used the people's hard earned income to give magnificent gifts to foreign kings to bribe favors from them in times of personal political need. For example, one of the Amarna letters describes a Babylonian king's gratitude over a recent Egyptian shipment of gold to help him sustain his regime: "The gold is abundant. Among the kings there are brotherhood, friendliness, peace and [good] relations. He is rich with precious stones, rich with silver, rich with [gold.]"[19] In Egypt, one Pharaoh boasted that gold was "the flesh of the gods."[20] The gods together with their chosen kings, consumed gold virtually as the daily bread of office-holding. And the Pharaohs wore it as their jewelry, their crowns, and decorated their palaces with it.

---

18. Murname, "Egypt, History of (Dyn 18–20)," 351.
19. Redford, "Amarna Letters," 175.
20. Frankfort, *Kingship and the Gods*, 46.

Pharaohs also fortified many colonial cities abroad and carried out frequent foreign military campaigns by reason of lust for more land or due to treaty obligation. All of this meant that Pharaoh, and the national government, had an insatiable appetite for tax revenue in the form of labor, gold, and silver. Israel was determined to have a very modest national government, one that did not use tax money for capitol cities or for standing armies. Several hundred years after Israel's settlement in Canaan, Nathan asked David whether the God of Israel had ever required a city or palace to be built. (2 Sam 7:1–4) This was a rhetorical question, for the answer clearly was no, as David knew. In addition, David was reproved for wanting to build a standing army by conducting a national census to determine how many men he could draw from. (2 Sam 24) Israel did not want either a building or an army to be a visible representation, or image, of their own system of government. The people, and their humble homes, fields, and flocks were the images that best represented their way of life.

Modern republican societies, like the one inaugurated on the American continent in 1776, similarly deplored concentration of wealth and power in a single ruler and representation of any such power in coins, statues, or national buildings and budgets. American revolutionary pamphleteers understood politics the way ancient Israelite republicans did. John Leacock, for example, wrote, "Cast off the idol god! Kings are but vain. Let justice rule, and independence reign." The Israelite idea that people should worship the law rather than rulers was expressed by John Adams: "In Republican Governments the Majesty is all in the Laws. They only are to be adored." Benjamin Rush viewed worship of kings in Britain in stark terms. He saw Britons as "animals in the shape of men cringing at the feet of an animal called a king." Richard Henry Lee wrote, "North America is not fallen, nor likely to fall down before the images that the king hath set up." Samuel West wrote, "The worst princes have been most flattered and adored . . . This idolatrous reverence has ever been the inseparable concomitant of arbitrary power, and tyrannical government." These revolutionary era writers clearly understood ancient Israel's political character. Samuel Cooper wrote, "The Hebrew nation . . . a free republic . . . consisted of three parts: a chief magistrate who was called judge or leader . . . a council of seventy . . . and the general assemblies of the people . . ." Peter Whitney wrote, "Kingly government is not agreeable to the divine will . . . (Israel) was a kind of republic . . . (it disapproved of) the idolatrous homage which is paid to the persons of kings."[21]

---

21. Nelson, *Royalist Revolution*, 137–41, 304–06.

The First Two Commandments

The casting of a molten image to signify the power of the magistrate required a transfer of the people's wealth like that which Aaron accomplished at Sinai when he asked for the contribution of jewelry from each family for a golden calf for use by the new government. Moses fortunately then was able to intercede and encourage the people to head back in the direction they originally intended to go.[22]

While the first commandment empowers the people through their elder representatives the way they were not empowered in Egypt, the second commandment describes and limits the power of the executive branch in a way Pharaoh's house was not limited in Egypt. The executive branch is not to be characterized by a strong or perpetually enduring house of leaders, but rather a "weak" (i.e. term-limited, and tax limited) judge-led government characterized by focus on short-term political goals outlined in the judge's call by the people. The first two articles of government together leave no doubt both about what the people wanted and what they did not want. They wanted a modest national government. They did not want a luxurious monarchy. Just as in the United States, the two articles taken together establish the supremacy of the legislative branch over the administrative branch. That priority is suggested in both constitutions not only through explicit language but by placement of the legislative article in the first position and the executive article in the second position.

The aim of the second commandment was to prohibit the accumulation of enough national wealth by the central government to pay a professional standing army to do the personal bidding of one individual. A strong magistrate in the ancient Near East was demonstrably not accountable to the people. Such a ruler essentially asserted a right to rule either because his father was the previous strongman or because other possible candidates for the job recently turned up dead. A secondary aim of the commandment was to prohibit substantial concentration of wealth in any other power center in the land, private or public, sacred or secular, merchant or pastoral.

The second commandment was a proto-type of the anti-sumptuary (plain living) legislation so prominent in the laws of early Rome, Sparta, the British colonies in New England, and the first hundred years of the government of the United States. Rulers in early Israel wore plain clothes and lived in plain dwellings, and after working hard for the people for several years went back to their plain lives with wives and children shepherding their flocks and manicuring their fields. This tradition of democratic plainness lived on into the period of kings as demonstrated by Elijah, who was fed by ravens, and as late as the time of John the Baptist, who was clothed with

---

22. Berman, *Created Equal*, 26, 142.

camel's hair and ate locusts and wild honey. (1 Kgs 17:6; Matt 3:4) The legal tradition of the second commandment prohibited a luxurious mansion for the chief magistrate, thus the pointed mention of King Ahab's bed of ivory and the warning to David by Nathan against building a permanent government office building. (2 Sam 7:1–4) The second commandment also frowned upon luxurious mansions of the private citizenry, those rural aristocratic courtiers of the king who "lay field to field" and never returned the land to its rightful owners. (Isa 5:8)

In order to project great power, a national ruler needs considerable wealth, and gets such wealth by taxing his own people's assets and labor or conquering other nations and expropriating that wealth for his administration. Sometimes a popular politician in a democratic system will make a bid to obtain wealth quickly in order to lard his personal estate, take power illegally, and pay his cronies to support him in office. Abimelech, the son of Gideon, did this during the period of Judges. He raided the city treasury, the temple of Baal-Berith, where the people of Shechem had entered into a local covenant of laws, hired his own mercenaries to run a rump government, ran roughshod over the city and the countryside for three years, and did it without the customary general election of the people or elders of the tribes, winning the temporary confidence only of one of the larger cities. (Judg 9) This is an example of how to break both the first and second commandments together.

It is inescapable that the second commandment ensured there would be no national taxation, no national coinage, no national military corvee (draft), no national civilian labor requirement, and no national political idol cast to glorify and finance any of those forbidden policies. Such a centralizing of power did not succeed until hundreds of years after the founding of the Israelite republic.

The presumption underlying the second commandment was that the people had power, wisdom, and resources to take care of their own needs locally. There were enough militia within the local clans and tribes of the homeland that Israel did not need the help of a national army to protect her borders from intrusion. Also, there were enough smart citizens in the tribes to enable the nation to govern itself without the help of political advice or direction from emperors of neighboring nations.

The second commandment is often seen as a prohibition of religious paganism, a polytheism characterized by the creation of molten representations of the religious gods of the people. The commandment certainly prohibited a luxurious national court populated by one or more molten gods representing the God of Israel or the gods of nearby hegemonic nations. In truth, as we have mentioned, any molten god statue represented the politics and economics of the nation more so than the religious worship of the nation. Still, in Israel there was to be no luxuriation of religion, meaning no large or small molten idols or graven statues for religious use any more than images of kings for political propaganda use. For Israel, any undue concentration of religious power on the national level was just as nefarious as the concentration of political and economic power represented by bulls or statues of politicians, or coinage or emblems representing the ruler. Creation of religious idols for private household use came under the prohibition of the second commandment law as well, as the story of Micah the householder during Judges makes clear. (Judg 18)

In sum, the "civil religion" of Moses and early Israel and of the first two commandments disapproved of worship politics and luxury politics, as well as worship religion and luxury religion. It favored "wisdom" politics and plain-living politics, as well as wisdom religion and plain-living religion. The political philosophy of Israel specified that human beings were endowed with capacity to learn about life and liberty and threats to life and liberty by means of a program of citizen literacy and legal education. Such a literacy program gave them the opportunity to be self-governing. Under worship politics, the people pay undue reverence to a well-heeled national leader and bureaucracy, as symbolized by a golden calf or bull. The royalist leader makes the decisions for them, which decisions most often benefit him and not the people. In worship religion they pay undue reverence to a religious leader like a Moses or an Aaron, or to a historical religious icon. The constitution specified that the foundational law was to be the only object she worshipped. Israel, however, as most large democracies, eventually went down the path of royalism, with its attendant religious and political idolatry.

At a later point of time in Israel's history, people worshipped Moses' bronze snake called "Nehushtan." They worshipped it either as a civic or a religious icon and seemed to believe they could be healed of various illnesses by it. This was a transgression of the second commandment as much as installing a national political idol of a foreign god or a nature god on Israelite soil, done by Aaron and, later, Jeroboam. The Israelite constitution essentially said that people are properly healed by God and science, not by a celebrity joy stick. Israel's job was to focus on individual observation, law, and written and oral history as objects of veneration instead. They were to govern themselves rather than be governed by others. In religion they were to develop the sacred within themselves, rather than looking for it in a special object or even in a charismatic leader. They were to dote instead upon the contents of a simple wooden ark containing the nation's covenant laws listing their rights to self-determination. They were not to look at the ark as an object of worship. What was inside the ark was to be read to them regularly, and excerpts from it worn on their bodies and posted on the lintels of their doorways to remind them of their importance. (Deut 6:6–9; Matt 23:5) The ark itself was a piece of wood. A bronze snake could be melted down and thus made to disappear entirely. The law was made to live forever in people's hearts and minds and in their communities.

14

Third and Fourth Commandments: Organizing and Regulating the Economy

The Third Commandment

> "Thou shalt not take the name of the Lord thy God in vain: for the Lord will not hold him guiltless that taketh his name in vain." (Exod 20:7)

IN EGYPT, IF THERE was a functioning free enterprise system, Israel did not have much access to it. Israelites as a group were conscripted, that is, forced into performing civilian government labor. If they would rather be miners, farmers, shepherds, canal diggers, boat captains, physicians, scribes, or whatever, that did not matter. Their single-purpose occupation was mandated by the state: either manufacturing bricks for construction of government buildings or producing straw for mixing with the bricks, all for the glory of the king of Egypt.

Once free of Egypt, Israel used what seems to us today to be strange language to prevent their own government from imposing labor requirements on citizens and to create free occupational choice and free enterprise. A law stating "Don't take the name of God in vain" sounds like a negative law limiting the range of conduct and speech of the people, but in fact it was just the opposite. It was a grant of power to individual adults allowing them to make things happen that they wanted to happen. When two people wanted to work together to generate income for themselves, they could go ahead and do so. Israel wrote a law whose intent was to ensure that the nature and direction of human social and economic activity was up to individuals voluntarily contracting with one another. Once two parties made an agreement, it was then legally binding without government permission or review. It was up to the two parties to make sure the actions were carried out so that the agreement, essentially a private law, was not made in vain, was not broken. The third commandment not only encouraged such a system of free enterprise, it made it the standard for all of the people of the nation to follow.

A law of contracts allowed Israelites to buy and sell, make employment agreements, establish trade arrangements, rent-out pasture and water, hire domestic help . . . all on their own say-so. Such agreements were witnessed, and made public in a sense, by use of the name of their national God Yahweh. Anciently, central governments had a big hand in granting organizational charters, regulating operations, and approving private contractual arrangements when such proposals were brought before the king and the nation's tutelary gods. Yahweh in Israel blessed these arrangements in advance as permissible within the Israelite frame of democratic government. Israel was essentially creating an honor system which allowed its own citizens to act on their own in the activities of daily life without government interference or the king's permission.

The law suggests that the state has no interest in getting involved in the contract or transaction as long as the parties are satisfied with the performance of their respective duties under the contract. Even when a problem arose, the free enterprise system provided a variety of methods of solving disputes short of government involvement. As late as New Testament times, Jesus was counseling citizens to make use of private mediation methods. (Luke 12:57–59) While the law of the nation and the nation's God Yahweh allowed great personal freedom in occupational and commercial activity, the third commandment made sure there would be a local government solution when private mediation did not work out. We will discuss below what happened when parties treated agreements lightly or in vain.

Pursuant to the third commandment, non-governmental individuals and agencies had freedom to operate broadly in the private sphere not just in economic relations, but in all human activity—all sectors of society where agreements between parties were to be recognized by the nation. This included social, political, militia, ecclesiastic/votive, and educational-scientific-scribal contexts. Thus, people could not only pursue whatever economic enterprise they wanted, they could also marry who and when they wanted, raise, educate and apprentice children, run for election as elders, defend and protect, officiate at religious ceremonies, and become teachers or historians. The third commandment was often interpreted so as to require individuals and agencies, governmental and private, to swear oaths of fidelity to the arrangements they were entering into. This was done to ensure the parties understood the seriousness of the arrangements, their heaviness, so they would not be treated lightly. Agreements were also generally to be made openly and attested, so enforcement could be facilitated. Most Biblical contracts were oral (1 Kgs 20:39–41), and were often witnessed by several listeners. (Ruth 4:1–11) But some had "paperwork" to back them up, as for divorce (Deut 24:1; Isa 50:1; Jer 3:8), and land purchase.[1] (Jer 3:8) Later in the history of Israel, Jesus protested what came to be an over-reliance on oaths and an under-reliance on actual character and reputation. But that did not mean Jesus wanted to negate the third commandment. He just wanted to clean up the people's behavior so their deeds matched their words.

It was in the interest of the confederation and its constituent tribes to encourage faithful execution of marital promises, political oaths of office, contracts between buyers and sellers, religious vows made at shrines, and evidences and predictions proffered about nature and about the future by priests, prophets and scribes in their activities. Ultimately, a system providing so much personal freedom could not easily continue if people could not be trusted to fulfill their promises. If Israel didn't want constant supervision of their daily activities by a government official, it was imperative that they faithfully take care of their personal business without much commotion. They had to police their own agreements. That took work. A freedom system is a hard work system.

Private legal contracts in the economic sphere were not uncommon in the ancient Near East. For example, wet nurse contracts, including provisions for breach of contract, were known from as early as 3,500 years BCE. The existence of this degree of free enterprise is evidence that there were other democratic societies in the ancient world, as we discussed in chapter 1. There were contracts of sale, contracts of hire, contracts of deposit of goods, herding contracts made with shepherds, debt contracts, ransom agreements, and contracts related to purchase and manumission of servants/slaves.[2] Israel likely expanded the number and kinds and ease of making of such agreements beyond what was available in neighboring countries by elevating them to a place of sacred importance in the source law of the confederation rather than just the common law or tradition of the region. The common law and tradition could be quickly negated when a strong new ruler came to power.[3] But the constitutional law could not easily be overturned. It required a huge amount of effort from all of the people to do so.

1. Wells and Magdalene, *Law*, 2:309.
2. Wells and Magdalene, *Law*, 2:33, 44, 52, 56, 86-87, 91, 106, 113, 234, 360.
3. Berman, *Created Equal*, 154; Hallo, "Writing in Antiquity," 820.

Israel's contract law mimicked that of the ancient Near East in a fundamental way. In both Israel and the ancient Near East the invocation/prologue used for private contracts mentioned the name of the local god. In both cases this mention did not have a religious or worship function, but rather a legal and civic function. An oath or contract using the name of a god meant it was legally binding under law. Although the parties were initially free to promise whatever they wanted, the power of the state could later be used to enforce it if promises were not delivered. Abrogation without cause could be prosecuted whether the agreement was social, political, or economic. The guilty party would suffer the "curse" of legal consequence administered by the state. This is true whether the oath was an evidentiary oath to establish guilt or innocence, or a promissory oath/contract, to guide future behavior, as in marriage, or to give consent in other civic matters.[4] For example, oaths in the ancient Near East and in the Bible were sworn at a shrine or temple in the presence of the divine (i.e., "before God") as a substitute for clear evidence or proof in a legal case.[5] If clear evidence later popped up, responsibility or guilt could be modified then.

Individuals in both Israel and other limited governments in the ancient Near East were asked to respect their engagement, marriage, divorce, and other domestic arrangements and abide by the laws enforcing them. In the ancient world in general, there were contracts related to betrothal, marriage, receipt of dowry by the groom, adoption, marriage between free and slave, divorce, and inheritance.[6] Divorce was hard to obtain in Israel because marriage vows, like contracts in general, were taken very seriously. Marriages were expected to be permanent, except in rare cases of nonfulfillment of basic responsibilities to one another. Other social promises related to the institution of marriage were to be fulfilled as well. One such case is known from the ancestral common law. Judah promised Tamar that she would shortly be able to wed a certain son of his, but he then neglected to fulfill that promise and came under condemnation for it. (Gen 38:1–26) This was an agreement that Judah flatly broke and Tamar was apparently justified in calling him to account for it in a rather spectacular way.

The difference between Israelite and Near East contract law was the sweep and depth of free economic activity Israelite citizens were given. For instance, Israelites could buy and sell land, while in many other nations they were limited to making tenant rental agreements. Also, political contracts made between leaders and their public partners were different in Israel

---

4. Wells and Magdalene, *Law*, 2:210, 277, 529.
5. Toorn, *Sin and Sanction*, 45–55; Levinson, "First Constitution," 1875.
6. Wells and Magdalene, *Law*, 2:81, 87, 129, 139-40, 160, 168, 257.

than in strong monarchies. There the king contracted with God and left the people out of the equation. In a hereditary monarchy, an aging ruler's accountability to the people was limited in a sense to one task ... his ability to sire a successor to the throne. If he couldn't live up to the task of producing another up and coming political celebrity, the people would ensure that his dynasty came to an end. In Israel, on the other hand, the chief magistrate contracted with the people to adhere to a few limited responsibilities to be closely monitored by the other contracting party, the people. The chief's limited duties under the political deal were solemnized by his oath of office and were then continually reviewed not just by one or two friendly factions familiar with the chief's activities, but by all of the hungry and grumbling people who collectively could murmur up a storm of discontent. An Israelite magistrate had to work like an ox to protect the people's freedoms. His job description was not limited to having productive sex.

Judges and kings typically swore to uphold the law when they took office and citizens held them accountable for doing so. For example, early political leaders swore in Israel to uphold the original constitutional law, or reconstitutions of the law, or special modifications/covenants of the law. They did this either at initial anointing ceremonies for nomination (1 Sam 9:16), or second phase anointing ceremonies for election/installation/investiture/coronation.[7] (2 Sam 2:4) In the time of Judges, the elders of Gilead administered a political contract with Jephthah. Both parties exchanged "words," or legal/oral testimony detailing the deal, which include allowing Jephthah to be judge in Gilead if he successfully repelled the Midianites. Jephthah uttered "all his words before the Lord in Mizpeh," which meant he acknowledged the obligations placed upon him in front of a legally convened court, likely of the elders themselves.[8] (Judg 11:8–11)

The political procedure that constituted a political oath for early kings was an acclamation phrase shouted by the people, "God save the King." (1 Kgs 1:39) This effectively meant, "Let the legal/political process (the truth finding processes instituted by God) judge the King and find him innocent of legal transgression, if that is possible." This acclamation phrase passed along to the King the expectation of the citizenry that he respect the laws of the land. In Deuteronomy (which likely reflects editing provided in a period after judges), the king swore not to "turn aside from the commandments to the right or to the left ..."[9] (Deut 17:20) Citizens in any period could chal-

---

7. Elazar, *Covenant and Polity*, 206. Objects/persons are anointed as a sign of their dedication to the deity, and the law provided by the deity; see Laws, "Anoint," 30.

8. See Meyers, *Exodus*, for the idea that "before the Lord" was an idiom for "at court."

9. The king appears to have to "swear" by the novel and quite strenuous method

lenge the leader if he strayed from the commandment constitution. Amos, for example, held political leaders responsible for the decline of society and subjected their names and their legacies to ridicule and harsh judgment. (Amos 1:3—2:16) Jehu lead a revolution against the house of Ahab due to the monarchy's many constitutional infractions.

On the other hand, political leaders themselves could put entire citizenries under oath to uphold the law, like Nehemiah did representing Babylon when he returned to Israel, and Solon did in Greece when a new law code was established there.[10] Moses put the people under such an oath on the plains of Moab before their crossing Jordan into Canaan. (Deut 29:12, 14; 31:12) When strong kings in the ancient Near East made international agreements with one another, those agreements were witnessed only in the name and sight of the gods of their countries alone, not by other political authorities in their realms or by their people. Moses invited the entire citizenry to be parties to the government contract and its laws—in actuality, to be witnesses to the covenant they were making among themselves—and to have God as a witness to their pledge of republican government. This was the same as saying those citizens were sovereign authorities like kings, each one with a sacred responsibility to be accountable for their actions to God, just as kings were accountable to a god.[11]

In the Bible, there is a theological rationale for the need to uphold oaths and agreements. God's name represents human freedom and responsibility, as represented by the history of successful flight from repressive Egypt and successful setting up of good government at Sinai. God delivered on his promise of freedom. His name thus really means something. It carries a punch. In like fashion, each citizen's name should be associated with freedom and good faith as well, since human beings are made in the image of God. An individual's very name and reputation is at stake whenever he or she makes an agreement. The name given by the parents to the child should carry a punch if the child is raised correctly. The name should evoke

---

of having to write out a copy of the entire law for his own reference, and refer to it often in administering the laws while he is in office. (Deut 17:18–19) This is not simply a copying and reading exercise, but a commitment exercise, like writing out and sharing one's marriage vows in today's world. The purpose of writing out the constitution is to show that his copy is no different than everyone else's copy. Thus, he cannot see the law any differently that anyone else, so his "heart" will not be "lifted up above his brethren." (Deut 17:20; Elazar, *Covenant and Polity*, 206) If he deviates from the constitution, it is understood he will not "prolong his days in the kingdom," that is, will be dismissed from office. It is not clear whether he has to accomplish the writing of the law before he is legally accepted in the office, or after, but likely before.

10. Berger, "From Hostage to Contract," 154–281; Laws, "Anoint," 30–31.

11. Wells and Magdalene, *Law*, 2:277.

trustworthiness. Thus, the third commandment enshrines both freedom *and* responsibility in foundational law. It requires that the people not take lightly such freedom to act privately and such responsibility to act faithfully. All such private agreements are sacred to the animating democratic spirit of Israel, as reflected in the constitutional law. The agreement and the oath accompanying it are sacred because they are the means by which each citizen can live an independent life, not a life dependent upon the state.

We are suggesting then that freedom to act is only the first half of the third commandment deal. Accountability is the other half. If private negotiation and mediation cannot bring a resolution to a dispute, a public judiciary must get involved as a last resort. The adjudicative agencies of society can and do get involved and make the ultimate decision. These agencies include village and clan elders, and specialized, often priestly, students of the law, and ultimately the specially trained national judges appointed during the period of kings. (Deut 17:8–9) The third commandment thus also serves much as the third article of the U.S. Constitution, that is, to set up a judiciary to deal with disputes over private agreements between autonomous, empowered citizens.

But there was a difference between the Israelite judiciary and the judiciary in monarchic societies. The judiciary in strong monarchies was often under the direct control of the executive branch. In Israel, there is evidence that the judiciary functioned independently of the chief magistrate. For example, priests did much of the judicial work, and they were not appointed, but had a hereditary right to those positions as Levites. Local justice was done by elected elders, but at higher levels it was accomplished by priests, Levites, and "the judge that shall be in those days." (Deut 17:8–9) In fact, Deuteronomy displays a "stunning silence" about the judicial function of the king."[12] The judicial court in Israel served to find the truth of the matter rather than seeing to it that the interests of the kings were served by the decision. The court thus gave real support to the two parties in fulfilling their private agreements in aid of one another.

It was appropriate that provision be made in the articles of organization and operation of government for government's position relative to activity in the socio-economic sector. The third commandment makes clear that Israelite society was to be predominately a libertarian-style polity in which private agreements rather than government mandates was to be the primary mode of regulation of human activity. The third commandment protected commerce and property against exploitation or over-regulation by government, and protected the parties to agreements by elevating the

---

12. Levinson, "First Constitution," 1880.

agreements themselves to the status of laws, holding all such agreements to a strict standard of adherence by each contracting party. For example, the third commandment required the honoring of debts, rather than the cavalier treatment of them. It essentially took a strict liability approach.[13] The notion of paying back what was borrowed was important enough in confederation society that a family member frequently had to enter into indentured servitude to work for a period of months or years to pay off a debt. The law generally required, "Exact every debt." (Neh 10:28–39) Parties can enforce their own agreements and take stern measures to procure what is rightfully theirs. Thus, the third commandment may be styled the "good faith" commandment. If persons enter into agreements with ill-intent, they will have to pay a price. We see, however, that the second commandment (placing limits on the wealth and power of the chief executive and authorizing debt relief) and the fourth commandment (anti-exploitation of labor and anti-slavery) balance this strict treatment of contracts with provisions for communitarian correctives to temper the libertarian way of doing things.

The third commandment is not only akin to the contract clause in the American constitution but also to provisions against expropriation of the peoples' property by the government found in constitutional law. Private parties can get their hands on others' property if debts are not paid, but the government cannot. The law, then serves essentially to protect not only the independent actionability of individuals and groups of individuals in the society, but also their privacy and property vis a vis the government as they go about managing their own business.

The Fourth Commandment

> "Keep the sabbath day to sanctify it, as the Lord thy God hath commanded thee. Six days shalt thou labor, and do all thy work: but the seventh day is the sabbath of the Lord thy God: in it thou shalt not do any work, thou, nor thy son, nor thy daughter, thy manservant, nor thy maidservant, nor thine ox, nor thine ass, nor any of thy cattle, nor thy stranger that is within thy gates; that thy manservant and thy maidservant may rest as well as thou. And remember that thou wast a servant in the land of Egypt, and that the Lord thy God brought thee out thence through a mighty hand and by a stretched out arm: therefore the Lord thy God commanded thee to keep the Sabbath day."[14] (Deut 5:12–15)

---

13. For strict liability, see Wells and Magdalene, *Law*, 2:376.
14. We use the Deuteronomy version of the commandment here because it make

If the third commandment unleashes relatively unrestrained activity in the private, non-governmental sphere in Israelite society, the fourth commandment balances that freedom, reins it in, puts a break on it. Trade and other work, including, likely, most of the work of government, shuts down for a day each week.[15] One recent commentator reminds, "Everybody stops work."[16] The aim of the law was to prevent over-rigorous labor requirements both by government (like that in Egypt) and by employers (like those in Israel). Wealth-building and the exercise of centralized power are set back on their heels. There is to be no physical labor, commercial labor, or regulatory activity. The restorative work of the family and the private institutions of health, education and welfare, crank up. The commandment seems to focus explicitly on the good of the persons being addressed and seems to want to leave no base uncovered, and so uses both positive and negative legal statements so as to make sure the people get a clear picture of what the law is trying to do.[17] Without the fourth commandment, the economy would get over-heated, private accumulation would go unchecked, laboring people would be exploited, debilitated, and fall prey to disease and disability, an aristocratic class would arise to govern in place of the people, and government would become muscle-bound.

We have mentioned that the extremely consequential first commandment setting up people's government and providing rights to political and religious freedom did not come out of thin air. It had earlier forms/precedents in Pentateuch history in covenants associated with Abraham, Isaac, and Jacob. The fourth commandment had similar importance to the people fleeing Egypt, and also had an earlier precedent as well. For example, the future law was put into practice in the situation of gathering manna in the desert before the migrants even got to Sinai and before they voted on the constitution.[18] (Exod 16:22–30)

Israel enacted the fourth commandment as a corrective to their life in Egypt, where it appears they were given no regular day of rest. Their brick-making days were long and hard, and then straw production was added to the labor requirement. Their forced labor situation put Israel perilously close to chattel slavery. It seems women and children were drawn into Pharaoh's

---

a more explicit link between working conditions in Egypt and the labor law for Israel in Canaan.

15. For example, the Bible makes clear that government military activity does not take place on the Sabbath. It is not until much later in Israel that exemptions take place when Israel's enemies attack them on the Sabbath that she responds in kind on that day.

16. Miller, *Ten Commandments*, 122.

17. Miller, *Ten Commandments*, 118.

18. Ibid.

forced labor system as well, since Moses asked for them to be included in his proposed three-day holiday retreat and rest pilgrimage. Labor exploitation of the Hebrew people likely did not start in the reign of Ramses II, who ruled for thirty-three years. It was characteristic of the term of Ramses II's father Seti I, who ruled for 13 years, and may have started earlier under Ramses I, who ruled for two years, and before that under Horemheb, the founder of the 19th Dynasty, who ruled for 28 years. The ascendency of a new dynasty was normally associated with a building program to undergird the new family's claim to power. The work program thus may have lasted 50 or more years, spanning some two and a half generations of the Hebrew people.

The commandment's reference to rigorous labor direction and exertion in Egypt provides clear legislative intent for the law. Things were never to be so bad for labor vis-a-vis the government in Israel as they were in Egypt. Constant work without significant rest anywhere in the ancient Near East mimicked penal labor and chattel slave labor. Yet, the Hebrews had not committed crimes and had not been captured in battle and held as slaves. The forced labor program for the Hebrew population was essentially a political labor program to wear down the bodies and minds of a people who threatened to undermine the despotic power of an insecure house of Pharaohs. Thus, the fourth commandment was certainly designed mainly to outlaw an over-rigorous approach to free labor in Israel of the sort that could hurt or wear down a particular group of people or particular individuals. It also likely limited traditional captive slavery as well, since this type of enslavement is rarely mentioned in association with the Israelite people.

But the fourth commandment had broader implications for the economic structure of society as well. The eastern Mediterranean was a region where many larger nation-states used an underclass to produce goods for them. In other nations, the ruling class could rest while the underclass worked the seventh day to make up the deficit in work the wealthy failed to provide. But in Israel there was no underclass to do the extra work, so all citizens had to work a full six days, and all had to rest on the seventh. At the end of each working day, and on the rest day, the citizenry had to make time for social, educational, political, and worship activities.

In other nations the ruling class also forced smaller neighboring nations to provide goods and services for them. Such a policy certainly would not be appropriate for an Israelite people who included all its residents and even visitors in one class of citizenry. In fact, the Israelite constitution, as we will see, did not allow for subjugation and colonization of weaker neighbors. There was no domestic underclass and no international colonial class allowable by law. Labor was forced only in the sense of the need for individuals and families to do all they could to survive in the absence of centralized welfare programs to save them from poverty. The New Testament Parable of the Talents shows that the length of the workday in later Israel was much like the length of the work day in the early American republic, some eleven hours long. (Matt 20:1–16) It likely was the same or longer in early Israel. In a free and egalitarian society, families, clans, merchants, pastoralists, agriculturists, militiamen, scribes, and elders had to work hard virtually all of the daylight hours six days of the week in order to survive economically and politically.

The economy worked not on a basis of force in Israel, but on a basis of passion for life, for self-government, and for economic self-sufficiency. One author writes that the drive for justice and compassion (that is, to prevent labor slavery) was by means of the fourth commandment "built into the system and regularized."[19] In Israel, the entire nation as one person needed to rest and recuperate on the seventh day in order to be able to efficiently continue on with their work.

While churches, or more properly, cult- or shrine-related communities and activities, played a role in Sabbath day events, most of such ritual and worship was performed at home. When the scripture says the Sabbath day is "for the Lord" ("layhwh"; Lev 25:4), this is tantamount to saying "for the people," or "for the law" because the God of Israel acted in the interests of ordinary people.[20] That is why Jesus taught that the Sabbath was made for people and people not made for the Sabbath. (Mark 2:27)

One Jewish scholar points to the direction we take here, that the Sabbath was not made strictly as a "go to church" day. He writes, "Unlike the day of atonement, the Sabbath is not dedicated exclusively to spiritual goals."[21] Isaiah, too, suggests the day is to be a day of human creativity, suggesting perhaps artistic and educational endeavors which make it a day of "delight," ("oneg") and pleasurable enjoyment. (Isa 58:13–14) That the day could be appropriately used for traveling to sit and learn at the feet of political constitutionalists familiar with law and history is suggested by a passage in Kings. (2 Kgs 4:22–23) Saadiah Gaon believed the day provided "opportunity for the attainment of a little bit of knowledge" and also "leisure to meet others at gatherings."[22]

Christians today worry about which day is the true Sabbath day, and therefore the proper day to worship God.[23] In New Testament times, many

---

19. Miller, *Ten Commandments*, 134.
20. Ibid., 137.
21. Heschel, "Palace in Time," 218.
22. Saadiah Gaon, "Beliefs and Opinions," 59.
23. Green-McCreight, "Restless," 223–236.

went to synagogue to hear Jesus speak about constitutional government on the sabbath day ("as was his custom"). They came on one day in particular to hear him deliver a very political message by re-iterating Isaiah's understanding that the purpose of the ten commandment law was to deliver captives from their tormentors. (Luke 4:16–19) That civic speech changed the world. And that particular change could not have happened without a free day for attending such a public forum. The importance of the fourth commandment in this light is that there *is* such a weekly day to discuss civic matters freely, not *which* day of the Roman or Greek weekly calendar is best suited for that purpose. Exodus 34:21 specifies that the Sabbath cessation of labor could not be interrupted even in critical times of plowing and harvest. A day for rest, education, and action is more important even than critical, time-limited agricultural activity. Cultural practice in Jesus' day went so far as to outlaw even medical activities related to restoration of good health. Jesus, however, was not one who believed that the requirements of the day of labor rest were more important than the health care needs of the people. (Luke 13:10–17)

While the Bible uses the noun form "sabbat" to describe the term "rest," it also frequently uses the verb form "sabat," which is a secular term that simply means "stop" or "cease." What is strongly suggested here by both forms is that the Sabbath day is not made holy merely by means of the particular *use* the day is put to, like worship. One scholar who focuses heavily on the religious use of the day, stumbles across this odd phenomenon and remarks, "How little we are told in any detail about what this sanctification of time involves."[24] The reason is that the day's emptiness (particularly, of bodily exertion and commercial exertion) is in fact its very purpose. The Sabbath is made special and holy by the mere fact of its existence . . . its availability to all people. It is a day where laboring people may be released from the rigors of their employers and from impositions by any other parties. The day is made good and holy not by means of the specific content of prayers uttered on the day, but by means of the day's legal existence and because of the freedom it gives to citizens. It is an axiomatic public labor and political law and that makes it holy to the people. It is the day of the citizen, the day of the worker. It almost seems that any particular good uses the day are put to are icing on the cake. But that is not quite the case.

The idea of holiness in Israel, as we discussed in part II, relates not only to freedom from forced labor but the attendant responsibility for citizens to exercise political and religious rights and achieve personal wellness with that freedom. They are to take care of themselves, and take care of their

---

24. Ibid., 120.

families, their communities, and their nation. Thus, there is a grand irony in their freedom to create and do whatever they want. There is much to do if the people want to remain free. They cannot merely lay down and not get up all day long on the Sabbath. They must put plenty of icing on the cake during the course of creating their own particular uses of the day.

It is clear that there are two parts of fourth commandment law: the command to work six days, and the command to rest one day. The first is a positive demand for the people to work during a specific time frame. The second is a negative demand for people not to work during a specific time frame. There is a distinct sense that the real focus, intent and motivating power of the seventh day is the existence of the extensive work week which precedes it and makes it necessary. The third commandment and the first half of the fourth commandment encourage a free enterprise system. The first half of the fourth commandment lets the citizenry know that the government expects them to work hard six days a week. The second half of the fourth commandment makes success in the first half of the commandment possible. It also makes the political success of the entire nation possible. The two parts of the fourth commandment thus constitute a national standard for the work week in Israel and a national standard for the political week in Israel. It is not an over-rigorous standard, but it is hardly an easy standard. It would have been understood as humanely vigorous, welcome, a good way to go for a democratic people who have lots of economic responsibilities to fulfill and lots of other responsibilities to attend to other than working. This is a law that fits a people who have a life outside of work.

The fourth commandment Sabbath "rest" law also authorized the laws of social welfare in Israel and kept big government at bay by instituting regular means for limiting poverty. The law mandating recovery/recuperation every seven days also authorized other recovery activities based on the number "seven." Those other release dates were based on the same principle of restoring balance and power to the citizens to carry on with democratic life. Workers rest every seven days to recover health and labor strength. Communities of the tribes rest economically every seven years, or seventy years, to allow the poor, the debtors, the landless, and even the land to recover from hard use by the managerial overlords.

Pursuant to the fourth commandment, legislation subsequently was enacted governing the release of the indentured (working to pay back debts) from bondedness and indebtedness. (Exod 21:2–11) Those who owed money or owed labor were released from those debts every seven years. The release from debt was from the full debt, not just the interest. (Deut 15:1–11) In fact, former servants were to be given a positive endowment of money upon release, as a manumission gift. (Deut 15:12–18) On the seventh year the land was to lie fallow so that it was not overworked and deprived of its nutrients. The poor could eat the after-growth that sprang-up spontaneously without human effort. During the fallow year, farmers and the community dined on stored preserves, like the migrants dined on stored manna in the wilderness. (Exod 23:10–11) Those families, clans, and tribes who once lost land could now in the 49th year regain the land they had to walk away from due to hardship and indebtedness. (Lev 25: 10, 13; Lev 27:16–25; Num 36:4) While ancient Near East kings might make a similar proclamation of "liberation" from debt ("andurarum"), such a gesture of release from poverty was dependent upon caprice and political calculation, and was not regularized as it was in Hebrew law.[25] Thus the fourth commandment moderates the demands of the third commandment for strict enforcement of the law of contracts. It is agreed that super strictness is ultimately not only tough for debtors but unjust, as it tips the scales heavily to favor creditors, who invariably demonstrate there is no limit to their greed.

---

25. Weinfeld, *Social Justice*; Miller, *Ten Commandments*, 148-49.

15

Fifth, Sixth, Seventh, and Eighth Commandments: Limiting National Government and Empowering Local Government

The Fifth Commandment

"Honor thy father and thy mother: that thy days may be long upon the land which the Lord thy God hath given thee." (Exod 20:12)

THE FOLLOWING IS A reasonable interpretation of the fifth commandment in light of its appearance and positioning in a highly politicized constitutional law document: "Respect family government rather than central government if you want your nation to maintain its independence." The socio-economic challenges faced by Hebrew families in Egypt provided real motivational context for this law, as we mentioned in the introductory section to part III. Parents in the forced labor communities of Pithom and Ramses, as everywhere in Egypt, had responsibility to clothe, feed, and shelter their own children. But Hebrew parents, in particular, lacked authority to provide their children with any significant educational and occupational opportunities. Parents could not effectively instruct children in the civic values embraced by their ancestors, since Pharaoh exercised control over much of the priestly legal and instructional apparatus of society and adults and children alike were required to respect the autocratic power of Pharaoh. Pharaoh also limited the field of work choices available to them to brick-making and straw production. Moses, sensitive to the plight of child labor in Hebrew communities and out of respect for their efforts, included children in his request for a three-day weekend away from work. Hebrew parents were not real governors in Egypt, but just flunkies to implement Pharaoh's demands.

Analysts of the fifth commandment concentrate mainly on children's obligation to honor and obey parents early in their lives and then to care for elderly parents when they themselves are middle aged. This line of interpretation has a long pedigree not only in the Christian but the Judaic community. Saadiah Gaon, the medieval Torah interpreter, emphasized the importance of obeying parents by noting that another of the commandments, the one on adultery, lent particular support to it. If adultery were not limited, he wrote, "No one would know his father" and thus the son could not "pay him reverence for raising him."[1] What is unstated in Saadiah's analysis is an acknowledgement that a major part of the reverence the son typically owes the father derives from the occupational direction painstakingly cultivated for him by the father to suit the child's particular abilities. That part of the equation was taken away from the father in Egypt. Every Hebrew child reaching a certain age in Egypt went into forced labor. Parental authority to groom a child for a productive, prosperous, and enjoyable adulthood later on was pointedly returned to Israelite families by the fifth commandment.

Focusing on the obligation of children toward their parents, as if the little group together occupied merely a humble little niche in the much greater scheme of social and governmental life, betrays a lack of awareness of domestic law in republican context in ancient as well as modern times. The focus on the children's responsibility is certainly an obvious and reasonable intent of the law, as we will discuss below. But the primary legal intent and content of the fifth commandment law is the obligation placed on parents to guide and control children until they reach the age of adulthood, and even well beyond. Even more specifically, the focus of the law is on the organization and operation of the huge local family government system normally very prominent in a republican polity. One important medieval interpreter of the Torah law, Judah Halevi, understood this. He wrote, "Honor your father and mother" is one of the "governmental laws."[2]

When Israel escaped Egypt, she gave parents legal authority to supervise all aspects of the upbringing, education, and occupational training of children. Parents were the officers of the system of local government in Israel. It is clear from the major law codes in the Torah/Pentateuch that parents and local elders exercised what legal scholars call the "police power"

1. Saadiah Gaon, "Beliefs and Opinions," 57.
2. Judah Halevi, "Kuzari," 64.

in society, essentially regulatory power over a wide range of human affairs, including social, economic, political, criminal, civil, militia, judicial, correctional, human service, health, educational and religious matters . . . in sum, the life-blood matters of the nation.[3] Parents served in other, but not necessarily higher, councils of government as well. A particularly respected parent/elder in the large Israelite farm household represented the family in clan and tribe level assemblies.

In ancient Israel, tribes were institutions like modern American state governments, clans were like county governments, and family estates were like city and town governments. In Israel, the fifth commandment delegated power specifically to the "paterfamilias," the legal and usually elder head of the grown children and grandchildren residing on the family land. The "house of the father" was not as small a unit of government as the nuclear family is today. It was a reasonably good sized one. It encompassed a household of three or more generations where the immediate family, together with in-laws, household employees and field and farm workers resided on the land.[4] (Gen 7:7) Abraham's household may have consisted of a good portion of the 318 militiamen he raised to rescue Lot, for example. Clan and household laborers likely built and maintained roads on family or clan property, and handled water and welfare issues like counties did in early America.

Since there was no elaborate national judiciary in early Israel, the father in particular, and likely both parents together, served as the adjudicatory agency of original jurisdiction in Israel's extensive rural areas. These courts operated in tandem with elder courts "in the gates" of villages and towns. The father had power to judge, sentence, and carry out criminal punishments of his own children and likely others in the extended family retinue. In the ancient Near East and early Bible settings, fathers could avenge a murder within the family by killing the murderer or by taking possession of all the murderer's property, or by accepting a ransom payment.[5] Fathers could enforce restitution for stolen goods at several times the value of the goods stolen, in order to discourage crime. (Exod 22:1; Luke 19:8) Fathers served as informers and prosecutors of rebellious children, and if they did not punish them themselves, could bring such children like a prosecutor

---

3. Under the constitutional law of the early American republic, parents had as much legal power to raise, educate, discipline, apprentice, contract for marriage, and specify religious affiliation as parents in ancient Israel did under the fifth commandment charter.

4. Wells and Magdalene, *Law*, 2:314.

5. Ibid., 33.

"before the elders."[6] (Deut 21:19) Fathers made marriage contracts for their children.[7] Fathers could pass along their own punishments to other members of the family.[8] Fathers could "sell" (really, place) daughters as "slaves" (indentured servants), essentially using them to pay off debts (and, incidentally, to provide helpful apprenticeships) or else to raise money for the family.[9]

The fact that the family was a government unit exercising the considerable power of the state in actual fact and not just in name, can be seen in particular Israelite laws relating to juvenile justice. Laws against "cursing" parents or rebelling against parents were not performed by a juvenile court, but by parents in the court of the family home or by parents serving as prosecutors in other local courts. Cursing was not simply a matter of using profane or abusive language in the presence of a parent. It was a matter of deliberate undermining of the family government system. (Exod 21:17) Striking a parent with intent to injure or kill was not seen as simple juvenile crime, but as sufficient treason or violent rebellion against the sovereign system of local government that the perpetrator was worthy of death. (Exod 21:15) Thus, the fifth commandment was an article of government of the highest importance in dealing with the survival of the Israelite state. This is made clear not just by these laws in Exodus, but by the mere fact that parents as authority figures were mentioned in the constitutional law, while kings were not. Parents were the real kings and queens in Israel.

Constitutionally, the Fifth Commandment provided parents with sovereign police power just as the Tenth Amendment of the U.S. Constitution provided state and local governments with similar power.[10] It is important to note that the national government dealt with international affairs both

6. Ibid., 426.
7. Ibid., 129.
8. Ibid., 271.
9. Ibid., 153.

10. The Tenth Amendment not only reserves the local police power to the states, but a great deal of that power to parents. American law gives a myriad of responsibilities and rights to parents with respect to governing children. These including disciplining, supporting, educating, protecting from harm (immunization, car seats), training in religion and law, controlling access to birth control and abortion (these rights have eroded in recent decades), approving marriage if under legal age to marry, approving and controlling buying and selling including of cars, deciding appropriate type of job and age for going to work, authorizing travel, exercising control over friends and associates, deciding what schools to attend, financing college, exercising control over earnings, and providing or not providing for inheritance. Other amendments to the U.S. Constitution speak to protecting the system of local government in other ways such as prohibiting quartering of soldiers "in any house" without consent in peacetime (Third Amendment), and unreasonable search and seizure (Fourth Amendment).

trade and military, but had limited involvement in domestic (i.e., "stateside") affairs. Those limited domestic affairs included construction of national roads, perhaps the keeping of a national granary for food storage, and perhaps maintaining a small shrine for the conducting of public ritual sacrifice for the welfare of the nation. The national confederate government had no constitutional power to raise, educate, or direct the labor of the youth of Israel. The power to deal with criminal, civil, employment, labor, welfare, education, and even ecclesiastic law, in addition to the usual social kinds of domestic law, rested with the parents of the children. The fifth commandment gave that responsibility to those most likely to do all they could to make those activities successful, the parents.

Much has been made of Israel as a coalition of tribes, but an even more extensive and powerful coalition of government units was evidenced at the family/clan level. Early tribal-level government was often as ephemeral or non-existent as the national government was. In the Bible, several of the twelve tribes dropped from view and mention during the period of Judges, for example. Canaan at the time of Moses was to a large extent a pristine frontier, and law was in the hands of the people who walked, cleared, and tilled that frontier. The land and its law was like the early American, gun-slinging, "lawless west." Government at village and town levels rarely reached outward far enough to exercise much control over rural family enclaves in either society. The fifth commandment gave local government shape and authority in those extensive "rural" areas just as Christian-mediated Biblical law and the distinctive local American law gave shape to local government on the American frontier. In both societies, the land and the plowshare, together with the families who worked the land, were the engines of progress. The sword (in ancient Israel) and the gun (in frontier America) were the agencies that protected such progress.

In Israel, the father's household government, with both parents as its administrators, for all intents and purposes had "total jurisdiction over its subordinate members."[11] Subordinate members included children, servants, hired laborers, and sojourners/visitors. Fathers like Abram took care to delegate power to wives to deal with important household matters, particularly to govern her own servants. (Exod 16:1–6)

In fact, the head of household had legal status as a government official, not only in domestic, but in external or international affairs.[12] According to legal documents governing life in Palestine in a time known as the Amarna Age shortly before the time of Moses, the doctrines of local family domestic

11. Wells and Magdalene, *Law*, 2:300.
12. Ibid., 271.

law included enforcement not only of criminal law and property law, but even took on a function normally reserved for national governments—entering into treaties with neighboring political powers.[13] The Bible notes not only that the patriarchal families of Abraham, Isaac, and Jacob also undertook such treaties, but families and clans even as late as the end of the period of Judges did. One example is when David with his wives and children made an agreement for their protection among the Philistines. (1 Sam 27) Extra-Biblical evidence, together with Biblical narrative, gives real coloring to the notion that families functioned as independent political entities in Israel and entered into coalitions with one another like larger tribal units did.

The family and clan had power to direct redemption-type welfare policies like Levirate marriage, debt and work remission, and land reversion. The fifth commandment, and laws pursuant to it, worked in tandem with the fourth commandment to form something like a U.S. county welfare system. The fourth commandment specified the programs of local aid (debt payment and debt relief, patterns of deployment of labor), and the fifth commandment specified the agency in charge of administering the programs.

The father/grandfather/elder essentially had the status of administrator of the political unit of the extended household estate by virtue of availability, administrative ability, or economic experience. These elders served in the community like the "patriarchs" of old (Abraham, Isaac, and Jacob). They owned land, ruled in their local domains, and lived long lives because they had plenty to live for. They made social decisions about marriage and land allotments relative to their numerous offspring. They provided dowry and accepted bride price gifts, educated, and trained and equipped their children and employees for work and defensive war. They sank wells, bought and sold mobile property, led religious worship ritual and activity, collected and paid taxes, conducted health care ritual and other healing practices, built roads, fed and cared for animals, conducted barter and banking activities, met in council with other patriarchs/elders, and administered local criminal justice and corrections. When they got together with other elders, they enacted legislation, decided war and peace, and decided legal matters relative to interpretation of both the common law of Syro-Palestine and the distinctive political and welfare law of Israel. In sum, landed elders exercised total police power of ancient Israel, the power to regulate life and death in the community.[14] The father, grandfather, or another elder of the household, perhaps an uncle, or a large landholder, may not have always been elected per se in a formal process as a city major or county official

---

13. Wells and Magdalene, *Law*, 2:272.
14. Reviv, *Elders in Ancient Israel*.

might be today, but likely had informal elective approval and likely could be relieved of his position if he did a poor job. Even Jacob, for example, was politically marginalized by his brash elder sons, as can be seen in the incident at Shechem.

Fathers/elders had to have a sophisticated understanding of the law in order to carry on such a variety of legal decision-making. There is a large body of legal material that fathers and elders had to be familiar with in order to carry out their function as government officials. The policies that derived from the Fifth Commandment and applied to the parental household included not just welfare law, but labor law relating to indentured labor, including child labor and hired labor. They also included gender laws, education law, inheritance law, marriage and divorce law, sexual conduct law, contract law, including creditor-debtor law, law related to use of the land, and militia law including exemption from mustering requirements.

Overall, the legal responsibilities of parents were so considerable that the later literary prophets used the strength and scope of such responsibility as a metaphor for the proper functioning of the entire society. God mentored the nation in the ways of self-government, just as parents mentor a child. When things were not going well in Israel during later times, the prophets described Israel as a wayward child who would not respect its parents—those parents essentially being the constitutional law and the God who inspired the law. (Hos 11; Jer 2) In this connection, the parents must not abuse this authority, just as the law and government must not abuse its authority. A New Testament citation underscores this: "Fathers, do not provoke your children." (Eph 6:4; Col 3:21)

It was not until those times when Israel gave-in to a system of powerful central government that the family system of government was undermined. Deuteronomy 28, for example, predicted the consequence of neglect of the constitution for the family system: "Thou shalt betroth a wife, and another man shall lie with her: thou shalt build a house, and thou shalt not dwell therein . . . Thy sons and thy daughters shall be given unto another people . . ." (Deut 28:30, 32)

One of the problems with central government was that it wanted to do for families what families traditionally did for themselves. For example, in the ancient Near East, documents have been uncovered dealing with responsibility for children to care for parents in their dotage, including providing for food, clothing, and a proper burial. These are in the form of contracts which tie fulfillment of such tasks to the receipt of an inheritance.[15] Much later, in New Testament times, we find Jesus still holding to

---

15. Miller, *Ten Commandments*, 182.

the ideal of fifth commandment family government responsibility for the aged. Jesus, for example, criticized the Pharisees for sidestepping the fifth commandment requiring honoring and supporting parents later in life. The Pharisees said that when a grown child devotes a "gift" (tax) to the national government or its high priest this "suffers him no more to do aught for his father or his mother" in the years of their infirmity. (Mark 7:12) This essentially shifted responsibility for caring for parents to the national government and whatever welfare or retirement system it had available for them. The Israelite citizen in Jesus' day was invited by at least some of the Pharisees to financially support the temple government and its rulers' programs rather than his own parents. This subverted local rule and family government and created something like an early example of a national welfare state, likely with approval or encouragement of the colonial master of the area, the emperor of Rome.[16]

Fathers and parents were so important to government in Israel that people swore oaths by parents as the most prominent authorities available in the land. For example, in the days of the patriarchs, individuals swore legal oaths by "the fear of my father," or the "fear of my mother." (Gen 31:53, 43) Family government was so important that families compiled genealogies of their ancestors that served like Mesopotamian king lists to notarize the family's history and importance in the region, and stake out their claims to land. Departed family officials were so deeply venerated that Israel had to pass laws condemning actual worship of ancestors. Those children who were deprived of fathers were cared for with a passion that went without parallel in non-democratic societies. This was because citizens in a democratic society knew what such persons, known as the "fatherless," were really missing. (Jer 24:3)

The Sixth Commandment

"Thou shalt not kill." (Exod 20:13; Deut 5:17)

If the first table of laws (whether four or five commandments) deals mainly with internal organization and operation of the national government and the private sector, the second table deals mainly with interaction of the national government with the citizenry as they go about their day to day activities. In particular, the second table laws place significant restraints on interference with the lives, property, and rights of the people. For its part,

---

16. Horsley, *Covenant Economics*, 99.

the sixth commandment grants a civil right of life to the citizenry, as against the usual tendency of autocratic government to take lives at its own pleasure.

On its surface, the sixth commandment seems to prohibit criminal murder—killing one's neighbor without cause, or taking life wrongly. However, if this narrow interpretation is expanded categorically or broadly, as an "apodictic" law must be, it encompasses the types of killing we believe the commandment is really reaching here. In the context of Israel's constitutional political values, which deal with the use and abuse of power, the sixth law is certainly aimed at prohibiting political murder—that is, killing for power. Killing to demonstrate or to get power is the same whether it is done by a citizen against a neighbor or by the national government against a citizen. Both involve power concerns between one party and another. Thus it would be inappropriate to interpret the commandment as prohibiting killing by the citizen in the countryside but not by the citizen in the urban government. The government is just an extension of the citizen and must abide by the constitution's values just as the citizen must.

Martin Luther, for one, did not feel that government was included in the prohibition of this commandment since its "right to take human life [is not] abrogated."[17] This argument places more trust in government than Israel and the Ten Commandments could countenance. Certainly the government by means of the constitutional policy-making process could authorize killings. For example, it could set the death penalty for a certain crime. In such a case the government could be said to have rightly acted on the matter. Perhaps this is what Luther was thinking of. But, if the chief executive, without the consent of the legislature, undertook any program of domestic killing like private revenge against a political enemy, or any program of international killing, that official was acting the part of a rogue and an outlaw in Israel. This latter kind of killing is what the sixth commandment was designed to prevent.

Using the same argument, the nation could go to war, but only if the legislature gave its blessing to do so. This is the proper context for viewing the New Testament statement of Paul: "Let every soul be subject unto the higher powers. For there is no power but of God. The powers that be are ordained of God." (Rom 13:1) In a democratic nation, like that of early Israel, and that of Rome to a lesser degree in the time of Paul, the principle power that exists is that of the legislative voice of the people. The legislature's decision is law, and not even a prophet or the God of Moses will go against it.[18] What may be implied in Paul's statement, and certainly is explicit in the

---

17. Simpson, "Thou Shalt Not Kill," 250.

18. Recall that God and Moses wanted the people to enter Canaan early and from

Ten Commandments, is that law decided by an autocrat rather than by the people requiring a people to go to war is not "of God."

The ethic with respect to physical violence in ancient Israel, despite what has been said and written by many who read the Bible uncritically or literally, is decidedly non-violent—that is non-aggressive, though not fully pacifist. The non-violent ethic is captured in a lyric of one of the Psalms: "Rebuke the company of spearmen . . . scatter thou the people that delight in war." (Ps 68:30) On the other hand, when the nation had to deal with serious military threats to its way of life, it knew what to do. The arms-bearing "men" of early Israel each had, or had access to, a sword, even if they had to convert a plowshare to get it. Israel would fight to the death against those individuals and forces who directly threatened her democracy and her citizens. In the meanwhile, the ardent desire of its early people and politicians was to prevent and avoid violence at almost any cost. By means of the sixth commandment, Israel's government was clearly and most certainly prohibited from hanging a law-abiding citizen from a tree or looking around for a weak neighboring tribe to conquer.

We can classify the sixth commandment into two main types of proscribed domestic civic killing. The first was cross-factional warfare or assassination aimed at capturing or overturning political power. One thinks of the struggle between Absalom and David and the Bible's many references to regicide in the books of Kings and Chronicles. One person aspiring to government power kills another who is desirous of the same power. This kind of killing was common in Egypt and its consequences are chronicled in the pre-Exodus Egyptian story of the life of Sinuhe. In Egypt, murder in and around the court of the king was so common it was institutionalized in folk lore by portraying the southern god Seth of Lower Egypt as a murderer. Regicide, or attempted regicide, was business as usual in autocracy, and even the heavens were reconciled to the practice.[19] The second type of political killing we point to here is government killing of citizens/neighbors, activated by a politician already seated in power. That would include killing to keep the leader or the leader's party in power when there was no serious threat to the republic, and violent suppression of individuals or groups opposed to the leader's policies.

Although it reared its head briefly at the time of the tyrant judge Abimelech in the early days, political assassination in order to obtain power did not occur regularly in Israel until the time of the monarchies in the

---

the south, but the people vetoed that idea with a resounding "No" and had their own way.

19. Frankfort, *Kingship and the Gods*, 19–20, 40–41, 145.

north and south. Then there were frequent acts of regicide by parties in the monarch's court. There is also evidence of persecution of the political party leaders know as prophets. Some prophets were imprisoned, others were murdered, all in order to maintain a corrupt leader in power or prevent further loss of popularity that the prophet was causing the king.

During Israel's early period of democratic republicanism, elections were peaceful and transitions in power accepted by all. However, after the death of the national judge Gideon, one of Gideon's sons, Abimelech, killed sixty-nine out of seventy of the other sons of Gideon in an attempt to promote his mother's political clan interests above his father's clan interests. He did this in order to make himself not just a limited power judge, but a powerful king.

This method of obtaining political power offended the confederate constitutional sensibilities of many of the people in the confederation. The last remaining of the persecuted sons of Gideon, Jotham, delivered a constitutional argument against Abimelech's methods to the citizenry gathered in assembly, before he disappeared into hiding. He pointed out the nation's long political tradition of electing individuals who were not particularly ambitious for political power. He also appealed to the confederation's tradition of peaceful popular election rather than violent usurpation. He argued that violence used in the electoral process was a certain indication that the candidate was not legitimate. He argued that if Abimelech's spicy new electoral process was a morally or constitutionally legitimate one, then all would be well among the citizens. But if it was a faulty process, even the citizens who had supported Abimelech would eventually feel the violent lash of Abimelech and come to understand that his rule was wrong. Jotham's predictions came to pass after three years of Abimelech's rule, which included a bloody civil war.

The regicide practiced by aspirants to power particularly in the north after division of the "united monarchy" of David and Solomon was a major step in the direction of the dilution of enforcement of the sixth commandment in Israel. At that time there were frequent changes in executive department leadership, but not through elections and peaceful transitions. One example will suffice here: "Pekahiah the son of Menahem began to reign over Israel in Samaria, and reigned two years . . . But Pekah the son of Remaliah, a captain of his, conspired against him, and smote him in Samaria, in the palace of the king's house . . . and he killed him, and reigned in his room." (2 Kgs 15:23–25) Hosea indicted the government for murders committed by government civil service employees, the priests. Those priests laid in wait like robbers to kill citizens on the way to Shechem, and such activity was noted as a transgression of the commandment covenant. (Hos 6:7–9)

The sixth commandment served as the cornerstone of the freedom of intellectual expression provided by the first commandment. Citizens who spoke out could not lose their lives for doing so, and so were emboldened to exercise their rights. The sixth commandment is almost a restatement of the first commandment in an extraordinarily earthy tone that all of the people could understand. If one might not understand the legal nuances of freedom of speech, all citizens in Israel at least could understand that under no circumstances were politics in Israel to involve killing. Fighting for power was not to be tolerated in Israel.

A ban on political murder provided the added benefit of curbing the despotic practice of confiscating the property of one's opponents and of entirely innocent persons in order to enrich themselves and their administrations. The Israelite constitution (by means of the second, fourth, and tenth commandments principally) limited concentration of wealth and promoted a relatively egalitarian economic lifestyle. Everyone was entitled to a subsistence living and politicians were not entitled to more economic resources than others just by virtue of winning office. They were certainly not entitled to use power to enhance personal fortune. The constitution purposefully required much personal risk and allowed for little personal reward as a part of the job of the national magistrate. One had to have a sincere and abiding affection for law, land, and liberty to even think of becoming a national "judge." In a truly democratic society, the store of wealth and power in the national government was little enough that it was not be worth the risk to life and limb to seize it.

Declining respect for innocent life near the end of the period of Judges is represented in the incident of the concubine who was raped and killed in the territory of Benjamin and also in the military response to this crime. This incident was an inter-tribal factor perhaps, that, along with the Philistine threat, led to calls for a stronger central government to prevent such events. (Judg 19) It seems that Israel was veering toward a constitutional philosophy that the best solution for domestic violence fomented by one party (the murder of one person) was similar or greater violence by the aggrieved party (the murder of many persons). This was the age-old philosophy of blood revenge that Moses and his party had worked so hard to banish from the culture of Israel. Because of the death of the concubine, the confederate tribes gave vent to a horrible civil war that virtually wiped Benjamin off the map. They took this course rather than gathering their senses and resolving the issue by means of negotiation and settlement.[20]

---

20. Miller, *Ten Commandments*, 255–57.

Fifth, Sixth, Seventh, and Eighth Commandments

As soon as the monarchy was set up, Saul, David, and Solomon all demonstrated the cogency of Samuel's concern about increasing levels of violence that would accompany a stronger national executive department of government. Saul become enmeshed in a number of jealousy-based attempts at political murder of his rival for political popularity, the young David. (1 Sam 24:12) David's own political killing of Uriah by placing him in harm's way, was a watershed Biblical event. The event was political rather than simply social, because it disrupted the governmental structure of the house of Uriah, and enhanced the governmental perquisites of his own lineage. For example, the liaison with Bathsheba produced the next king of Israel, Solomon. The leader of David's own political party, Nathan, could not avoid accusing him of great hostility to the constitution at this point. David sidestepped what could have been more serious repercussions by admitting his guilt.

How does one square the idea of a pacifist Bible with the fact the Bible is full of "surely ye shall die" statements aimed at its own citizens? The Bible usually uses this kind of phrase to punctuate admonitions against constitutional backsliding, and, as such, it speaks in most cases metaphorically. People may lose their lives upon conquest of the homeland at some point, but in the meantime they lose their eternal lives, meaning the connection with their intelligent and valiant ancestors, and also their spiritual and political souls. Even when the phrase is used to condemn a criminal, it is most often used metaphorically. For example, David answered Nathan's parable about a rich man taking a poor man's lamb, by saying such a man "shall surely die" for his theft. David himself interprets his own statement by admitting that the thief is not to be literally killed but is rather required to repay the poor man four-fold for the crime, which will probably kill him economically at least for a time. The dying may also be an expression of the criminal's mortification after he comes under prosecution by the local authorities who know him.

Nathan then declares that David is the rich man of the parable, because he has taken Bath-sheba from the poor man Uriah. This is certainly a much greater crime than theft of a lamb, as David is partly responsible for Uriah losing his life, and not just the taking of Bath-sheba to be his own wife. David is a public official and is subject to the laws like any other and even to greater scrutiny than most. Even so, David does not lose his life. When David admits some culpability, he suffers public humiliation instead as his crime is known and remembered "before all Israel." (2 Sam 12:13) He is the Israelite equivalent of the American Bill Clinton. The English expression "I could have died when they found out" renders the meaning of the

Israelite phrase fairly well. It is a phrase used in a culture that works hard to use shame and guilt to help control individual behavior.

The sixth commandment prescribed both domestic (as in the case of potentially warring tribes) and international political and military neutralism and general pacifism. The solution to both domestic and international aggression was enlightened self-defense and negotiation, but not adventurism of any sort like that practiced by the great kings of the Orient. One author writes, "The great kings divided . . . the entire civilized world, each dominating its vassals . . ."[21] Israel was prepared to defend its people and its lands against such attempts at domination, but did not seek, at least in the early period, to take people, lives and lands from others. Egypt had the strongest central government of all the kingships in the Near East, and thus easy access to a menacing killing machine. Pharaoh was known as the king of kings in the eastern Mediterranean. The king of Babylon wrote to one Pharaoh, observing "Canaan is your land its kings are your servants." The object of the adventurism was usually riches to fill the king's coffers.

During Israel's long stay in Egypt, she became familiar with the regular imperial campaigns of the houses of Pharaohs into surrounding territories, including Canaan. Their campaigns abroad were waged at great cost of Egyptian lives and treasure. Some campaigns were waged at home against Egyptian people as well. For example, early in the 18th Dynasty, Ahmose I (1570–1546) fought against the Hyksos rulers of Egypt in a civil war and also crushed their Egyptian supporters. Ahmose also warred against Kush (Ethiopia). Egypt tripled its colonies in Nubia by the time of Thutmose I (1524–1518), who also adventured as far north as the Euphrates. Co-regents Hatshepsut and Thutmose III adventured into Punt, on the eastern coast of Sudan. Thutmose III conquered Canaan in 1482, which inspired a long-term, organized resistance there well before the children of Israel returned to their homeland around 1250. Thutmose IV fought a confederation of local kings at Megiddo in Canaan and conducted an expensive siege of seven months there. He eventually secured the Syro-Palestine coast, much of the interior of Palestine, and in 1473 went as far north as the Euphrates.

Much of the endemic violence in Canaan was the result of a vicious cycle of depredations made between Mitanni in the north and Egypt in the south, each overrunning the other's colonial possessions and toying with the lives and properties of local Canaanite populations. Egypt's imperial ambitions were rolled back somewhat during the time of Amenhotep IV, also known as the monotheist Akhenaten, who ruled during the Amarna period (1400–1350) shortly before the start of the 19th dynasty of Seti and

---

21. Redford, "Amarna Letters," 176.

Ramses. Seti I, however, campaigned abroad in imitation of earlier dynasties. Ramses II, the Pharaoh of the Exodus, escalated the level of his father's militarism, making six campaigns to the north, crushing unrest in Palestine, and increasing fortifications there. Colonials were subject to conscription into Pharaoh's army and Pharaoh also used tax money to purchase the services of mercenaries. This is the international marauding that Israel saw and knew and the fact that her homeland was suffering was not lost on her. She was aware of the warring activity in Canaan even while she was in Egypt, since some of her own tribal cousins, known as Apiru rebels in Palestine, were directly involved in anti-colonial activity there.[22]

Once free of Egypt and formed into a convoy of freely roaming tribes constituting a large and strong confederacy, Israel took care not to act like a new imperialist on the block. Israel skirted nations she might have conquered during the "40 years" of wandering in the wilderness before entering Canaan. Israel, by dint of Yahweh's intent for her to take possession only of ancestral lands in Canaan, was given limited "East Bank" territory to be hers and was told to keep her hands off other territories. For example, God told Israel "to pass through the coast of your brethren the children of Esau, which dwell in Seir . . . meddle not with them; for I will not give you of their land, no, not so much as a footbreadth . . ."[23] (Deut 2:4–5) There was no provision in the Israelite constitution allowing them to annex land they historically had no claim to. In fact, there was a provision prohibiting it . . . the sixth commandment. In much the same way, citizens of the early United States worried that they needed a constitutional amendment to obtain Louisiana, which space of land was not a part of their original colonial charters.[24]

Once in Canaan, Israel engaged militarily with only those Canaanite city-states that would not accommodate her re-settlement program and its self-government focus. City-states in the area, apparently well known for their political murderousness, included Hittites, Amorites, Canaanites, Perizzites, Hivites, and Jebusites. Israel was to avoid or confront and destroy them "that they may not teach you to do all the abhorrent things that they do for their gods . . . " (Deut 20:18) These tribes were likely loyal either to Pharaoh or to a northern or eastern emperor, and equally likely utilized a government system of local puppet monarchy that could quickly be turned to serve an emperor's desire to destroy them. Their "gods" were the Egyptian dynasty's rulers and the "abhorrent things" were the molten and graven

22. Murname, "Egypt, History of (Dyn. 18–20)," 348–49, 351; Redford, "Amarna Letters," 177–78; Pritchard, *Atlas*, 24, 26–27.

23. Elazar, *Covenant and Polity*, 202.

24. Shinkoskey, *American Kings*, 22–23.

symbols of despotic political government that they regularly paraded about in their cities and into their battles.

The sixth commandment also sets in place Israel's die-hard policy prohibition against a national census, which policy David offended and paid for dearly. It also provided authority for Israel's policy against a standing army, which held up until the time of Solomon. The sixth commandment proscribed national conscription of local labor into the ruler's militia even when an impending conflict was of a defensive nature. In the days of Judges, individual tribes decided whether they would commit forces to protect the confederacy, and in the time of Deborah several of them refused to send troops for confederate use. In addition, raising of the militia could not be done by wholesale means, since many exemptions were given. (Deut 20:5–8) Also, war preparation was to be undertaken by civilian authorities, not military. In the case of war preparations, the law specified, "The priest [not the commander-in-chief] shall approach and speak unto the people." (Deut 20:2, 9) The war power was with the legislative body, not the chief executive. The law spoke to the citizenry using the plural, or corporate "you." "When thou goest out to battle . . . and seest . . . a people more than thou . . ."[25] (Deut 20:1) This emphasized that the people as a whole were to make judgments about threats and responses. A verse in Proverbs underscores this passionate concern for broad legislative input to war decisions: "For by wise counsel thou shalt make thy war: and in a multitude of counselors there is safety." (Prov 24:6)

By the time of Saul, there was a shift in militia policy to where the national government could conscript soldiers rather than merely ask for voluntary participation. It was said, "When Saul saw any strong man, or any valiant man, he took him unto him." (1 Sam 14:52) Indeed, this is one of the characteristics of ancient "kingship," the ability to have a stronger hand in military affairs vis a vis the local tribes. The Hebrew verb translated "take" meant forceful expropriation. For example, Samuel warned the people that a "king," i.e., a strong magistrate, "will take your sons, and appoint them for himself, for his chariots, and to be his horsemen; and some shall run before his chariots." (1 Sam 8:11)

Democracy guards against conscription because a regular army can be turned against its own people and can also be used to conquer other nations without the consent of the citizenry, at great cost to life and national treasure. The history of representative governments shows that democracies rarely seriously war against one another, unless, like Greece and Rome, they do so in the declining stages of their constitutional law systems and in

---

25. Elazar, *Covenant and Polity*, 208–209.

the midst of a head-long rush toward autocracy. A good example of peaceable neighbors sporting representative systems of government in modern times is Canada and the United States.[26] But in the declining stages of Israel's history, and certainly in twentieth century America, national power concentrated in the executive branch began to aggressively and offensively project power outward and menace governments both nearby and far away. Israel and Judah menaced Edom, Moab, and Syria, and America pushed for expanded hegemony in the Caribbean, Latin America and the Pacific, and later Europe, Asia and Africa.

Israel committed to the use of its iron resources for cultivation rather than war. It needed its industry to be employed in life-giving work rather than life-taking work. At the time of Samuel, Israel had virtually no armament iron-works available to her tribes and had to rely on neighbors for those services. (1 Sam 13:19–23) Israel had clearly beaten her wilderness swords into plowshares after the Canaan settlement, and her legitimate constitutional advocates continually admonished her to do so in order to put national policy emphasis on the promotion of life and prosperity. (Isa 2:4; Mic 4:3; Joel 3:10) Exhortations toward peace were common in the law and the prophets' literature. (Lev 19; Ezek 33; Gen 12:3) Early on, the Yahweh of the Exodus effectively moved Israelite society away from any flirtation with the war gods of Egypt. This happened when Moses nipped in the bud Israel's tentative tilt toward molten kingship and therefore Israel's ability to finance an army. He did this by destroying the molten calf and thus repudiating the debt owed to Egypt. By means of numerous examples of dealing with health issues in the wilderness and numerous references to leaving behind them the varied communicable diseased of Egypt, Israel committed instead to the public health god of Moses, rather than the war gods of Egypt and Canaan.[27] Yahweh was a restrained God, one who counseled Moses to negotiate tirelessly with Pharaoh, accede endlessly to the murmurings (opposition) of the people in the wilderness, and forgive those who spitefully used him.

The sixth commandment applied, as we have said above, to parties vying for government power, government in its dealings with its own people, and government relations with neighboring countries. But we must also admit it was also a broad law for inter-family and inter-clan domestic tranquility, providing for a right to life for citizens of the nation vis a vis their own neighbors. It ensured that the confederation of tribes were to be committed to a culture of preservation rather than exploitation of life. This law demanded

---

26. Doyle, "Liberalism," 50–64.

27. We will view the public health implications of the tenth commandment in the section devoted to that law.

that Israelite society be devoted to the pursuit of healthy living and long life for its citizens. As such, it also enacted a broad proscription against several other types of killing often tolerated in ancient Near East societies.

Because Israelite democracy set its sights upon political and economic and social enfranchisement of all its citizens, and hoped for contributions from all of them, it was vital to ensure that no individual life no matter how marginal or defenseless was taken for any vain or ill-considered reason. For this reason, Israel prohibited social killing of disabled, disfigured or unwanted infants, and religious killing by sacrifice of children. Even killing of trees during war time was prohibited pursuant to the sixth commandment.[28] (Deut 20:19-20) There is evidence that all of these practices were limited or proscribed in fundamental ways in Israel.

In the ancient Near East social killing was usually done by "exposure," simple placing of the infant in the wild on its own to die, either because of economic conditions, illegitimacy, adulterous conception, or some other threat to the child's future.[29] Hagar exposed her child to the elements and wandered a ways away to let it die when she could not provide water for it. God's suggestion to her that she should take the child up and keep looking for water was effectively an early statement that issues related to survivability of children even under extreme conditions could be handled with due diligence and good faith. (Gen 21:14-21) However, cultures around Israel were not always as solicitous of the lives of children. An Anatolian source (from Ephesus, in modern Turkey) indicates that often newborns were put through a type of physical ordeal to see if they were strong enough to survive. Infanticide and child abandonment were widespread in ancient China.[30] A legal text from 217 BCE in China bestowed on parents the right to kill newborns that were deformed, but denied them the right to infanticide merely because they already had too many children.[31]

Child sacrifice was practiced as a supposedly powerful, semi-magical method of religious manipulation of the gods or as a method of obtaining political or military advantage. Abraham learned from God that there should be no sacrificing of children to obtain the favor of God, a humanitarian advance that had lasting effects later in Israel. In Abraham's family, God was ever more firmly established as a patient and forgiving one, rather

---

28. Miller, *Ten Commandments*, 238.

29. See Berman, *Equal Justice*, 66, 143, 147. In the ancient Near East epic Atrahasis, the monarchy promotes infant sacrifice/exposure for purposes of population control; see Berman, *Equal Justice*, 23. Exposure is still rampant in Semitic societies at the time of Muhammad 600 years after Jesus Christ.

30. York, *Health and Wellness*, 88, 93.

31. York, *Health and Wellness*, 92-93.

than a vindictive one, solicitous of the people's privacy, property, and their very lives. However, killing for the purpose of demonstrating the faith, or dependability, or honor of a political ruler continued to be a practice in the area not only in the time of Moses but well into the time of Judges. The King of Moab practiced it to enhance his chances of favorable outcome in war, as did the outlaw judge Jephthah.[32] (Judges 11:31, 34) Israel banned its practice. (Lev 18:21, 20:1-5; Deut 12:29-31)

The sixth commandment dampened the tradition of blood revenge, whereby family members could pursue and kill a suspected felon. That pattern of vigilante justice was inadequate in the case of accidental or negligent homicide or cases in which the identity of the murdered was in dispute or unknown. The sixth commandment substituted a more scientific and humane procedure for determination of guilt and execution of punishment. Cities of refuge were set aside where fleeing felons could obtain respite from pursuing relatives until an objective trial could be held. (Num 35:9-28; Deut 19:1-13)

Because the sixth commandment surely applied to simple spiteful killing of one citizen by another, it is appropriate here to look at the Hebrew word "rasah," sometimes translated "kill," sometimes translated "murder." Another way of expressing the same act is "to strike" ("naka") or "to strike the life" ("nepes"). If one strikes another with a wood, stone, or iron object, the intent is to cause serious harm or death.[33] Intention is important as well. The legislative policy enacted pursuant to the constitutional law distinguishes between accidental (Num 35:23), or with hatred (Num 35:20) and/or premeditation. (Num 35:20, 22) One author writes, "Killing a person [even negligent manslaughter] was an act of such extraordinary weight that it could not be reconciled through the sacrifice of an animal."[34] The individual had to live in a city of refuge until the death of the current high priest in order to release the stain of his act.

The ancient Israelite article of democratic law against killing was also effectively a prototype of the U.S. Constitution's prohibition against cruel and unusual punishment, of which killing of dissenters or rivals is certainly the most cruel and unusual of all.[35] Nations around Israel were notorious for physical mutilation practices, like the putting out of eyes. (Judg 16:21) Israel

---

32. The Vikings practiced child sacrifice much later as well; see 10/31/13 NBC News Science.

33. Miller, *Ten Commandments*, 223; Hamilton, *Pentateuch*, 194-95.

34. Miller, *Ten Commandments*, 227.

35. Both ganging up on an adversary (Deut 25:11-12) and mutilation is considered bad in Israel. For example, even a serious felon cannot be treated to more than 40 lashes. (Deut 25:1-3; Miller, *Ten Commandments*, 246)

avoided such mutilation practices. The sixth commandment thus mimicked the type of prohibitions against torture found in the field manual of the U.S. armed forces. Israel's sensitivity to humane treatment of citizens, and even to animals, played out in laws like the provision of moderation in the practice of flogging (Deut 25:2–3), kind treatment toward animals (Exod 34:26; 23:11–12), exemption of the relatives of criminals from punishment (Deut 24:16), precautions against accident (Deut 22:8), and humane treatment of workers, captives, resident aliens, and defenseless persons like orphans, widows, and the blind. (Exod 23:12; Deut 27:17–18)

The doctrine of Jesus of Nazareth was distinctly pacific as well. When Jesus stated that the great commandment was to love the neighbor (and even the enemy) rather than hate and kill the neighbor, he was merely re-iterating Leviticus 19:18, "You shall love your neighbor as yourself." Jesus began his teaching about the law in the Sermon on the Mount with the sixth commandment. (Matt 5:21–24) He cautioned his listeners not only to refrain from actual killing, but to take measures to purge themselves of the anger which could eventually lead to violence. An anger-filled emotional state, Jesus said, made of a person a hypocrite when he went near an altar to leave a gift for the God of non-violence. Elements of the Christian political world during the tenth century effectively installed a version of the sixth commandment as a guiding principle of international relations. The Peace and Truce of God movement introduced once again a Mosaic and early Christian democratic, pacifist doctrine into the affairs of bickering nations.[36]

The Seventh Commandment

"Thou shalt not commit adultery." (Exod 20:14; Deut 5:18)

The topic of adultery in its various forms is strangely pertinent to a discussion of limited government in any era of time. It is therefore not surprising there is an article of government devoted to it in the ancient Israelite constitution. Bluntly put, common adultery subverts local government strength and stability, as it breaks up the social unit responsible for administering a great many government functions. The duties of the family jurisdiction of government then have to be handled elsewhere, such as in clan, tribe, or national government. For example, when adultery occasioned family breakup, the father's estate did not descend easily among his children. It was contested, diluted, or fully diverted away from the ancestral lineage, and perhaps into the hands of the state.

---

36. Bauer, *History*, 590, 642.

Adultery in the households of government officials at mid-levels of government was an equally devastating phenomenon in human social and political terms, but on the national level it was subversive of the very foundations of democratic law and government. We will look at the peculiar varieties of aristocratic-type adultery in Egypt which the seventh commandment sought to prevent in the households of chief executive officers in Israel. Narrative stories about Bible patriarchs, negative statements about strong monarchy made by the Bible's prophets and scribes, and extra-Biblical sources springing from the ancient Near East, combine to suggest three particular "adulterous" practices common among strong kings: court incest; taking of additional wives from the domestic population; and intermarriage into royal families of neighboring nations. Each of these social practices worked against republican government.

A peculiar politics of incest helped sustain Egyptian dynasts on their thrones. Pharaohs, in order to stand apart from the people, claimed to have the blood of gods in their veins. But it was not enough that one particularly grand ruler from time to time should claim this. The royal court perpetuated the myth of the right of divine dynastic succession of the ruler's offspring whether those new rulers were good or bad, sane or insane. They did that by seeing to it that a young Egyptian prince married within the family—a cousin, or even a sister—and thus kept the dynasty's divine blood line pure. Israel's 400 year stay in Egypt allowed them to understand the role that royal court incest marriages played in making repressive autocracy possible in that nation.

During the time of Israel's stay in Egypt, Queen Hatshepsut solidified her claim to the throne by wedding her half-brother Thutmose II. Their daughter then married *her* own half brother (and cousin) Thutmose III.[37] Dynasties legitimized these kinds of activities by publishing theo-political propaganda about the activity of the gods in heaven, who were said to have pulled off similar marriages, sometimes in collaboration with earthly consorts. In one case of long currency in Egypt, for example, the court published an account about the deceased King Pepi from an early dynasty. The court reminded the people that the great Pharaoh Pepi was actually the son of the goddess Nut. Pepi's own living son thus had the blood of the gods in him as well. The dynasty's court officials, apparently, were not content to bring one of their own members to power based on that one amazing happenstance alone. After his death, it was reported that Pepi went on to impregnate his goddess mother in heaven. This happy circumstance provided Pepi with a type of rebirth of his own life in heaven. It also strengthened the dynasty's

---

37. Murname, "Egypt. History of (Dyn. 18–20)," 349.

connection with the divine realm, since Pepi apparently was taking an active role in heavenly power circles. In addition, it seems the earthly dynasty now had their own patron god in heaven worthy of worship on earth, Pepi himself.[38] Israel, for her part, wanted no truck with such monarchic political propaganda, and took detailed care to abolish sexual relations with family members and near relatives.[39] (Lev 18:6–18)

On the other hand, royalists were not always averse to sexual contact with ordinary mortals if it served their purposes and inclinations. The sexual escapades of Egyptian kings is described in a piece of ancient Egyptian literature known as the Tale of the Two Brothers.[40] Popular monarchs in the Near East were infamous for holding contests or banquets to find "fair" women to take from ordinary families into their harems. This sort of promiscuous and adulterous sexual activity undertaken for aesthetic or pleasurable purposes by monarchs and aristocrats corrupted traditional socio-sexual values in the population. It set a bad example for ordinary families who were trying to inculcate the dream of stable family land ownership and long-term marital happiness in their children and grandchildren.

At times, royals looked among the females of a newly captive or conquered people to take additional consorts.[41] The Bible's Genesis narrative demonstrates the propensity of strong kings to "take" beautiful women from neighboring or traveling families and add them to their harems. They might even go so far as to take women from lawful marriages, perhaps disposing of the husbands along the way as well. This was such a well-known phenomenon in Egypt and Canaan that Abraham and Isaac both had to disguise their beautiful wives as sisters to insure against losing their lives. The patriarch prophet leaders went to great lengths to remain alive in such an environment in order to have any hope of fulfilling the promise of a great democratic civilization in Canaan.

Israel herself was not immune from the "taking" variety of royal court adultery. King David arranged the death of Bathsheba's husband in order to try to cover up his adultery with her and allow their future marriage. (2 Sam 11–12) The practice of adding additional wives was not only adultery against the king's first wife if the new wife was single, but was adultery against the legitimate husband if the new wife was already married. The law in Deuteronomy against kings taking additional wives can be seen as a

---

38. Frankfort, *Kingship and the Gods*, 177.
39. Ibid., 43.
40. Assman, "Egyptian Literature (Survey)," 381.
41. The Bible's own Esther was taken in such a manner as the wife of the Persian king.

curb on royal court murder and manipulation of the households of ordinary citizens to be sure, but also necessary to curb the likelihood of bad-seed hereditary monarchy as well. Not all capture marriages turn out as captivatingly as David's marriage to Bathsheba.

The ruler's sexual conduct was absolutely important to regulate by law in order to sustain democracy for still another reason. It was customary in the ancient Near East for kings to keep a stable of government/temple concubines who could only be impregnated by him. Extra wives and concubines served a highly politicized purpose, and that is why the seventh commandment outlawed them. Emperors in the ancient world took multiple wives, even dozens or hundreds of them, in order to guarantee a male successor. Making sure that the concubines were devoted to a sacred purpose—that is, only to the king—helped perpetuate the myth of a divine lineage.[42] The king's production of a male offspring ensured the continuation of his dynasty and prevented a lurch toward republicanism.

The third major category of political adultery that the seventh commandment ended in Israel, at least for a few hundred years, was the practice of international royal intermarriage. Kings typically sealed a military alliance by means of marriage to help ensure compliance with the alliance terms. One king inspired confidence that he would come to the military aid of another by giving a beloved daughter to be the wife of the other king. If he did not come to the distressed king's aid, his daughter could easily be hurt or killed or used to extort his compliance. A strong king needed many wives to give him many daughters for the purpose of making many alliances to keep his many sons in power. If he did not have the daughters to get the job done, he would have to enter into the marriages himself. This sort of dynamic explains why Amenhotep II married two Babylonian princesses, two Mitannian princesses, and one from Arzawa.[43]

In a democratic nation like Israel, there was a strong legal and ethical prohibition against alliances for a variety of reasons. The principal reason was that it allowed the foreign nation to usurp the authority of the homeland legislature to decide the matter of war. It placed the war power in the hands of a single foreign king who might need the weaker nation's armed forces at a moment's notice. Elazar, supporting our view here, sees the restriction in Deuteronomy 17 against taking many wives as "both anti-hedonistic and anti-foreign alliances."[44]

---

42. McMahon, *Women Shall Not Rule*.
43 Murname, "Egypt, History of (Dyn. 18–20)," 349 .
44. Elazar, *Covenant and Polity*, 206.

During her several hundred year-long stay in Egypt, Israel had first-hand knowledge of the Egyptian practice of international alliance-making, to the detriment of local communities seeking independence from imperial control. Thutmose IV, for example, married a daughter of the king of Mitanni, and this diplomatic adultery helped greatly with the suppression of rebellions of Palestinian locals against the two superpowers.[45] Ramses II himself continued the practice of diplomatic adultery marriage. He married "no fewer than two Hittite Princesses."[46] Israel had no desire to work with other nations to suppress local populations of independence-starved people in such a way. Neither did they want to be one of the populations suppressed in such a way, and hence the seventh commandment.

The tactic of international adultery alliance was used directly against Israel as a nation. After David conquered Edom, Hadad, the crown prince of Edom, took refuge in Egypt and married a member of the royal family. (1 Kgs 11:14–22) This gave Egypt an ally to use as a buffer against the new Israelite government.[47] Solomon, for his part, offended his nation's constitutional tradition against adulterous marriages by making political intermarriages with other royal houses, for which he is roundly condemned by the Bible. (1 Kgs 11:1–3; 1 Kgs 3:1–2)

The literary prophets railed against international alliances during the period of kingship. Long after Israel's kings began entering into military alliances with other nations and embroiling her people in debilitating wars not of their own choosing, political constitutionalists like Isaiah pointed back to the original intent of the seventh commandment and the horrible consequences of not holding to it. He wrote, "Associate yourselves, O ye people, and ye shall be broken in pieces . . . Take counsel together and it shall come to naught." (Isa 8:9–10) Here, the English words "associate yourselves" and "take counsel together" refer to making a foreign alliance. Isaiah also writes, "Say ye not, 'A Confederacy' . . .," that is, don't argue for an alliance. Isaiah was familiar with ancient Near East law and history. He understood, as one modern legal analyst of the period states, that "Protection of the [treaty] partner's dynasty [for example, against a usurper] was a standard treaty obligation."[48] Thus, an alliance not only committed a partner to helping a neighboring king repel an external threat, but to keep his own children on the dynastic throne and thus thwart republicanism in that nation. It would

---

45. Murname, "Egypt, History of (Dyn. 18–20)," 349–50.
46. Redford, "Amarna Letters," 175.
47. Ward, "Relations with Canaan,"405.
48. Wells and Magdalene, *Law*, 2:284.

require Israel to protect and defend a form of government it historically was seriously averse to.

The oft-repeated anthem restating the First Commandment, "You shall not worship other gods," (2 Kgs 17:37) is not primarily aimed at restricting private devotional worship of a different named god. A much more political goal is intended her. Worshipping other gods meant yoking the nation to other political systems not their own. International treaties were signed under the name and the blessing/curse of the national tutelary gods of the signing parties. The vassal nation surrendered part of its sovereignty to the king of the suzerain nation. The first and seventh commandments provided that Israel was to rely on its own democratic-oriented God for public policy rather than the oligarchic or monarchic gods of other lands. The land she was given was sufficient for the purpose not just of survival but of complete independence and neutrality among the nations.

The connection between the first and seventh commandments leads one author to name a sub-title in his chapter on the Seventh Commandment as "Breaking the First Commandment as the Sin of Adultery."[49] Another way of say this is that the Seventh Commandment is a re-iteration of the First Commandment in more specific prohibitional terms. If part of the meaning of the first law is to enjoin strict construction of the following laws, the meaning of the seventh commandment reinforces strict legal construction of the constitution in sexualized terms. God announces that he is a "jealous" God, (Exod 20:5; 34:14) like any partner in a committed marriage. God is hoping that the other party, the people of the nation, will keep their commitment to the democratic law. Covenanting with others gods, as at Peor, or in the case of the Golden Calf, which temporarily yoked them to Egypt, is seen as prostitution, lusting, whoring, harlotry, even animalistic "neighings." (Deut 31:16; Jer 13:27)

This very political concern was in evidence even before Israel entered Canaan to settle there. Moses warned his people to pay strict attention to the commandments "lest thou make a covenant with the inhabitants of the land, and . . . go a whoring after their gods . . ." (Exod 34:15–16) Much later, the prophets made it clear that surrounding nations actively and successfully invited Israel into such political adultery, and thus alienated Israel's affection from its democratic God. Ezekiel writes, "Thou has also committed fornication with the Egyptians thy neighbors . . ." (Ezek 16: 25–26) Also, "Thou hast played the whore with the Assyrians . . . thou hast moreover multiplied thy fornication in the land of Canaan unto Chaldea (Babylon)." (Ezek 16:28–29) Again, "The Babylonians come to her in the bed of love . . ."

---

49. Miller, *Ten Commandments*, 281.

(Ezek 23:17) With these actions, Israel gets in bed with the politics of other nations. The problem with alliance is that alliance partners are inevitably unfaithful. Ezekiel is clear about this: "I will raise up thy lovers against thee ... and I will bring them against thee on every side." Clearly enough, Assyria and Babylon came up on every side and conquered both the northern and southern kingdoms of Israel. Obadiah added a commentary on the matter: "All the men of thy confederacy have brought thee even to the border; the men that were at peace with thee have deceived thee and prevailed against thee." (Obad 7)

Often political adultery (backsliding away from strict constitutional law) starts with wide-spread physical adultery, particularly when male citizens cavorted around with women from other cultures. When Israel's citizens interacted socio-sexually or even socio-economically with strong monarchic cultures, they tended to assimilate accompanying political and moral values. The seventh commandment prohibition against adultery explains the Israelite policy against sexual mixing and inter-marriage with non-citizens of Israel. Sexual relations with Midianites before entering Canaan led to eating sacrifices with them—that is, experiencing and perhaps growing fond of their political traditions by partaking in their civic festivals.[50]

Israel also committed political adultery, or constitutional slippage, not due to any outside force, but just by virtue of growing ignorance of her own history. One commentator calls the adultery metaphor "emblematic" of general Biblical subversion of the laws.[51] We have seen above why so. The seventh precept of Israelite government is given much of its interpretive color as an article of government importance by the prophet Jeremiah. For Jeremiah, "Backsliding Israel committed adultery." (Jer 3:7) In another passage, Jeremiah wrote, "Surely as a wife treacherously departeth from her husband, so have ye dealt treacherously with me, O house of Israel." (Jer 3:20) The seventh commandment is a provision of law requiring judges in Israel to hold to the original strict construction of the constitution, instead of backsliding toward monarchy. Later generations are to stick to democracy. Deuteronomy states this clearly: "The Lord made not this covenant with our fathers, but with us, even us, who are all of us here alive this day." (Deut 5:3) New generations covenant like the original Exodus group to decide their own fates, not give them over to a highly sexualized monarch. The seventh commandment is clearly, then, a constitutional anti-backsliding commandment. There is to be no political adultery in the form of paying extensive national taxes to be deposited in a national bank at the disposal of

---

50. Wildavsky, *Moses as Political Leader*, 87, 180–81.
51. Bosman, "Adultery," 273.

an autocrat, or in the form of paying tribute to a foreign ruler who lords it over homeland voices screaming in dissent.

For reasons suggested above, the traditional neighbor-to-neighbor interpretation of the seventh commandment's prohibition is not without merit, although it falls well short of covering the constitutional waterfront. Faithfulness in social and sexual commitments to the spouse helps ensure effective and lasting family formation and ongoing family economic solidarity. According to this view, the law provides a spouse with a right to a continuing committed relationship and it provides children with a right to a stable mechanism for support and upbringing. It must be added that society at large has an obvious financial stake in stable families, since illegitimate children and orphans may burden tribal or national treasuries. The parallel between local adultery and subversion of constitutional law is thus more organic than it is metaphorical. When spouses separate, local government suffers and the burden of supporting children, as well as keeping law and order, defaults to a broader jurisdiction of government. Ultimately, the national temple treasury had to store food and clothing for distribution to the dissolute or poverty-stricken. The greater the burden placed on the temple treasury, the larger the call for national taxation, government bureaucracy, and strong rulers to tame the bureaucracy.[52]

Individual infidelity to one's marriage partner is an obvious concern because it subverts the system of family government we reviewed above under the heading of the fifth commandment. New marriages essentially create new local governing units, which Israel hopes will demonstrate stability and longevity and undergird the viability of the nation. Fidelity to family success is the backbone of local political function in a democratic society. Thus, a pledge of fidelity to one's spouse is not just a social pledge, but a political pledge of commitment to democratic government. The same is true of the pledge the chief magistrate makes to defend the constitutional law of the land and adhere to limits on the office's power. Any stepping outside of constitutional boundaries is thus infidelity to God, government, one's own national history, ancestors, and freedom. Restrictions on divorce protect the viability of local government and prevent the advent of despotism. Those restrictions come under the heading of seventh commandment law.

Divorce in ancient Israel was meant to take place only on a fault basis, not for any light reason. Adultery was one of the few clear grounds for divorce, but clearly the union did not necessarily have to end because of it. Divorce was also made rare in law by making it expensive. If a husband in the ancient Near East wanted a divorce for anything other than sexual

---

52. Ward, "Temples and Sanctuaries" (Economic Functions), 371.

misconduct, he had to repay the dowry, the bride's wedding present from her father. The dowry was owned jointly by both during marriage and he had use of it, but she assumed full possession of it upon divorce. The dowry was usually larger than the wedding gift given by the groom's family to the couple. The husband usually had to make other divorce-related payments as well.[53]

Any political divorce desired by Israel from any of her foundational principles was intended to be similarly rare. In fact, Israel held tightly on to its covenant of political marriage to democratic principle for nearly 300 years, from the time of the Exodus to the time of its first elected "king," or strong magistrate—Saul. Israel liberalized its national constitution at that time, and then, throughout the next 300 years in the north, and 400 years in the south, liberalized it even further, with predicted consequences coming glaringly into public view before the final destruction of both kingdoms.

The Eighth Commandment

"Thou shalt not steal." (Exod 20:15)

One way to approach interpretation of this law is to ask what would be the most valuable possession that could be stolen from an Israelite citizen. It most certainly would be the land. The next pertinent question would be, what entity or person would be the most likely to steal it? Absent invasion and conquest by a foreign government, one would have to say that the national government in Israel or in any ancient nation was the most likely culprit, as the story of Naboth's vineyard pointedly recounts in the Bible.

In Egypt, most land was owned by the royal family and its political patrons. Younger generations of both Egyptians and Israelites could not inherit what their parents did not own. Many had access to the land only as tenant farmers renting the land and paying their rent with a portion of the crops they grew. Without ownership of land, which in ancient times was essentially the means of production, the people had little profit from their labor and little political clout. This situation was intolerable to Israelites, who had unfettered land ownership in Canaan before descending into Egypt.

One of the great waves of Egyptian government expropriation of private land from the people is told in the Bible's own story of Joseph at Pharaoh's court. Only those few landholders at that time who were left with their own land—the priests—were outside the reach of the new government land policy. (Gen 47:26) And many of the priests were government employees

---

53. Wenham, "Divorce," 170.

themselves, so they were by definition exempt from any government raid on their lands. Unfortunately, once Israel left Egypt and headed for Canaan, she did not leave behind her land woes. Once she claimed ancestral lands in Canaan, she had to defend them against expropriation by nearby monarchs who did not like peasant land ownership. One scholar notes, "All of the arable land of a Canaanite city-state belonged to its king." Much of his land was then "granted as hereditary estates to a military aristocracy in return for its martial and other services to the crown . . . other estates were granted to high-level bureaucrats in payment for their governmental duties . . ."[54] Tenant farmers also earned a partial living serving in the king's mercenary infantry.[55] This economic structure constituted a great part of the "idolatry" that Israel wished to avoid when she reclaimed her homeland. In a system of idolatry, the masses worship the wealthy governing class and fall all over themselves supporting royal right to great expanses of land, luxurious castles, mounds of gold, and fair maidens galore. Israel was determined not to fall into the class-based society that Canaan had built to mimic Egypt.

Israel showed its distaste for this entire system by totally reversing the whole arrangement. The common people got all of the land and the government got nothing. Upon entry into Canaan the elders of the families, clans, and tribes distributed the land fairly to all of the citizenry, likely under authority of the second commandment, an article of government prohibiting a luxurious government court. The eighth commandment then prohibited the government from taking the land of the people in Israel in a time of economic or political hardship in Israel as it had in Egypt. The tribes, farmers and herders owned all the land and its rights and dictated terms of its distribution, use and inheritance. Priests, because they were government employees in Israel as elsewhere, by law could not own arable land. (Num 18:21–24) Also, Israel's king had no land reserved for him in Israel. (2 Sam 7:4–7) David, for example, had to capture land for his capitol city and purchase parts of it out of personal funds. (2 Sam 5:6–10; 2 Sam 24:21–24) The estate of this second king of Israel was so minimal that during a moment of political difficulty in his reign, it was disclosed that one boat carried all of David's belongings. (2 Sam 19:18) The constitution of Israel thus effectively banished the thought of the government ever expropriating the people's most cherished property.

There were several ways for the government to steal land from the people in the ancient Near East. These included moving landmarks (Deut 19:14; Job 24:2); fire-sale purchase of private fields by the government from

---

54. Chaney, "Coveting," 310.
55. Pritchard, *Atlas*, 24.

distressed owners, as in the case of the Joseph story; and attainder, the practice of condemning one's political enemies under some pretense and then taking his property for use as the king's personal property, as Ahab did with Naboth's field. (1 Sam 8:14) Israel could not constitutionally condemn land by eminent domain as Egypt could and did. Moses demonstrated the kind of government restraint with respect to heritable private land that later rulers in Israel found it necessary to follow. The confederacy of Israel in the wilderness had considerable power to do as it pleased wherever it went. Moses, however, stressed the policy that the national government could not take land from ordinary people struggling to maintain political independence: "When thou comest nigh over against the children of Ammon, distress them not, nor meddle with them: for I will not give thee of the land of the children of Ammon any possession; because I have given it unto the children of Lot for a possession." (Deut 2:19) On the other hand, once settled in Canaan wealthy bankers and land owners legally could take land in Israel in pledge when small landowners went into debt or purchase it when the owner was in more dire need. Even so, Israelite land law mandated that land had to be returned to descendants of its original owners on an every 50-year cycle.

Marvin Chaney likes an interpretation of the tenth commandment against coveting that we believe applies just as well to the eighth article of Israelite government. He writes, "I propose that the tenth commandment [in our view here, the eighth commandment]... forbade forms and practices of land consolidation so aggressive and coercive that they deprived a family of fellow Israelites of their ancestral plot of arable land and the subsistence and social inclusion that it supported."[56] In support of his claim, Chaney sites Moran's finding of legal language from second millennium Ugarit, written in Akkadian dialect, which deals with the transfer of immovable property. Those documents frequently refer to "house and field," the same order as listed in the tenth commandment.[57] This same order is observed in the writing of the literary prophet Micah. (Mic 2:2) The pairing is also found in a variety of other Biblical sources. (1 Kgs 21; Gen 39:5; 2 Kgs 8:13; Jer 32;15; Isa 5:8). In fact, the term "house" itself typically means "foremost a plot of arable land."[58] House and field were clearly made sacred by means of the Israelite constitution. We agree with Chaney that the foundational law prohibited taking of land, but find a different prohibition in the tenth commandment than land theft.

---

56. Chaney, "Coveting," 309.
57. Moran, "Conclusion of the Decalogue," 543–54.
58. Chaney, "Coveting," 309.

An interpretation of the eighth commandment favored by many scholars is that it prohibited kidnapping. In the Bible, references to stealing of persons refer either to theft/sale of indentured servants or theft of free persons. If these were intended targets of the commandment, and we think so as well, then the eighth commandment gives authority not only to stop slave traffic but also to release indentured servants after a reasonable time, even if the debt they owe was quite high. Release from indenture was a type of early form of bankruptcy protection, as it protected a debtor from being enslaved over a long period of time. Theft of persons could also be done by the government. This was known in the ancient Near East as corvee—mandatory civilian employment in the government, or mandatory conscription into the army. It is likely that the eighth commandment was understood to prohibit both of these kinds of theft of persons in early Israel. During a period of constitutional slippage in Israel, Saul conducted a military draft, and Solomon a civilian draft, but these policies were criticized by the constitutional specialist prophets who took note of them in their histories.

No doubt the eighth commandment provided authority for prohibition of a variety of other forms of Biblical era theft: theft of war booty (Josh 6:18—7:26); theft of tax donations/gifts/vows made to the government-temple complex (Deut 23:21-23; Acts 5); taking of goods left in the safekeeping of another citizen (Exod 22:7-13); taking too much free grain—a type of welfare fraud (Deut 23:24-25); charging interest on loans, or charging high rates of interest (Exod 22:25; Lev 25:36; Deut 23:20; Ezek 18:8); allowing the animals of another owner to pasture with and get incorporated into one's own flock (Job 24:2); taking a pledge in the first place, taking an inappropriate pledge as collateral, or keeping a pledge inappropriately long (Job 24:3; Deut 24:6—25:4; Neh 5:1-13; Job 24:9); withholding wages for too long (Deut 24:12-13; Lev 19:13); and adulterating grain or rigging scales used to weigh grain or money (Lev 19:35-36; Deut 25:13-16; Hos 12:7-8; Amos 8:4-6; Mic 6:10-11; Prov 11:1; 16:11, 20:10, 23)

After the Israelites left Egypt and finished their long preparation for entering Canaan, they settled available land and once again became "people of inheritance," capable of passing along private property to their descendants. (Deut 4:20) The constitutional tradition of maintenance of land in the family lineage was codified into law in a different form in Leviticus. Here the law says the original owner or a kinsman can buy back sold land at any time. This means his selling of land is really just rental of its produce to another until the original holder wants it back. (Lev 25:25-28) Jesus' statement that "the meek shall inherit the earth" assured his audience of his commitment to the original constitutional paradigm of the inalienability of land. (Matt

5:5) In Jesus' mind it was proper that there be a re-enfranchisement of the poor and powerless according to eighth commandment law.[59]

The eighth commandment also speaks against raids on the national treasury by tyrant rulers who spend gleefully in order to get power and keep themselves in power. Aaron was the prototype, and Abimelech an early example after settlement. Theft of the treasure of the government by overspending or unauthorized spending is surely a form of economic and political crime or treason. On the other hand, confiscation of the treasuries and properties of illegitimate rulers and restoration of constitutional rule is justifiable in Israel, as in the case of Jehu's overthrow of Athaliah.[60] (2 Kgs 11:1–20)

---

59. Berman, *Created Equal*, 104.

60. It must be said that Jehu's bloody methods were decried by the prophet Hosea.

16

Ninth and Tenth Commandments: Mandating Justice and Literacy, Citizenship and Public Health

The Ninth Commandment

"Thou shalt not bear false witness against thy neighbor."
(Exod 20:15; Deut 5:20)

IN EGYPT, THE ISRAELITE tribes experienced injustice in ways both large and small. The fact that Hebrews were "an abomination" to the Egyptians meant they were hated by the 19th Dynasty, that is by Seti and Ramses and others in their courts. (Gen 46:34) We saw how Pharaoh killed the firstborn of Hebrew males, and how another Pharaoh later drafted their adult males into long-term forced labor. There is no Biblical evidence that groups other than Hebrews were forced to work on Pharaoh's building projects, and that meant Hebrews had an inferior position in Egyptian law with respect to other ethnic or clan groups living there. That is injustice.

Israel's new confederate government did not intend to give special legal protection to the rulers of society in either the government or in the private sector (the merchant establishment, large landowners, and bankers), as the Egyptian government did. The laws protected Potiphar's wife, but gave short shrift to Joseph's claims, for example.[1] The ten commandments, with the specific help of the ninth, were intent upon promoting proper judgment (i.e., governmental oversight) of the stranger, the widow, and the fatherless child. (Exod 22:21–22) If justice was properly and regularly guarded for

---

1. Miller, *Ten Commandments*, 369–370.

these hapless groups, it was likely that all other groupings of Israelites would get justice as well.

Moses himself experienced judicial injustice on a very personal level. The story about his interceding to help a Hebrew being abused by an Egyptian was not inserted in the Exodus story just to take up space. It was inserted to make a point—to provide historical and legal context for an important law, the ninth commandment enacted at Sinai. Moses killed a man in a fight and was forced to flee Egypt likely because a Hebrew could not get a fair hearing in court against an Egyptian, in much the same way African Americans in post-civil war America could not get a fair hearing against whites in court.

Whether Moses committed accidental or negligent manslaughter, or justifiable homicide by virtue of self-defense, or second degree (non-premeditated) murder, is not the point, and not really our concern here. The point is that Moses seemed to believe that he had to flee for his own life under the circumstances. Moses fled essentially to a place where he could be safe until a certain point in time. For Moses, this turned out to be until the high priest in Egypt, Pharaoh himself, died and gave way to a new administration. But Moses did not return to live a normal, quiet life as a criminal released back into the community might try to do. He brought with him a passion for free intellectual life, private enterprise and private property, health and wellness, local government, and peace and justice for all. He wanted his fellow Hebrews to have the same kind of life he was able to build for himself in the free society of Midian.

The ninth commandment provided a sort of refuge for the poor, the landless, and those accused of misdeeds in Israel, a refuge by which they could be made safe both in place, in time, and in fact. They could not be treated like second class citizens like they were in Egypt. The commandment authorized the government to utilize cities of refuge in Israel, cities that functioned much like Midian served Moses upon his flight from the scene of his alleged crime. That was safety in place. The law prescribed that the exiled accused could live safely in time until the Israelite high priest passed away. If this practice was customary in the ancient Near East, perhaps it was so because the government's memory of the alleged crime receded or dissolved once the leading judicial light of the nation was no longer there to nurse his hatred of the villain. Perhaps there was a tradition of providing pardon or amnesty at the end of the term of one high official, or at the start of the term of another, as in republican America. Or perhaps new administrations made amnesty arrangements with well-known criminals in order to curry favor with the people. In New Testament times, amnesty was given to a hardened criminal, while Jesus, who had not broken any serious law, suffered instead. (Matt 27:15–26)

Ninth commandment law provided political safety to hounded individuals in direct point of fact, because it constructed a judicial standard that said there should be no false witness tolerated in an Israelite court. Witnesses would have to stick to the facts, and not give vent to insecurity, wounded pride, or hatred. False witness was often associated with Pharaoh's dealings with Hebrews. Ramses' father decreed in advance of any actual crime that Hebrews intended to overthrow the dynasty. (Exod 1:10) There was no court-room authentication of such a plot, nor could there be, but that did not stop Pharaoh from mandating a preventative policy with respect to the Hebrews by killing the firstborn males of Hebrew women. In Deuteronomy 19, the law setting up cities of refuge is linked to the law requiring true witness. (Deut 19:16–20) This tends to tie together the two constitutional purposes we have outlined here for the ninth commandment.

In order to help prevent a despotic Egyptian kind of justice system from developing in Israel, the new government also set up an anti-discrimination law: "Thou shalt not abhor an Edomite; for he is thy brother: thou shalt not abhor an Egyptian; because thou wast a stranger in his land." (Deut 23:7) Israel had lived reasonably well in Egypt for 300 years before the House of Seti began to discriminate heavily against them. Israel remembered the discrimination, but also remembered the better days. The anti-discrimination law in Deuteronomy was likely enacted pursuant to the ninth commandment, which aims at truth and justice as the standard for legal proceedings, rather than biased testimony and cronyism. Truth and justice presumably could be had at one time or another in both Edom and Egypt.

Israelite law also prohibited bribery (1 Sam 8:3; Amos 5:12; Ps 26:10), and required multiple witnesses for felony crime (Deut 17:6). These were laws oriented toward the discovery of actual present reality rather than distorting reality or punishing possible future disloyalty or crime. These two policies were enacted pursuant to the ninth commandment. The commandment also did away with group responsibility for crime, the time-honored method of tyrants and despots in exterminating dissident groups. A democracy was conditioned upon equal justice for all. In Israel, there were no enemies of the state except those who would exterminate people or deny them their rights.

Seti's court pronouncement about a Hebrew political plot was virtually a false prediction regarding the intent of the Hebrew population to be disloyal to the current administration, after 350 years of being loyal to other Egyptian dynasties. It was this type of false witness in Egypt that was known generally in the ancient world as political propaganda. Israel enacted a law to invalidate any such disinformation not substantiated using adequate procedure and adequate science. That law is the law found in Deuteronomy 18 dealing with false prophecy. False prophecies in Egypt or Israel or anywhere were essentially official lies about individuals or groups of people. Those statements of deliberate fantasy were twisted by sophistry, or weakly supported assertions, into official reality, which could then be used to justify repression or murder. Eventually, such a dissolute approach to government administration came to Israel as well. Jeremiah lamented, "Everyone deals falsely." The official propaganda line with regard to government domestic and foreign policy was that all was well, everything was going just fine. Jeremiah wrote, "They [say] . . . peace, peace, when there is no peace." (Jer 6:14) Here, politicians tried to assure the people that their policies were working well, when in fact the whole nation was about to explode.

The prophets of Israel railed continually against bad government in Israel, which basically meant unjust, bloated, or discriminatory government. The operation of government, for good or for evil, was known in the Bible as the process of "judgment." That is because one of the most important functions of government was to resolve disputes and keep the peace between citizens. Jesus taught that "judgment" was the first priority of law and government. (Matt 23:23) Another New Testament passage echoes this concern: "Doth our law judge any man, before it hear him, and know what he doeth?" (John 7:50–51)

The Bible's concern about injustice is particularly sharp in its focus on national government injustice, as we have mentioned above. Two stories in the Old Testament/Hebrew Bible provide instruction related to the ninth commandment's focus on government lies and injustice. In the case of David and Uriah, and Jezebel and Naboth, the matters are not taken up *in court* but *at court*, that is, in courtly circles. These episodes, in Brueggemann's view, demonstrate "royal reality with its penchant for distorted public policy." David manipulated reality by trying to make Uriah appear to be the father of Bathsheba's child. (2 Sam 12:7–12) Jezebel purchased false testimony against Naboth in order to deprive him of his land.[2] (1 Kgs 21:19–24)

Truthful witness is necessary for justice in government administration. We have suggested that false witness is power-related. It is an attempt to elevate one party's power status and diminish another's. Martin Luther mentions the following in his Large Catechism: "One may accuse and malign a poor, innocent man and crush him by means of false witnesses, so that consequently he may suffer punishment in body, property, or honor."[3]

---

2. Brueggemann, "Truth Telling," 293.
3. Miller, *Ten Commandments*, 347.

In other words, the purpose of the hate crime of false witness is to deprive someone of life, liberty, money, or good reputation. Placed in the context of the typical socio-economic stratification of ancient society, we may well imagine that powerful political or economic interests could use patronage power and financial power to manipulate one or two witnesses so as to be able to achieve a desired outcome in court. For example, they could pay off witnesses with bribes or call in favors. Ahab and Jezebel did so in order to falsely accuse Naboth. They extinguished first his civil rights by suborning perjury and falsely convicting him of treason. They then took his life and his estate, so that it could not be inherited by his children.

When the monarchy took away Naboth's property, they eliminated the possibility that his offspring could effectively participate in the democratic system as responsible landholders. He took away the future prospects of hundreds and thousands of people that would come forth from the loins of Naboth and his wife and consigned them to abject poverty. All this was done so the king could have a farm plot conveniently located near his own property. Psalms lamented the devastating power of the "lying lips of a prince." (Prov 17:7) The ninth commandment, in tandem with the eighth against theft, was designed to prevent just this sort of occurrence, the hated monarchic practice of extinguishing the civil rights and nationalization of the property of political opponents. Naboth, after all, appealed to what was well known to be the original construction of the eighth commandment, arguing that the king could not legally take his property.[4] Much later in Israel, government returned with a vengeance to the activity of destroying community figures who made ethical or constitutional challenges to royal leadership. The government of Judea, for example, committed judicial murder of Jesus by means of false witness. (Matt 26:59–68)

The ninth commandment was broad enough in its support of accurate observation and reporting of reality to extend its policy reach to providing authority for compulsory education, scientific history telling, and accurate interpretation of constitutional law, before that tradition suffered abuse. (Amos 5:10) The ten commandment text itself drew attention to the history of tribal misery in Egypt in its own prologue. It gave sound witness as to the precipitous descent of a large and once enlightened regime into political corruption. If people were reminded about how Pharaoh perverted justice in Egypt, they would know that Israelite kings could do so as well. The citizenry in a democracy must be open to learning and must not "hate instruction." (Ps 50:17) When they studied and understood history, they

---

4. The provision against attainder in the American constitution mimics the intent and purpose of the eighth and ninth commandments of ancient Israel.

could provide accurate witness not only in small matters at court, but in big matters like the fitness of a ruler or the constitutionality of a particular government policy.

The Tenth Commandment

> "Thou shalt not covet thy neighbor's house, thou shalt not covet thy neighbor's wife, nor his manservant, nor his maidservant, nor his ox, nor his ass, nor any thing that is thy neighbor's." (Exod 20:17)

> "Neither shalt thou desire thy neighbor's wife, neither shalt thou covet thy neighbor's house, his field, or his manservant, or his maidservant, his ox, or his ass, or anything that is thy neighbor's." (Deut 5:21)

We begin with Jesus' re-casting of the tenth commandment into what has become known in the Christian world as the love commandment, the duty to "love thy neighbor as thyself."[5] Jesus uses the love commandment in his story of the rich young man. When the rich man asks what he can do to obtain eternal life, Jesus answers with the second table of the Decalogue. After listing the commandments against murder, adultery, stealing, false witness, and honoring father and mother, in that order, he ends with the statement "love thy neighbor as thyself."[6] (Matt 19:19)

Jesus' interpretation of the tenth commandment is a clear reflection of the interpretation we offer here, especially in light of what he says next. Jesus goes far beyond today's normative understanding of the commandment law as a personal religious moral code whose purpose is to regulate human moral conduct. Instead, he teaches that the Decalogue invites participation in a broad based cultural movement—attending to the poor, sick, and marginalized, and learning self-government principles traditionally associated with a political system known as a "kingdom of God." (Matt 19:20–21) Participation in such a movement, Jesus believes, would put a person in "perfect" relationship to the law. Jesus here politicizes the tenth commandment, and indeed all those before it, by placing them in context of doing democracy. Doing democracy requires sacrifice of individual resources for an important community cause, an anti-luxury lifestyle where

---

5. Fuller, "Decalogue in the New Testament," 36–40.

6. Some religious traditions, such as Lutheran and Catholic, break up the tenth commandment into two parts, having melded the two earlier commandments on other gods and images together. Some also place the fifth commandment in the second table of laws, as Jesus seems to do here.

accumulating and consuming is replaced by learning and lobbying. He asks the rich young ruler to sell all he has, give the proceeds to the poor, and join the apostles' good citizenship and good government renewal movement. If he gets involved in community action under Jesus' leadership, he will fulfill the wide scope of obligations outlined in the constitutional law for citizen participation in the democratic process.

The purpose of the tenth commandment is to make people into citizens rather than subjects. If they are actively promoting and defending the interests of their neighbors by giving to the poor, joining a movement to educate the people in the history of their own nation, and healing the infirmities of an ignorant and lethargic citizenry, they will help Israel recover lost ground. This ground was lost over several hundred years when Israel turned over the sovereignty of her people and their local institutions to kings both domestic and foreign.

In Egypt, Israel could not be particularly good citizens in the sense of supporting and promoting the neighbor's interests. They did not have extra economic substance to give to neighbors. For example, they had to borrow to make even a three-day holiday journey outside of Goshen. Also, Pharaoh had long ago enlisted perhaps the best and brightest of their younger generation to be overlord "officers" to push them ("afflict" them in the terminology of Exod 1:11–12) to greater and greater levels of brick-making. Those officers were likely used as informants to pass along to Egyptian taskmasters information about which Israelites were working hard and which were not. Ordinary good citizenship was transformed so that it could be manipulated in the interests of the king rather than the neighbor. The object of citizenship in Pharaoh's system was to divert resources and intelligence to his use rather than to the people's use.

Once Israel settled in Canaan, citizens intuitively understood it was not their job to stick their noses into the private social and occupational concerns of their neighbors and use that knowledge to undermine them. In fact, they were not to contribute to the failure of the neighbor in any way, and were to take great care with the persons and property involved in the neighbor's estate. The citizen's job was to let the neighbor govern his household as he saw fit, within the limits of clan and tribal law.

Under tenth commandment law, citizens would now inform neighbors in the sense of educate them rather than inform *on* them in the sense of report on their activities. They would notify neighbors of their rights and responsibilities in a self-government system, rather than tutor them in any extravagant responsibilities to a king. For example, citizens in Israel were required by law to write the constitutional law on the gates and posts of their properties and homes. This would educate not only their own servants, workers, and children, but would educate neighbors and warn travelers that the liberal law of the land was enforced and respected on the premises. Such a requirement underscores the idea that family elders served a legal role much like that of a modern county recorder, attorney or sheriff in keeping and administering the law.

A more humane approach to citizenship activity hardly needed much encouragement from God or Moses. At Sinai, the elders of Israel enthusiastically ratified the tenth commandment requirement that citizens be supportive of one another's interests and rights rather than destructive of them. In particular, the tenth article required that citizens stand up for one another against any attempts by their own national government to interfere with, or covet, their lands, their families, and their flocks.

The God of Sinai wanted citizen resources and initiatives to flow in a different direction. Instead of upward to the king and his palaces to one who already had enough to meet his needs, those resources should flow outward, laterally to other citizens who really needed help. This way, the bulk of government activity was administered on a personal/household level by people who knew individual needs and could meet them effectively from their own pockets. In addition to authorizing a local government legal office, the tenth commandment, together with the fourth commandment, thus authorized a locally-administered system of welfare services.

The tenth commandment is one of eight that are listed in a negative way. It says "don't do this" rather than "do this." We have discussed above in our section on the second commandment that the specific intent of the negative form of the law was to limit the power of the audience being spoken to, rather than strengthen the power of that audience which the positive form seems to do. In the nine laws outlined above, the main audience being spoken to is the people acting through the offices of the national government. The overall document is, after all, a charter for the operation of the national government. In Israel's experience, the central government was the entity needing restriction, much more so than the tribes, clans, or average citizens, whose activities were, of course, also included in the scope of the law. It was only the national government, typically ensconced in a richly endowed capitol building located far away from the great body of the population, that historically ignored or usurped local power, so it was naturally the highest priority target of the law. Since clans and families were governmental units, leaders of those units also had to respect the same law, which called them to help rather than hinder the decent aims of the neighbor.

In keeping with our emphasis on the correct audience intended by the term "you" or "thou" in each of the ten laws, the tenth law specifically prohibited the national government from coveting the persons and property of its neighbors, meaning the citizenry. Much emphasis in traditional interpretation is placed upon whether the commandment merely speaks to inner desires, whether it also extends to taking preliminary steps to expropriate, or, finally if it actually deals with taking or stealing the neighbor's property. For example, the words "covet" and "take" are frequently used together. (Deut 7:25; Josh 6:18; Josh 7:21) In most societies of the ancient Near East, the government did the bulk of the "coveting" by taking a periodic census of the population. This enabled the ruler to find out whose property was available to include in his "taking" programs. Taking then occurred by means of forced labor or taxation of a portion of the income (crops, animals) of the king's subjects. International taking occurred by means of conquest and tribute imposed upon the conquered nation.

One author astutely mentions, "Where one encounters instances of coveting in the Old Testament, they are largely acts of royalty and the wealthy." Further, "Coveting is not a problem of the poor . . . insofar as the biblical story . . ." In this author's view, the intent of the tenth commandment law was to curb the taking of moveable assets, as the reference to wives, servants, animals, and any thing else suggests.[7] Coveting is primarily an activity of greedy kings either who hammer on their own citizens or on the citizens of foreign lands. Israel learned this not only in Egypt, but later in its own national experience. Ben-Hadad of Syria, for example, besieged King Ahab's capitol city of Samaria. A message was sent from the invading king to Ahab, stating "Thy silver and thy gold is mine; thy wives also and thy children, even the goodliest, are mine." (1 Kgs 20:3) This is personal and political greed openly and lustily announced. This sort of open taking by a national government of the same "objects" enumerated in the tenth commandment was prohibited in Israel by its constitution. National taxation was prohibited at Mt. Sinai by means of the tenth commandment and did not surface for the first time in Israel until the time of monarchy 250 years later when Saul "took" men into his army, and David and Solomon later enacted civilian labor and money taxation. National taxation became so oppressive in the time of Solomon's son Rehoboam that the northern half of the country revolted against the south.

On the other hand, there was much that could be done by government and the citizenry to protect the neighbor. Citizens protected and promoted the interests of the neighbor by participating in assemblies to elect good leaders and make good policies. They protected and promoted the interests of the neighbor by returning lost animals, (Exod 23:4–5) releasing workers indentured for debt after a short period (usually a maximum of seven years,

---

7. Miller, *Ten Commandments*, 396.

not the fourteen years Jacob was forced to serve Laban; Gen 29), and returning purchased property to descendants of its original owners at the time of the 50-year Jubilee. The tenth commandment was essentially the "commonwealth" law, which required all citizens to understand that the safety and solidarity of the neighbor's property and family were as important to the community as one's own. No one person or class of persons was lower than another so that an upper class member or a powerful politician could invade his property and family and take it for his own. The government's interests were not higher than the individual family's interests.

We mentioned above that the third commandment gave authority to privacy rights in Israel. The tenth commandment did this as well. It did so by authorizing laws protecting homes and personal property against search and seizure by creditors who wanted to take a particular pledge item. (Deut 24:10–13) This was an early type of foreclosure protection. In Israel, a privacy law also served an important public health function. Both children and adults raised in Egypt looked back on their former land as a place where there was much sickness and debilitation, a place where seasonal communicable diseases were passed along in crowded public places, especially in the forced labor populations of certain cities. (Lev 26:25)

Government officials and ordinary citizens settling in Canaan were to avoid social contact, and certainly sexual contact, with the neighbor's wife. This served as a sort of preventative quarantine that curbed the spread of disease. The purity laws of Exodus and Leviticus enacted pursuant to the tenth commandment were designed to prevent the recurrence of Egyptian-style plagues. (Lev 26:25) Sexual promiscuity with neighbors resulting in plague was a scenario demonstrated early on in Israel's experience at Peor in the wilderness. There Israel committed "whoredoms" and suffered a plague killing 24,000 people, many of whom were not likely a part of the cavorting. (Num 25)

Epilogue

WE HAVE SEEN THAT there existed a democratic tradition in the ancient Near East that Moses' Israel drew from to assist them in the creation of their own representative system of government. This tradition included the lengthy history of the very ancient ancestors in Mesopotamia, the largely oral history of more recent ancestors who settled in Canaan after migration there from Mesopotamia, and the republican experience of contemporary neighbors like Midian. But no amount of oral history telling or passing down of documents through tribal elders and scribes could add the coloring to the historical background of the Ten Commandments that oppression under the House of Seti provided. Israel cried out in anguish because of it, and knew personally, every one of them, what they needed to do to create a more just society. They needed to get out of Egypt, and they needed a place of their own where they could make laws to their liking. One final ingredient used in the recipe to create a humane new government seems to have been Moses' personal oracle from God. This revelation at Sinai linked Israel and her present troubles in Egypt to an answer found in the spirit of humane government that had brooded over all the land and waters of the earth from the beginning. It made Israel believe its troubles were not unique, and that a solution existed to solve the problem.

We also reviewed the fact that the Bible is the story of all aspects of the lives of a confederation of tribes wanting peace and freedom for their peoples. The "salvation" that the book trumpets is not religious salvation principally, but a time-tested and humane solution for dealing with social life, work life, political life, and one's own highly individualized physical and mental health and happiness as well. The Bible's occasional focus on individualized religious prayer and ritual merely supports rather than dominates its laser-like focus on civic life, with its attendant intellectual and political freedoms, including free religious expression. In order to provide support for this overall thesis, we outlined six major Biblical philosophical themes relating to freedom and self-government. We suggested that as a text the Bible is a documentary history that pulls from numerous first hand historical accounts and literary genres. Its compilers and editors worked over these documents to reflect their own views on the constitutional law originally set up to guide the nation of Israel.

The whole story of the Bible is swaddled in God-talk, not because Israel felt they were in church wherever they went, but because God-talk was the cultural language of the ancient world. Amazingly for us, as we look back, God-talk was also the language of early science. God was particularly interested in political science, or power relationships, in every setting imaginable. Because God was the master scientist, everything that humankind accomplished was attributed to God, as if God had accomplished it all. It was humankind, however, together with nature and its unseen movers and forces, that actually did the heavy lifting. Modern religious institutions have not taken a serious and intelligent approach to the Bible with their congregations. They have positioned God outside of the civic arena, something that would have brought a hush to a crowd of ancient people. Modern faith-based interests have given the Bible's broad-reaching descriptive vocabulary a narrow religious interpretation intended to guide theological belief rather than democratic political action.

The ten articles used to structure Israel's national government and guide its relationships with its autonomous constituent tribes, clans and families resulted from specific circumstances in Egypt that they wanted to guard against in Canaan. These circumstances included the absence of several things: free intellectual life, a free economy, self-directed labor and leisure time, stable family relationships, long life, national independence, land stewardship, justice, and public health and wellness measures for all of the people. For that reason, Israel enacted constitutional precepts and legislative policies in those areas once free of Egypt.

The first and second government commandments set parameters for the limited power to be exercised by the national government, while also granting basic freedom to the people. It specifically prescribed a mechanism for decision-making on the national level by setting up legislative and executive/administrative functions, both of which were accountable to the people. The legislative and executive departments exercised the judicial function until the time when an independent judicial branch was set up.

The third and fourth commandments freed the private economy, which consisted mainly of the labor and commerce involving individual families, while also setting boundaries on the use of labor in the free economy. The third commandment also authorized the judicial function. The fifth, sixth, seventh and eight commandments gave local government all the basic police powers—the ability to regulate all social, political and economic relations, including power to regulate local lives, properties and lands. These powers encompassed all critical issues related to protection of life, property, and liberty, including the power to call out the militia for war. The sixth and seventh articles also spoke to foreign policy in a firm way that all could understand. It made clear that war policy and foreign policy were decided by tribes, clans, families, and individuals and were merely administered by the chief magistrate. The ninth and tenth commandments set parameters for the operation of local government: the philosophy and method for accomplishing criminal and civil justice and for deciding health, education and welfare policy and programs. The ninth and tenth commandments also gave authority for locally mandated education in law and science, and application of that knowledge in the work done by individual citizens, local court and correctional agencies and the communities of the realm.

Appendix I

Comparison of Government Charters of Ancient Israel and the United States

A. The Legislative Power and Strict Construction

Israel's First Commandment

Exod 20:3—Thou shalt have no other gods before me. (First commandment ratified by Israel)

Exod 3:16—Go and gather the elders of Israel together (First commandment given to Moses)

Deut 31:9-13—Observe to do all the words of this law . . . as long as you live in the land.

Interpretation—Have no other gods than the God who empowers the elder representatives to make decisions for all of the people. Do not mess with the fundamental constitutional law. The commandments are to be strictly interpreted and not altered.

U.S. Article I

Article I, Section 8—The Congress shall have Power . . . To make all Laws.

Article V—Amendments . . . (must be) ratified by the Legislatures of three fourths of the several States, or by Conventions in three fourths thereof . . .

> Article VI, Section 3—The Senators and Representatives before mentioned, and the Members of the several State Legislatures, and all executive and judicial Officers, both of the United States and of the several States, shall be bound by Oath or Affirmation, to support this constitution . . .

Interpretation—The legislature, not the executive, makes the laws. Both of these first articles of government enact legislative supremacy, essentially people's government, representative government, republicanism . All government officials at all levels must support the constitution as written. It is to be extremely difficult to alter the constitution.

B. The Executive Power

Israel's Second Commandment

> Exod 20:4—Make no graven image

Interpretation—The people shall not make the national elected magistrate into a long-term celebrity who uses a precious metal bull symbol to represent his considerable power. They must not allow him to run people's lives in place of the more intellectually balanced and numerous legislature. The government shall not tax the people to set up a well-heeled national treasury used to finance the leader's wars. The people must always remember the idol made of gold bullion that Aaron agreed to cast to back the new government at Sinai, and that Moses convinced the people to destroy.

U.S. Article I, Section 9, and Article II

> Article I, Section 9, Paragraph 4—No Capitation, or other direct, Tax shall be laid . . .
>
> Article I, Section 9, Paragraph 7—No Money shall be drawn from the Treasury, but in Consequence of Appropriations made by Law . . .
>
> Article I, Section 9, Paragraph 8—No Title of Nobility shall be granted by the United States . . .

Interpretation—The national government is to be limited as to its overall funding, and the chief executive is to be banned from spending money without an act of Congress authorizing the spending. Also, no aristocratic class shall be set up or encouraged by the government whereby a king would be chosen from the nobility to run the country.

> Article II, Sections 2 and 3—The President shall be Commander in Chief of the Army and Navy . . . and recommend to [the Congress'] Consideration such Measures as he shall judge necessary and expedient . . .

Interpretation—The chief executive has power to decide military matters once war has been initiated by the Congress (Article I, Section 8, Paragraph 11). But he can only recommend legislation to the Congress, not decide the legislation himself.

C. The Judicial Power

Israel's Third Commandment Empowering the Private Sector and a Public Judiciary

> Exod 20:7—Thou shalt not take the name of the Lord thy God in vain . . .

Interpretation—The people shall be free to make all manner of agreements with one another and solemnize them by using the name of God (essentially in the name of the government), particularly in social and economic matters. Those agreements will have force of law, unless disputed or broken (taken in vain), in which case a public judiciary shall intervene and make a decision.

U.S. Constitutional Provisions Empowering the Private Sector and a Public Judiciary

> U.S. Article I, Section 10—No State shall . . . pass any . . . Law impairing the Obligation of contracts . . .

> U.S. Article III, Section 1—The judicial Power of the United States, shall be vested in one supreme Court, and in such inferior Courts as the Congress may . . . establish.

> U.S. Article IV, Section 4—The United States shall guarantee to every State in this Union a Republican Form of Government . . .

> U.S. Amendment 10—The powers not delegated to the United States by the Constitution . . . are reserved to the States . . .

Interpretation—The national government shall guarantee the existence of a vigorous local private sector in the states whereby citizens and groups can make agreements with one another. Those contracts shall hold legal sway until and unless taken lightly, in which case the local courts formed under the powers reserved to the states can intervene and decide matters.

D. The Nation's Workforce

Israel's Fourth Commandment
Concerning Work and Rest

> Exod 20:8 Remember the Sabbath day to keep it holy. . . . six days shalt thou labor . . . the seventh day . . . thou shalt not do any work . . . Deut 5:15 And Remember that thou wast a servant in the land of Egypt . . .

Interpretation—A period of rest after a standard work week is mandatory in Israel, in order that the citizenry should not be slaves in Israel as they were in Egypt. Rest is "holy," that is, necessary, right, healing, humane, empowering. A democratic citizenry have much in the way of education (secular and sacred), political assembly, and community service to accomplish outside of economic labor alone.

U.S. Constitutional Provisions
Concerning Work and Rest

> U.S. Article I, Section 9, Paragraph 8—No Title of Nobility shall be granted by the United States . . .

> U.S. Amendment XIII—Neither slavery nor involuntary servitude . . . shall exist within the United States . . .

> U.S. Article IV, Section IV—The United States shall guarantee to every State in this Union a Republican Form of Government . . .

> U.S. Amendment 10—The powers not delegated to the United States by the Constitution . . . are reserved to the States . . .

Interpretation—There will be no upper class, and therefore no servant underclass in the United States to exploit and make work longer and harder than others. Also, there is no longer to be an institution of non-citizen slave property. The national government must assure that the states maintain these democratic republican standards using the local police power they have to regulate life, liberty and property within their boundaries.

E. The Autonomy of Local Government

Israel's Fifth Commandment

Exod 20:12—Honor thy father and thy mother . . .

Interpretation—Family government has the bulk of the "police" power in Israel, the sovereign ability to lay down the law for children, and likely also for hired workers, debt workers, apprentices, and sojourners within their estate boundaries. The national government must stay out of the way of parents.

U.S. Amendment X

The powers not delegated to the United States by the Constitution . . . are reserved to the States . . .

Interpretation—The national government must stay out of the decision-making way of state and local government. Parental government is the pattern and pillar of local society in both colonial and republican America.

F. The Right to Long Life

Israel's Sixth Commandment

Exod 20:13—Thou shalt not kill.

Interpretation—There shall be no domestic political killing, no executive department war-making, no standing army, and no mandatory military conscription by the government in Israel. Neither shall Israel's citizenry kill except at times and in ways prescribed in law decided by the people.

U.S. Constitutional Provisions Protecting Life Domestically and Internationally

Amendment V—No person shall be held to answer for a capital, or otherwise infamous crime . . .unless on a presentment or indictment . . . nor shall any person be . . . twice put in jeopardy of life or limb ... nor be deprived of life, liberty, or property, without due process of law ...

Article I, Section 8, Paragraph 11—The Congress shall have Power ... To declare War ...

Article I, Section 8, Paragraph 12—The Congress shall have Power ... To raise and support Armies, but ... (not) for a longer Term than two Years ...

Article I, Section 8, Paragraph 16—The Congress shall have Power ... for governing such Part of (the militia) as may be employed in the Service of the United States ...

Interpretation—There shall be no domestic political killing, no executive department war-making, no standing army, and no mandatory military conscription by the government in the U.S.

G. Socio-sexual Conduct Among Government Officials

Israel's Seventh Commandment

Exod 20:14—Thou shalt not commit adultery.

Interpretation—Israel's national magistrate shall not make political marriages with the nobility of other countries, shall not make international alliances, shall not take additional wives from among the citizenry, shall not make an incestuous marriage in order to marry within a politically favored family, and shall not betray the trust of the original marriage partner. Neither shall Israel's citizens commit any such kind of adultery.

U.S. Constitutional Provisions Against Political Adultery

Article I, Section 9, Paragraph 8—No Title of Nobility shall be granted by the United States ...

U.S. Article II, Section 2, Paragraph 2—(The President) shall have Power, by and with the Advice and Consent of the Senate, to make Treaties, provided two thirds of the Senators resent concur ...

Interpretation—There shall be no system of marriage which confers special political status on any citizen. The chief magistrate cannot make treaties and alliances on his own. A super-majority of Senators must find reason to do so and must bless the policy. The nation must maintain its independence and the citizenry must maintain its ability to decide its own policies and not be regulated by a foreign power.

H. The People and Their Lands

Israel's Eighth Commandment

Exod 20:15—Thou shalt not steal.

Interpretation—There shall be no government taking of private property—especially land. Neither shall there be any taking by employers, bankers, or private citizens of the property and land of citizens and especially the property of the poor, unless subject to humane laws specifying their return. In particular, there shall be no charging of interest, withholding of wages, and moving of boundary markers.

U.S. Constitutional Provisions Against Government Theft

Amendment V—Nor shall private property be taken for public use without just compensation.

Interpretation—There shall be no government taking of the land, the means of production, nor personal property and effects without proper payment and process.

I. The System of Justice

Israel's Ninth Commandment

Exod 20:16—Thou shalt not bear false witness against thy neighbor.

Interpretation—There shall be a proper system of justice and due process for treating fellow citizens, including truthful testimony concerning the neighbor at court and non-malignant conversation about neighbors among the citizenry. The justice system shall utilize reputable witnesses at trial, cities of refuge for accused felons, and judges who refuse to accept bribes.

U.S. Constitutional Provisions Protecting and Promoting Justice

> Amendment 5—No person shall . . . be deprived of life, liberty, or property, without due process of law . . .

> Amendment 6—In all criminal prosecutions, the accused shall enjoy the right to a speedy and public trial, by an impartial jury . . . to be confronted with the witnesses against him; to have compulsory process for obtaining witnesses in his favor . . .

> Amendment 7—In suits at common law, where the value in controversy shall exceed twenty dollars, the right of trial by jury shall be preserved . . .

Interpretation—Justice activity is to be performed in the open and subject to equitable methods which give the benefit of the doubt to the accused, so that citizenship rights cannot easily be destroyed.

J. Citizenship Requirements

Israel's Tenth Commandment

> Exod 20:17—Thou shalt not covet thy neighbor's house, thou shalt not covet thy neighbor's wife, nor his manservant, nor his maidservant, nor his ox, nor his ass, nor any thing that is thy neighbor's.

Interpretation—Israel's government and citizens shall protect the private property and promote all of the interests and rights of the neighbor. Thus, Israel shall require diligent citizenship activity from its people, including protection of the health of the many. This shall be accomplished by banning sexual contact with and limiting undue socializing with the neighbor, by respecting the quarantine of impure (diseased) persons and animals, and avoiding contact with clothing and other personal effects of householders and workers. Israel shall also require circumcision as a public health measure for the prevention of the spread of sexual disease. Israel shall welcome immigrants to its system of republican government, and shall treat all naturalized citizens as equals under the law. There shall be laws to enforce an anti-sumptuary, anti-luxury, anti-nobility system of plain living among the citizenry. These laws shall preclude the government and any of the citizenry from excessive accumulation of property from out of the hands of the other citizens.

U.S. Constitutional Provisions Respecting Immigration and Citizenship, and Protecting the Property, Health and Welfare of the Entire Citizenry

Article I, Section 8, Paragraph 4—The Congress shall have Power . . . To establish a uniform rule of Naturalization . . .

Article I, Section 9, Paragraph 1—The Migration or Importation of such Persons as any of the States now existing shall think proper to admit, shall not be prohibited by the Congress prior to the Year one thousand eight hundred and eight . . .

Amendment XIV—No State shall make or enforce any law which shall abridge the privileges or immunities of citizens of the United States, nor shall any State deprive any person of . . . property, without due process of law; nor deny to any person within its jurisdiction the equal protection of the laws.

Amendment XV—The right of citizens of the United States to vote shall not be denied or abridged by the United States or by any state . . .

Interpretation—Immigration is to be encouraged in order to help occupy and fortify the land and the system of government. All citizens shall have the same rights and responsibilities as all others. The government shall not take away any citizen's property or rights.

Appendix II

A Note on the "Public Display" Controversy

THE ARGUMENT THAT THE Ten Commandments are religious in nature is given weight by statements such as the 2015 Oklahoma Supreme Court decision which ordered removal of a Ten Commandments monument. The court opined, "The Ten Commandments are obviously religious in nature and are an integral part of the Jewish and Christian faiths."[1] This kind of rationale for legal decision-making regarding monuments is outdated in light of the new evidence of the secular content of the Decalogue we provide in this book.

The argument that the Ten Commandments are more than just religious laws—the so-called "historic purpose" argument—and thus can be displayed in public places, is carried further and given much more weight by the interpretation presented here. We argue that the ten laws are civic, constitutional law, and that they promote and organize a specific kind of political system rather than a particular kind of religion. Those laws do not organize or support any system of private or public worship at all. In fact, we have shown that an establishment of Israelite religion would violate the first and second commandments, which together give authority for the opposite—separation of private shrine activity from state government activity, and separation of public ritual from the large number of public secular duties of government.[2]

Priestly oracles, prayers, incense burning, national holidays and sacrifices, and the like, were characteristic of all ancient governments, no matter whether autocratic or democratic, and no matter whether those

---

1. MSN News, June 30, 2015.

2. Public ritual is common in modern America, as in all countries. For example, America uses non-denominational prayer in Congress and other public settings and uses the Bible for swearing in the President.

governments controlled religion or separated it from the public sphere. But none of these activities is referenced in the Ten Commandments or controlled by the commandments. That is because those ten articles of government treat the organization and operation of government, not the organization and operation of religion.

The Bible's earliest reported characters and events provide a backdrop for a civic/secular interpretation of the commandments and serve to introduce the intent of the commandment law. For example, the Bible makes a claim that the limited government system of early Israel was but a continuation of the democratic republicanism known at the time of the Garden of Eden, the time of Noah, and the time of Abraham and his immediate offspring. The inhabitants of the Garden lived lawfully and without intimidation from an internal political faction until Cain introduced one. Noah was committed to government by non-violence, as an antidote to the violence that held sway prior to the flood. Abraham lived deferentially with all his neighbors under a code that required him to extend tolerance to all who protected his own right to self-determination.

Some American legal commentators and courts argue that the Ten Commandments exclude non-monotheistic religions and atheistic belief and thus are discriminatory and can not be used as a standard for blind justice. But the Bible text itself, and especially the foundational civic law of Israel, make no claim to limit science or curb polytheism. Ancient Israel was manifestly committed to the scientific "wisdom" tradition of the day and tolerated many dozens of named gods on its own soil as long as those gods spoke well of republicanism. Jeremiah complained that a different deity or shrine was represented on every street corner of Jerusalem. Moses invited religious denominational and political variety in the "wilderness" narratives, and later government officials did so during Judges and Kings. In addition, there are numerous iterations of ten commandment law given prominence in non-monotheistic and arguably non-theistic settings such as Confucian and Buddhist societies, which buttresses the idea of their civil content.

What Israel did not tolerate was an autocratic political system in its midst, and "worship" of, that is, alliance with, foreign governmental systems whose political ethics and national deities were not as humane as those of Israel. Israel endorsed, sponsored, favored, promoted, and demanded rule of law by means of its commandment system of government, but did not endorse, sponsor, favor, promote, or demand any system of private religious worship.

In fact, the Ten Commandments, including the first table of four or five, are so secular in intent and purpose that they have been used extensively in the West as the principal articles for civil government. This was the case under the system of colonial government in North America prior to the American Revolution and in times and places in the early westward settlement of the United States. The Ten Commandments came to the fore once again somewhat later as inspiration for liberal and humane public policy during the period of the 1880s and 1890s, when oppression of workers became common during the era of the Robber Barons. Their prominence continued in the speeches and literature of the first two decades of the twentieth century, the so-called Progressive Era, when political candidates and government leaders sought to make reforms in economic and political policy.[3] This is the same kind of historical context out of which the constitutional law of Israel arose immediately after flight from Egypt. Movements in both societies were civic, political, economic, and constitutional, and only tangentially religious.

In the America of both colonial and early republican periods, and even the later Progressive Era, the commandments were poorly understood as to the breadth and depth of their actual civic content. The champions of their relevance did not know how to make the argument we make here, not having had access to the extensive published biblical research of the past 150 years. Nevertheless, reassertion of those ancient laws became a pointed and relevant reminder of the spirit of Western liberal constitutional government and political science. The governor of the state of New York, and later Chief Justice of the United States Supreme Court, C. E. Hughes, wrote that Americans were "a people who . . . will make the governments of the states and the United States square with the eternal principles of the Ten Commandments and the Declaration of Independence."[4]

---

3. Langston, "The Ten Commandments and American Ideals."
4. *The New York Times*, September 4, 1907.

Bibliography

Albertz, Rainer. *A History of Israelite Religion in the Old Testament Period: From the Beginnings to the End of the Monarchy*. Translated by John Bowden. Louisville: Westminster John Knox, 1994.
Anderson, Bernhard. *Understanding the Old Testament*. 3d ed. Englewood Cliffs, NJ: Prentice Hall, 1975.
Aquinas, Thomas. "The Moral Precepts of the Old Law." In Brown, William, ed., *The Ten Commandments: The Reciprocity of Faithfulness*, 51–60. Louisville: Westminster John Knox, 2004.
Assman, Jan. "Egyptian Literature." In *Anchor Bible Dictionary*, D.N. Freedman, ed., 6 vols. New York: Doubleday, 1992, 2:381.
Avalos, Hector. *Illness and Health Care in the Ancient Near East: The Role of the Temple in Greece, Mesopotamia, and Israel*. Atlanta: Scholars Press, 1995.
Barr, James. "Politics and the Bible." In *Oxford Companion to the Bible*, Metzger, Bruce and Michael Coogan, eds., 599–601. New York: Oxford University Press, 1993.
Bauer, Susan. *The History of the Medieval World: From the Conversion of Constantine to the First Crusade*. New York: W.W. Norton, 2010.
Berger, Raoul. "From Hostage to Contract." *Illinois Law Review*, 35:154–281.
Berman, Joshua. *Created Equal: How the Bible Broke with Ancient Political Thought*. Oxford: Oxford University Press, 2008.
Boehm, Christopher. "Pre-Classical Democracy – Prehistory." In Isakhan, Benjamin and Stephen Stockwell, *The Edinburgh Companion to the History of Democracy*, 29–39. Edinburgh: Edinburgh University Press, 2012.
Bosman, Hendrick. "Adultery, Prophetic Tradition, and the Decalogue." In Brown William, ed., *The Ten Commandments: The Reciprocity of Faithfulness*, 267–74. Louisville: Westminster John Knox, 2004.
Bright, John. *A History of Israel*, 4th ed. Louisville: Westminster John Knox, 2000.
Brown, William, ed. *The Ten Commandments: The Reciprocity of Faithfulness*. Louisville: Westminster John Knox, 2004.
Bryce, Trevor. *Letters of the Great Kings of the Ancient Near East: The Royal Correspondence of the Late Bronze Age*. London: Routledge, 2003.
Brueggemann, Walter. "Truth Telling as Subversive Obedience." In Brown, William, ed., *The Ten Commandments: The Reciprocity of Faithfulness*, 291–300. Louisville: Westminster John Knox, 2004.

Burgess, John. "Reformed Explication of the Ten Commandments." In Brown, William, ed. *The Ten Commandments: The Reciprocity of Faithfulness*, 78–99. Louisville: Westminster John Knox, 2004.

Calvin, John. *Institutes of the Christian Religion*. Translated by Ford Lewis Battles, edited by John T. McNeill, 2 vols. Library of Christian Classics. Philadelphia: Westminster, 1960.

———. *John Calvin's Sermons on the Ten Commandments*. Edited and translated by Benjamin W. Farley. Grand Rapids, MI: Baker Books, 1980.

Chaney, Marvin. "'Coveting Your Neighbor's House' in Social Context." In Brown, William, ed., *The Ten Commandments: The Reciprocity of Faithfulness*, 302–17. Louisville: Westminster John Knox, 2004.

Cody, Aelred. "Priests and High Priest." In *Oxford Companion to the Bible*, Metzger, Bruce and Michael Coogan, eds., 608–11. New York: Oxford University Press, 1993.

Cole, Susan Guettel. "Temples and Sanctuaries – Greco-Roman." In *Anchor Bible Dictionary*, D.N. Freedman, ed., 6 vols. New York: Doubleday, 1992, 6:380–82.

Collins, Raymond. "Ten Commandments." In *Anchor Bible Dictionary*, D.N. Freedman, ed., 6 vols. New York: Doubleday, 1992, 6:385.

Coogan, Michael. *The Old Testament: A Historical and Literary Introduction to the Hebrew Scriptures*. New York: Oxford University Press, 2006.

Dever, William. "Temples and Sanctuaries – Syria-Palestine." In *Anchor Bible Dictionary*, D.N. Freedman, ed., 6 vols. New York: Doubleday, 1992, 6:376–80.

Dauphinais, Michael and Matthew Levering. "Law in the Theology of St. Thomas Aquinas." In Brown, William, ed. *The Ten Commandments: The Reciprocity of Faithfulness*, 45–50. Louisville: Westminster John Knox, 2004.

Doyle, Michael. "Liberalism and World Politics." In Mingst, Karen and Jack Snyder, eds. *Essential Readings in World Politics*, 4th ed. New York: Norton, 2011.

Ehrman, Bart. *The New Testament: A Historical Introduction to the Early Christian Writings*, 3rd ed. New York: Oxford University Press, 2004.

Elazar, Daniel and Stuart Cohen. *The Jewish Polity*. Washington D.C.: University Press of America, 1985.

Elazar, Daniel. *Covenant and Polity in Biblical Israel, Vol. 1: Covenant Tradition in Politics*. New Brunswick, NJ: Transaction, 1995, 1998.

———. *People and Polity: The Organizational Dynamics of World Jewry*. Detroit: Wayne State University Press, 1989.

"Elder." In *Encyclopedia Judaica*, Jerusalem: MacMillan, Vol 6 (1971), 578–81.

Frankford, Henri. *Kingship and the Gods*. Chicago: The University of Chicago Press, 1948, 1978.

Fuller, Reginald. "The Decalogue in the New Testament." In Brown, William, ed., *The Ten Commandments: The Reciprocity of Faithfulness*, 33–44. Louisville: Westminster John Knox, 2004.

Gonzales-Ruibal, Alfredo. *An Archaeology of Resistance: Materiality and Time in an African Borderland*. Lanham, MD: Rowman & Littlefield, 2014.

Gordis, Robert. "Primitive Democracy in Ancient Israel." In *Poets, Prophets, and Sages: Essays in Biblical Interpretation*. Bloomington: Indiana University Press, 1971.

Gottwald, Norman. *All the Kingdoms of the Earth: Israelite Prophesy and International Relations in the Ancient Near East*. New York: Harper & Row, 1964.

———. *The Politics of Ancient Israel*. Louisville: Westminster John Knox, 2001.

BIBLIOGRAPHY

Green-McCreight, Kathryn, "Restless Until We Rest in God: The Fourth Commandment as Test Case in Christian 'Plain Sense' Interpretation." In Brown, William, ed., *The Ten Commandments: The Reciprocity of Faithfulness*, 223-36. Louisville: Westminster John Knox, 2004.

Hallo, William W.. "Writing in Antiquity." In *Oxford Companion to the Bible*, Metzger, Bruce and Michael Coogan, eds., 820-23. New York: Oxford University Press, 1993.

Halpern, Baruch. "Kingship and Monarchy." In *Oxford Companion to the Bible*, Metzger, Bruce and Michael Coogan, eds., 423-16. New York: Oxford University Press, 1993.

Halbertal, Moshe. "God's Kingship." In *The Jewish Political Tradition, Vol. 1: Authority*, Walzer, Michael, et al., eds., 128-32. New Haven: Yale University Press, 2000.

Halevi, Judah. "The Kuzari 3:11." In *The Jewish Political Tradition*, Vol. 1: Authority, 60-65. New Haven: Yale University Press, 2000.

Hamilton, Victor. *Handbook on the Pentateuch*. 2nd ed. Grand Rapids: Baker Academic, 2006.

Hazony, Yoram. *The Dawn: The Political Teachings of the Book of Esther*. Jerusalem: Shalem, 1995, 2000.

———. *The Philosophy of Hebrew Scripture*. Cambridge: Cambridge University Press, 2012.

Heschel, Abraham. "A Palace in Time." In Brown, William, ed., *The Ten Commandments: The Reciprocity of Faithfulness*, 214-22. Louisville: Westminster John Knox, 2004.

Hooker, Edna. "The Significance of Numa's Religious Reforms." *Numen, v10 n2* (1963), 87-132.

Horsley, Richard and Tom Thatcher. *John, Jesus and the Renewal of Israel*. Grand Rapids: Eerdmans, 2013.

Horsley, Richard. *Covenant Economics: A Biblical Vision of Justice for All*. Louisville: Westminster John Knox, 2009.

Jayne, Walter Addison. *Healing Gods of the Ancient World*. Whitefish, MT: Kessinger, 2010.

Josephus, Flavius. "Against Apion," *Vol. 1*. Translated by L. Feldman. Cambridge: Harvard University Press, 1961.

Kent, Charles. *Israelite Laws and Legal Precedents: From the Days of Moses to the Closing of the Legal Canon*. New York: Charles Scribner's Sons, 1925.

Knight, Douglas A. "Tradition History." In *Anchor Bible Dictionary*, D.N. Freedman, ed., 6 vols. New York: Doubleday, 1992, 6:637.

Langston, S. "What Make the Bible Meaningful: The Ten Commandments and American Ideals," *Society of Biblical Literature Forum*, np, May, 2008. http://sbl-site.org/publications/article.aspx?ArticleId=773.

LaSor, William Sanford. "Temples." In *Oxford Companion to the Bible*, Metzger, Bruce and Michael Coogan, eds., 731-34. New York: Oxford University Press, 1993.

Laws, Sophie. "Anoint." In *Oxford Companion to the Bible*, Metzger, Bruce and Michael Coogan, eds., 30. New York: Oxford University Press, 1993.

Levinson, Bernard. "The First Constitution: Rethinking the Origin of Rule of Law and Separation of Powers in Light of Deuteronomy." *Cardozo Law Review*, 27:4 (2006), 1853-88.

———. *Legal Revision and Religious Renewal in Ancient Israel*. Cambridge: Cambridge University Press, 2008.

Luther, Martin. "How Christians Should Regard Moses." In Brown, ed., *The Ten Commandments: The Reciprocity of Faithfulness*, 68–77. Louisville: Westminster John Knox, 2004.

Magdalene, Rachel and Bruce Wells, eds. *Law From the Tigris to the Tiber: The Writings of Raymond Westbrook*. Winona Lake, IN: Eisenbrauns, 2009.

McMahon, Keith. *Women Shall Not Rule: Imperial Wives and Concubines in China from Han to Liao*. Lanham, MD: Rowman & Littlefield, 2013.

Metzger, Bruce and Michael Coogan, eds. *Oxford Companion to the Bible*. New York: Oxford University Press, 1993.

Meyers, Carol. *Exodus*. New York: Cambridge University Press, 2005.

Mieroop, Marc Van De. *A History of the Ancient Near East*. Oxford: Blackwell, 2004.

Milgrom, Jacob. *Leviticus: A Book of Ritual and Ethics*. Minneapolis: Fortress, 2004.

Miller, Patrick. *The Ten Commandment*. Louisville: Westminster John Knox, 2009.

Moore, Michael S. *WealthWatch: A Study of Socioeconomic Conflict in the Bible*. Eugene, OR: Pickwick, 2011.

Moran, William. "The Conclusion of the Decalogue." *Catholic Biblical Quarterly* 29 (1968) 543–54.

Murname, William. "Egypt, History of (Dyn. 18–20)." In *Anchor Bible Dictionary*, D.N. Freedman, ed., 6 vols. New York: Doubleday, 1992, 2:348–53.

Nelson, Eric. *The Royalist Revolution: Monarchy and the American Founding*. Cambridge: Harvard University Press, 2014.

Nissen, Hans. *The Early History of the Ancient Near East, 9000–2000 B.C.* Translated by Elizabeth Lutzeier. Chicago: University of Chicago Press, 1988.

Prichard, James, ed. *The Harper Collins Concise Atlas of the Bible*. New York: Harper Collins, 1991, 2006.

Propp, William H. "Golden Calf." In *Oxford Companion to the Bible*, Metzger, Bruce and Michael Coogan, eds., 257. New York: Oxford University Press, 1993.

Redford, Donald. "Amarna Letters." In *Anchor Bible Dictionary*, D.N. Freedman, ed., 6 vols. New York: Doubleday, 1992, 1:175.

Rehm, Merlin. "Levites and Priests." In *Anchor Bible Dictionary*, D.N. Freedman, ed., 6 vols. New York: Doubleday, 1992, 4:297–310.

Reviv, Hanoch. *The Elders in Ancient Israel*. Jerusalem: Magness, 1989.

Robertson, John. "Temples and Sanctuaries–Mesopotamia." In *Anchor Bible Dictionary*, D.N. Freedman, ed., 6 vols. New York: Doubleday, 1992, 6:372–76.

Ryken, Leland. "The Bible as Literature." In *Oxford Companion to the Bible*, Metzger, Bruce and Michael Coogan, eds., 461. New York: Oxford University Press, 1993.

Saadiyah Gaon, "The Book of Beliefs and Opinions," In *The Jewish Political Tradition*, Vol. 1: Authority, 55–60. New Haven: Yale University Press, 2000.

Sakenfeld, Katharine. *Numbers: Journeying with God*. Grand Rapids, MI: Eerdmans, 1995.

Shinkoskey, Robert Kimball. *The American Kings: Growth in Presidential Power from George Washington to Barack Obama*. Eugene, OR: Resource, 2014.

———. *Biblical Captivity: Aggression and Oppression in the Ancient World*. Eugene, OR: Resource, 2012.

———. *Do My Prophets No Harm: Revelation and Religious Liberty in the Bible*. Eugene, OR: Resource, 2011.

Simpson, Gary. "Thou Shalt Not Kill—The First Commandment of the Just War Tradition." In Brown, William, ed., *The Ten Commandments: Reciprocity of Faithfulness*, 249–65. Louisville: Westminster John Knox, 2004.

Smith, W. *A Dictionary of Greek and Roman Antiquities*. London: John Murray, 1875.

Spencer, John. "Golden Calf." In *Anchor Bible Dictionary*, D.N. Freedman, ed., 6 vols. New York: Doubleday, 1992, 2:1065–69.

Stockwell, Stephen. "Before Athens: Early Popular Government in Phoenicia and Greek City-States." In *The Secret History of Democracy*, Isakhan, Benjamin and Stephen Stockwell, eds., 35–48. New York: Palgrave Macmillan, 2012.

Stockwell, Stephen. "Israel and Phoenicia." In Isakhan, Benjamin and Stephen Stockwell, eds. *The Edinburgh Companion to the History of Democracy*, 71–81. Edinburgh: Edinburgh University Press, 2012.

Toorn, K. Van Der. *Sin and Sanction in Ancient Israel and Mesopotamia: A Comparative Study*. Assen, Netherlands: Van Gorcum, 1985.

Trigano, Shmuel. *Philosophy of the Law: The Political in the Torah*. Jerusalem: Shalem, 1991.

Vaux, Ronald de. *Ancient Israel: Its Life and Institutions*. Translated by John McHugh. Grand Rapids, MI: Eerdmans, 1997.

Walzer, Michael. *Exodus and Revolution*. Basic Books, 1985.

———. *In God's Shadow: Politics in the Hebrew Bible*. New Haven: Yale University Press, 2012.

Walzer, Michael, Menachem Lorberbaum, Noam Zohar, and Yair Lorberbaum, eds. *The Jewish Political Tradition, Vol 1: Authority*. New Haven: Yale University Press, 2000.

Ward, William. "Egyptian Relations with Canaan." In *Anchor Bible Dictionary*, D.N. Freedman, ed., 6 vols. New York: Doubleday, 1992, 2:405.

———. "Temples and Sanctuaries – Egypt." In *Anchor Bible Dictionary*, D.N. Freedman, ed., 6 vols. New York: Doubleday, 1992, 6:369–72.

Weinfeld, Moshe. *Social Justice in Ancient Israel and in the Ancient Near East*. Jerusalem: Magness, 1995.

———. "The Transition from Tribal Rule to Monarchy and Its Impact on the History of Israel." In Elazar, Daniel, ed. *Kinship and Consent: The Jewish Political Tradition and Its Contemporary Uses*, 151–66. Washington D.C.: University Press of America, 1983.

Wells, Bruce and Rachel Magdalene, eds. *Law from the Tigris to the Tiber: The Writings of Raymond Westbrook, Vol 1: The Shared Tradition, Vol 2: Cuneiform and Biblical Sources*. Winona Lake, IN: Eisenbrauns, 2009.

Wenham, Gordon J. "Divorce." In *Oxford Companion to the Bible*, Metzger, Bruce and Michael Coogan, eds., 169–71. New York: Oxford University Press, 1993.

Wildavsky, Aaron. *Moses as Political Leader*. Jerusalem: Shalem, 2005, 2008.

Wolf, Umhau. "Traces of Primitive Democracy in Ancient Israel." *Journal of Near Eastern Studies*, VI (Jan–Oct). Chicago: University of Chicago Press, 1947.

York, William. *Health and Wellness in Antiquity through the Middle Ages*. Santa Barbara, CA: Greenwood, 2012.

Name Index

Aaron, 12–13, 32, 43, 44, 55, 106, 127, 130, 146, 149, 198
   ascension of, 38
   building political base, 57, 58
   challenging Moses, 54
   depiction of, 57
   given the priesthood, 31, 33
   golden calf and, 21–22, 56–58, 60–61, 63
   governmental duties of, 34
   Moses sharing power with, 16–17, 47, 58–59, 63, 107
   as national priest, 38
   priestly line through, 31–32
   ritual leadership of, 22–24
Abel, 58
Abiathar, 107
Abimelech, 12, 30, 76, 89, 129, 139, 146, 150, 176, 177, 198
Abiram, 29, 44, 47, 48, 55
Abraham, 7, 11, 52, 77, 95, 125–26, 129, 188
Adams, John, 49n8, 148
Adams, John Quincy, 59n2
Ahab, 28, 70, 89, 124, 127, 144, 150, 196, 203
Ahimelech, 34
Ahmose I, 180
Ahtaliah, 85
Akhenaten, 12
Alexander of Pherae, 146
Amalek, 50, 75

Amenhotep II, 189
Amenhotep IV, 180
Amos, 31, 158
Amun-Re, 12
Ananias, 63–64
Antiochus Epiphanes IV, 146
Aquinas, Thomas, 1, 2
Arcadius, 146
Aristotle, 31
Athaliah, 198
Augustus, 125

Bathsheba, 179, 188–89
Barr, James, 6
Ben-Hadad, 207
Bright, John, 82
Brueggemann, Walter, 202
Bush, George W., 114n3

Caleb, 34, 73, 86
Caligula, 146
Calvin, John, 2–3
Chaney, Marvin, 196
Cincinnatus, 47, 51n11
Clay, Henry, 59n2
Clinton, Bill, 179–80
Confucius, 112
Cooper, Samuel, 148
Cyrus, 9

Dathan, 29, 44, 47, 48, 55
Dauphinais, Michael, 1–2

231

Name Index

David, 24, 28, 31, 34, 94, 95, 106, 127, 130, 148, 150, 172, 195, 207
- and Bathsheba, 179, 188–89, 202
- election of, 91, 92
- secular-sacred separation under, 23
- storing weapons at the temple, 40
- undermining second commandment, 128

Deborah, 75, 76, 77, 86, 90, 95

Ehud, 76
El, 19
Elazar, Daniel, 189
Eldad, 47, 55, 127
Eli, 34, 107, 127
Elijah, 70, 98, 149
Esther, 188n41
Ezekiel, 104, 191
Ezra, 116

Frankfort, Henri, 11, 125

Gad, 77
Garfield, James, 51n11
Gideon, 12, 51–52, 57, 64, 70, 76, 89, 91, 123n1, 129, 142, 177
God
- access to, 108
- in charge of government and politics, 6
- concern of, for common people, 131, 135
- encouraging self-government, 42, 77, 83, 105–7, 132
- ethics of, as leader, 136
- first political act prescribed by, 131
- goal of, 108–9
- identity of, 131
- intermediaries for, 132
- kingship of, 136–37
- name of, 158
- omnipotence of, 6
- political interest of, 26, 135–36
- presence of, 134
- role of, 111
- things of, 1
- voice of, people hearing, 26–27
- as witness to legal document, 19

Gordis, Robert, 82, 85

Hadad, 190
Hagar, 184
Hamilton, Alexander, 60, 63
Harrison, William, 51n11
Hatshepsut, 180, 187
Herod, 130
Hezekiah, 85, 90, 94
Hilkiah, 67
Honorius, 146
Horemheb, 162
Hosea, 116, 177

Isaac, 11, 52, 95, 188
Isaiah, 51, 90, 98, 145–46, 163, 190

Jackson, Andrew, 60, 66
Jacob, 11, 52, 58, 95, 173
Jefferson, Thomas, 49n8
Jehoash, 85
Jehu, 124, 127, 158, 198
Jephthah, 31, 76–77, 91, 185
Jeremiah, 51, 70, 116, 192, 202
Jeroboam, 13, 64, 91, 103, 124, 139, 146
Jesus, 145, 155
- civic speeches of, 164
- cleansing the temple, 65–66
- encouraging private mediation, 154
- pacifism of, 186
- parables of, 130, 163
- recasting the tenth commandment, 204
- on sidestepping the fifth commandment, 174

Jethro, 18, 22, 27, 48, 53, 71, 126
Jezebel, 202, 203
Job, 112
John the Baptist, 149–50
John of Patmos, 104–5
Johnson, Andrew, 51n11
Joseph (OT), 14, 52, 58, 194
Josephus, 31, 69
Joshua, 34, 74, 75, 77, 86, 95, 116, 132
Josiah, 12, 67, 94, 116, 128, 129
Jotham, 70, 76, 177
Judah, 156
Judah Halevi, 168

Korah, 47, 48, 54, 55, 59, 142

Leacock, John, 148
Lee, Richard Henry, 148
Levering, Matthew, 1–2
Levinson, Bernard, 68–69
Luther, Martin, 2, 175, 202

Madison, James, 49n7, 49n8, 51n11, 89n36
McKinley, William, 51n11
Medad, 47, 55, 127
Melchizedek, 126, 129
Micah the householder, 35, 146, 151
Miriam, 44, 54, 55
Moran, William, 196
Moses, 5, 7, 14, 95, 130, 132, 142, 149, 158, 167–68, 178
   access to, 27
   administering law enacted at Sinai, 41–55
   appointing leaders, 18
   as author of the Torah, 103
   blessings by, 73
   bronze snake of, 151
   calling elders into session, 15, 27–28
   on citizens' government participation, 30
   as constitution-maker, 41, 43, 56–57
   constitution of, 17
   death of, 74
   democratic practices of, 27
   desiring a democratic people, 22
   elders' support for, 16
   as elected magistrate, 41, 44
   emergency powers of, 43, 44, 46, 47, 53, 55
   on entering Canaan, 45
   farewell address of, 67, 71–74
   favoring democratic republicanism, 5
   feeling under-qualified for his position, 50–52
   first political act of, 27–28, 131
   golden calf and, 21–22, 56–63, 183
   governmental duties of, 34, 42
   governmental philosophy of, 26
   and government's role in religion, 12–13
   judicial injustice and, 200
   land policy and, 73
   as leadership example for Israel, 45, 47, 76, 106, 122
   leadership qualifications of, 16
   leadership stages for, 41–46
   as logistical coordinator, 43
   murmurings against, 29, 41, 54, 86, 92
   no-confidence proceedings against, 46
   non-violence of, 47, 52
   people's relationship with, 45, 46, 132
   personality of, 47–55
   Pharaoh and, 15
   portrayal of, 47, 50
   as prophet, 22, 40
   as revolutionary leader, 41, 43
   relinquishing power, 42, 44, 53, 55
   revelations to, 42
   secular leadership of, 22–23, 24, 45–46, 131
   seeking office, 41, 42–43
   sharing power with Aaron, 16–17, 58–59, 63, 107
   sorting out governmental roles, 23, 122–23
   as statesman, 16
   term of office for, 28–29
   tribe of, 16
   weaknesses of, 16

Naboth, 194, 196, 202, 203
Nathan, 25, 94, 130, 148, 150, 179
Nehemiah, 158
Nelson, Eric, 137n6
Nixon, Richard, 87
Noah, democratic governance and, 11

Obadiah, 192

Pepi, 187–88
Phalaris of Acragas, 146

Pharaoh, 43, 70, 201. *See also* Ramses II
  citizens approaching, 27
  divine right of, 118
  political actions of, 29–30
  political personality of, 52
  socio-political culture of, 119–20

Ramses I, 162
Ramses II, 5, 15, 118, 130, 139, 162, 181, 190. *See also* Pharaoh
Rehoboam, 74, 91, 128–29, 130, 139, 207
Rush, Benjamin, 148

Saadiah Gaon, 163, 168
Samson, 76, 89 [QY: Note Sampson on 76]
Samuel, 33, 67, 74, 75, 77–78, 86–87, 94–96, 107, 127, 129, 132, 138, 179
Saul, 12, 23, 28, 34, 79–80, 91, 94–96, 124, 129, 179, 194, 197, 207
Seti I, 14, 162, 181
Solomon, 25, 60, 64, 95, 98, 107, 124, 127n9, 128, 179, 190, 197, 207
Solon, 158
Spinoza, Baruch, 18, 32
Steven (NT), 62

Tamar, 156
Theodosius, 146
Thutmose I, 180
Thutmose II, 187
Thutmose III, 180, 187
Thutmose IV, 180, 190

Uriah, 179, 202
Urukagina, 12, 125
Uzziah, 12, 129

Valentinian, 146

Washington, George, 47, 49n8, 51n11, 63, 91
Wellhausen, Julian, 104
West, Samuel, 148
Whitney, Peter, 148
Wildavsky, Aaron, 29, 54, 76
Wolf, Umhau, 85, 91

Zadok, 34, 129
Zedekiah, 28, 70, 90
Zipporah, 54

Subject Index

Aaronic priesthood, 36–37, 40, 123
Adams (John) administration, 67
adjudication, 92–93
adultery, 120
    breaking up the social unit, 186–87
    fifth commandment and, 168
    limited government and, 186
    political, 192
    biblical language and, 10
alien state, 6
Amarna Age (Egypt), 59, 171–72, 180–81
America. *See also* United States
    British crown in, 125
    frontier in, 170
amnesty, 200–201
Analects (Confucius), 112
Anchor Bible Dictionary, 97
ancient Near East
    chief magistracy in, 123–24
    concubines in, 189
    construction projects in, 147
    coveting in, by the government, 207
    democracy in, 7, 11
    divorce in, 193–94
    economic issues in, 99–100
    elders in, 42
    financing governments in, 61
    governments in, stealing land, 195–96
    imperial power in, 9
    national idols in, 58, 111, 137
    priesthood in, 32, 34, 58
    private legal contracts in, 155–57
    republican government in, 131
    rulers in, 27, 145–46
    rulers' accountability in, 149
    secular documents in, 19
    social killing in, 184
    treaty documents in, 20–21
anointing, 92, 157
anti-autocratic societies, 9
anti-discrimination law, 201
anti-sumptary legislation, 149
Ark of the Covenant, 36–37, 82
assassination, 176–77
assembly, 75, 83, 84–85. *See also* congregation; elders, gathering of
attainder, 196
augures, 39
authority, source of, 17
autocracies
    incest and, 187
    regicide and, 176

Baalism, 107
backsliding
    penalty for, 179
    political, 142, 192
banking, 59–60
Benjamin, tribe of, 74, 75, 77, 81, 86, 178

Subject Index

Bible
  body counts in, 10
  characters in, socio-political goals of, 99
  civic faith in, 101, 106
  communitarian context of, 99
  community-wide issues in, 99–100
  concern of, for peace, 105
  on culturo-political violence, 106
  economic issues in, 99–100
  literary analysis of, 102–4
  literary themes of, 105–6
  non-religious interests in, 97–98
  philosophic/scientific issues in, 100
  as political document, 100, 105
  political images in, types of, 6
  prayers in, 98
  religious packaging of, 112
  rooted in concrete realities, 97
  secular focus of, 98
  secular themes in, 101
  social concerns in, 98–99
  themes in, 124
Book of the Dead, 3
bribery, 201
burnt offerings, 114

Canaan
  absolutist city-states in, Israel confronting, 70, 181
  conquest of, 80
  democracy in, 11–12, 19
  as frontier, 171
  Israel's entry into, 28, 45–47, 49–50, 55, 72, 86
  land policy in, 18, 37, 133, 195
  tribal alliance in, 125–26
  violence in, 180–81
canonical criticism, 104
captains, 81, 95
case law, 19
caste system, 33
census, 182
central bank, 59
central government, obligations of, 59
centralism, 25
chieftains, 73
child abandonment, 184

child labor, 167–68
children
  lives of, 184
  responsibility of, 168
child sacrifice, 184–85
Christianity, abuses of, based on misinterpretation, 5
Chronicles, books of, 103, 128
church-state separation, 12. *See also* secular-sacred separation
circumcision, 15, 87
cities of refuge, 121, 185, 200
citizens
  functioning as a whole, 28, 44, 83–84, 86
  as kingdom of priests, 30–32
  names of, 158–59
  participating in a democracy, 47–48, 53, 108
  participating in government, 87
  political enfranchisement for, 30–32
  supporting each others' interests, 205–6
city-states, development of, 9
civic law, Ten Commandments devoted to, 19
civic prophets, 108. *See also* prophets
civic religion, 117
civil life, biblical images of, 6–7
civil rights, 138–40
civil service, examinations for, 31
clans, 169
class distinctions, 22, 71, 162
Cluniacs, 12
coins, rulers on, 145–46, 149
commandments, 116
community, elders establishing, 15–16
confidence votes, 29, 46, 83, 92, 96, 138, 142
conflict, pervasiveness of, as theme in Bible, 105–6
congregation, 83–84, 116. *See also* assembly
consensual government, 27
constitutional an-iconism, 53
constitutional government
  Numbers and, 44–45
  three legs of, 145

constitutional provisions, mass ratification of, 71
constitutional republic, image of, 7
constitutions
    boundaries for, 107–8
    interpretation of, 141–42
contracts, 119
    law of, 154–57, 166
    political, 156–57
    types of, 155
corruption, 76–77, 86–87
corvee, 100, 150, 197
council of elders, 28. *See also* elders
court incest, 187
covenants, 11
coveting, 122. *See also* tenth commandment
crime, group responsibility for, 201
cronyism, 37, 128
curses, in treaty documents, 20

Dan, tribe of, 89
Davidic dynasty, restoration of, 85
death of the firstborn, 43
debts, release of, 38, 88, 165
Decalogue. *See* Ten Commandments
democracy, 73
    citizens' participation in, 47–48, 53
    congregations conducting activities of, 116
    conscription and, 182–83
    desired end of, 63
    doing of, 204–5
    early versions of, 11–12
    elements of, 12
    founders' beliefs and, 140
    history of, in ancient world, 4
    indicators of, 12
    Israel as, 135
    Jesus placing democracy in context of, 204
    leaders in, 51
    royalism and, 151
    separation of powers in, 44
    spirit of, 108
    start-ups of, 45
    treaty documents and, 20–21
    tribal confederations and, 13

    threats to, 139
democratic federation, 135
democratic group behavior, early evidence of, 8–9
democratic republicanism, 4, 5, 27, 28, 48–49, 51, 105, 137, 177
democratic societies
    battles for, 10
    sons in, 33n13
Deuteronomy, book of, 38, 67–74, 92, 129, 142
dignitaries, temporary, 81
disease, 112
divination, 39, 69
divorce, 193–94
documentary hypothesis, 104
domestic arrangements, 156
domestic law, 17, 168
dowry, 194

economic assistance, source of, 71
economic democracy, 70–71
economic law, 17
"edah," 82–84, 87
Eden, democratic life in, 9
education, 69, 71, 203–4, 205–6
Egypt
    aristocratic-type adultery in, 187
    finance system of, 60
    independent provinces in, 11
    Israel's debts to, 60–63
    labor practices in, 61, 119, 153
    land policy in, 194–95
    oppression in, 4
    priesthood in, reduced privileges for, 12
eighth commandment, 3, 120–21
    kidnapping and, 197
    land ownership and, 194–98
    original construction of, 203
elders, 24
    councils of, 17, 118
    election of, 15
    function of, usurped, 28
    gathering of, 27–28, 42, 43–46, 83, 88, 131, 134–35
    handling day-to-day government, 87–88

elders *(continued)*
   hierarchical system of, 87–88
   issued addressed by, 88–90
   judicial council of (seventy), 43–44, 84, 90, 141
   jurisdiction of, 172–73
   legislative power of, 144
   local, police power of, 168–69
   organization of, 15–16, 133
   power and, 18
   presiding, overridden by legislature of the whole, 86
   problems addressed by, 134
   roles of, 90–91
   title of, way of assuming, 88, 91
   women as, 90
elections, 11, 43–44, 75, 76, 85–86, 91–92, 132, 177
emergency law, 18
enthronement psalms, 128
Ephraim, tribe of, 81
eschatological image, 6–7
Esther, book of, 101
ethics, 48
exceptionalism, 6
executive branch, 50, 149
exile, biblical language and, 10
Exodus, book of, 10, 14, 142
expression, freedom of, 137–39, 178. *See also* speech, freedom of
extispicy, 39

false witness, 202–3
family
   government and, 167, 168–74
   as political authority in Israel, 16, 80
   stability of, society's interest in, 193
family estates, 169
fathers, jurisdiction of, 169–73
fetiales, 39
fifth commandment, 3, 16, 30, 35, 119–20, 134
   delegating power, 169
   family government and, 167
   intent of, 168
   and Israel's survival, 170
   laws related to, 173
   police power and, 170

   welfare system and, 172
first commandment, 3, 118, 123, 124, 126
   banning worship of foreign gods, 144
   constitutional revisionism and, 141–42
   foreign policy and, 142–43
   government function of, 135
   intent of, 144
   legislative branch and, 132, 136, 137
   national government organization and, 19
   political goal of, 191
   precedents for, 161
   protecting civil rights, 138–40
first fruits offerings, 114
fleeing, biblical language and, 10
form criticism, 104
fourth commandment, 1, 3, 119
   on concentration of wealth, 178
   communitarian correctives in, 160
   compassion and, 163
   economic activity and, 161, 162
   economic structure and, 162
   free enterprise and, 165
   justice and, 163
   labor law and, 19
   precedent for, 161
   social welfare and, 165, 172, 206
   two parts to, 165
freedom
   establishing, 135
   Sabbath and, 164–65
   uses of, 164–65
free enterprise, 154, 155, 165
free soil domains, 9

gates, as meeting places, 85, 87, 169
genealogies, 174
Genesis, book of, 11, 14, 103, 106
Gilgamesh, story of, 10
gods
   contracts and, 156
   having no other, 141–42, 144–45
   invocations of, 141
   types of, 110
God-talk, 210

Subject Index 239

Golden Calf, story of, 21–22, 38, 48, 56–66, 149, 183
government
    administered on family/clan level, 35
    bi-partite, 84
    citizens' participation in, 87
    consensual, 4, 27
    family/clan-level approach to, 80, 83
    financing of, 21
    as house of prayer, 66
    organization of, 17, 19
    roles of, 23–24
    strong national financing of, 61
    tri-partite, 84–85
    wisdom-style of, 119
    worship-style of, 118–19
Greece, ancient, civil service exams in, 31
groups, democratic behavior of, early evidence of, 8–9

Hasmoneans, 32–33, 124, 129
head of household, legal status of, 171–72
health care, 164
hereditary priesthood, 32–33
Herod, house of, 65
highland areas, governmental forms in, 9
history
    definition of terms and, 112
    telling of, 103–4
Hittites, governance and, 11
holiness, 116–17, 164–65
holy day celebrations, 115
home rule, local, 11
hospitality, 26
humans
    activity of, boundaries for, 108
    as agents of control, 111–12

idolatry, 2, 57, 59, 62, 70–71, 90, 118, 127, 146, 147, 195
idols, national, 58, 59
Iliad, 10
impeachment, 46, 47, 54, 86–87
incense, burning of, 115

incest, 120, 187
India, magistrates in, 13
infanticide, 184
innocent life, declining respect for, 178
intellectual expression, freedom of, 107
inter-marriage, 144, 187, 189–90
international relations, law and, 17

Israel, 9, 17, 18
    addressing political issues, 45
    alliances of, with other nations, 191–92
    attributing activity to God, 111
    authority in, lines of, 123, 139
    budget for, 33
    central government in, 25, 34–35, 150
    civic religion of, 117
    compact of, with God, 83
    contract law for, 154–57
    debts of, 59–63
    decentralization in, 82, 125
    as democracy, 135
    democratic republicanism and, 5
    divine kingship in, 128–29
    divorce, 193–94
    education in, 71
    elections in, 91–92, 177
    families in, under Pharaoh, 167–68
    family as political authority in, 80, 83. *See also* family
    first national sacrificial rite of, 126
    focus of, 151–52
    forced labor of, 14, 61, 138, 147, 153, 161–62, 168, 205
    foreign relations work by, 80
    governance of, 4, 5, 24–25
    hereditary monarchy in, 4, 128–30
    historical memory of, 46, 70, 139, 140
    histories of, 103–4
    and the House of Seti, 14
    humane practices of, 186
    judicial function in, 92–93, 159
    juvenile justice laws in, 170
    land for, 181
    land policies in, 84, 195–96, 197

Israel *(continued)*
  legislative department supremacy in, 28
  military decision-making in, 49–50
  military engagements of, 181
  modesty of, in national government works, 148
  molten monarchy of, 57
  monarchy in, accounts of, 103
  Moses setting precedent for, 45, 47, 76, 106, 122
  national government limited in, 80
  national priesthood of, 34–35
  national taxation in, 207
  national treasury for, 64, 59–60
  non-violence ethic in, 176
  organizing national government, 43–46
  placing trust in wealth, 63
  political autonomy of, 15–16
  political capitol in, separate from sacral center, 127
  political contracts in, 157
  political system of, 132
  private law in, 5
  re-establishing government in, 142
  religious liberty in, 107
  rivaling city-states, 26
  setting up a democratic republic, 4
  sovereignty in, for tribal councils of elders, 118
  three crowns in government of, 94–96
  tribes of, 4
  turning to republicanism, 125
  Tyre and, 12
  work week in, 165
  worship in, 116

Jefferson administration, 67
Jewish revolts, 66
Jewish War (66–73 CE), 66
Joshua, book of, 126
Judah
  southern kingdom of, 106
  tribe of, 81
judges, 36, 43, 82, 95, 127, 157

Judges, period of, 9, 24, 32, 34–35, 64, 89, 129
  decline during, 77
  elections during, 91
  leadership during, 76
  libertarian assessment of, 79
judgment, 123, 202
judicial function, 39, 68–69, 92–93
justice, 39, 103, 170, 199–204

kidnapping, 197
killing, 175–86
kingdom of God, 204
kingdom (nation) of priests, 35, 48
kings, 95
  additional wives for, 187, 188–89
  distrust of, 69–70
  divine leadership and, 26
  eschewing of, 107
  secular relationship of, with his people, 125
  swearing to uphold the law, 157
Kings, books of, 103, 128
kingship, 77–78

labor, individualized direction of, 119
land. *See also* Canaan, land policy in; Egypt, land policy in; Israel, land policy of
  distribution of, 133
  ownership of, 120–21
  rest for, 165–66
law, worship of, 148
leaders
  institutional power of, 68
  titles for, 95
  working for the people, 28–29
leadership
  confidence votes on, 29
  ethics of, 48
  forms of, 8
  idolatry and, 118–19
  lack of, 77
  limitations on, 10–11
  Mosaic qualities of, 50–55
  term of office for, 53–55
legislative branch, supremacy of, 48–49
Levirate marriage, 70, 80, 182

Levites, 33, 36–37, 127
  commandment law and, 37–38
  education of, 37
  land policy of, 37
  membership in, 31
  public policy regarding, 123–24
Levitical laws, 24
Levitical priesthood, 36–37, 40
liberation, imagery of, 7
life, value of, 183–84
literary criticism, 104
local home rule, 16
localism, 25
lowland cities, governmental forms in, 9
luxury politics, 151
luxury religion, 151

magistrates, 68, 72, 74
marriage, 156. *See also* inter-marriage;
    Levirate marriage
  Egypt's practices for, 120
  political, 70, 194
  widows and, 80, 88, 120
mediation, 154
men (of Israel / of a city / of a region / of
    Judah), 83–84, 91, 92
Meribah, 28, 29, 44, 46, 74
Mesopotamia
  decentralization in, 125
  political institution in, 11
  sacred-secular separation in, 12
micromanagement, 53
Midian, 15, 22, 76
migration, imagery of, 7
military, civilian control of, 72
militia, raising of, 43, 169, 182
ministers, 91
Mitanni, 11
mo'ed, 75
molten images, 56–57, 123, 127, 137,
    140, 147, 149–51. *See also*
    Golden Calf, story of
monarchies, 137
  citizen discontent with, 10
  elders and, 90
  judiciary in, 159
  political contracts in, 156–57
  regicide and, 177

scribe-priests in, 37
  treaty documents and, 20–21
monarchs, sexual activities of, 188
morality, individual, 1, 2, 3
Mosaic priesthood, 123
moveable assets, 207
murder, political, 175, 176–79
murmurings, 29, 41, 54, 86, 92

Napthali, tribe of, 81
national bank, 64
national gods, 137
national idols, 58
national writings, 104
neighbors, 205–8
neutralism, 180
New England, 7
ninth commandment, 3, 121
  education and, 203–4
  justice and, 199–204
  providing political safety, 200–201
nobles, 81
non-violence, 52, 120, 176
Numbers, book of, 44–45

oaths, 156, 157–58, 174
Odyssey, 10
officers, 133
openness, governmental, 27
oppression, biblical language and, 10
originalist constitutional theory, 68
Oxford Companion to the Bible, 97, 103

pacifism, 180
paganism, 150–51
Palestine, imperial power in, 9
Parable of the Talents, 163
parents
  caring for, 173–74
  police power of, 168–69, 170
  responsibilities of, 167–73
patriarchs, 95
peace, advocacy of, 183–84
Peace and Truce of God movement, 186
Pentateuch, 103. *See also* Torah
  kingship portrayed in, 70
  legislative action in, 28
people, legislative power of, 144

Persia, magistrates in, 9
Pharaohs
    building projects of, 147–48
    imperial campaigns of, 180
    wealth of, 147–48
Pharisees, 33
Phoenicia, democracy in, 11–12
pilgrimages, 115–16
plagues, tenth, 43
pluralism, political, 107
political marriage, 54, 68, 70, 194. See also inter-marriage
political murder, 175, 176–79
political opponents, forgiveness of, 54
political propaganda, 145, 147, 151, 188, 201–2
politics, ambition and, 51–52
polygamy, 120
Pontifex Maximum, 128n10
poverty, release from, 166
power
    abuse of, 175
    ambition for, 47
    coveting of, 122
    overturning, 176
priesthood, 34–35. See also priests
    as civic position, 36
    covenant of, 68
    hereditary, 32–33
    public, 12–13
    varieties of, 36–37
priestly leadership, 22
priests, 24. See also priesthood
    apprentices of, 31, 32
    characteristics of, 31
    in Deuteronomy, 69
    duties of, 30–32, 37–40, 95, 98, 113–14
    freedom for, 139–40
    guardians of the Ten Commandments, 37–38
    justice function of, 39
    kingdom of, 30–32, 35, 48
    making law, 34
    sacrifices and, 114–15
    as scribes, 37, 38
    virtuous reputation and, 39
prime ministers, 95

prince/priest pairs, 128
princes, 91
privacy rights, 208
private property, 12
prologue to Ten Commandments, 140–41
property, rights and, 12, 71
prophecy, false, 202
prophetic image, 6
prophets, 106
    appointed, 90
    attacking priests, 39
    categories of, 94–95
    God speaking through, 105
    good vs. bad, 132–33
    interpretation of, as religious figures, 98
    persecution of, 177
    as political party leaders, 42, 94, 96
    role of, 7, 42
public health, 17, 23–24, 39, 43, 113, 121
public policy, local, 16
punishment, 185–86
purification offering, 115
purity laws, 113, 121

redaction criticism, 104
regicide, 176–77
religion
    as political science and natural science, 110–11
    regulation of, 12
    teachings about, 110
religious freedom, 13, 107, 126, 137, 138, 209
religious idols, 151
religious killing, 184
representative governments, war and, 182–83
repression, 29
republic
    constitutional responsibility for, 45
    early American, 47, 49n8, 64, 126, 163, 169n3
    founding spirit of, 111
    hedging against national taxation, 37

Subject Index

seventh commandment and, 144
republican government, 131. *See also* democratic republicanism
    coalition building in, 59
    domestic law and, 168
    Israel's turn to, 125
    representatives in, 90
    rulers' powers and, 148
rest day, 119
rest laws, 165. *See also* Sabbath
Revelation, book of, 10
revenge, 178, 185
Rex sacrorum priesthood, 38
ritual,
    public, 114
    as rationalist science, 110
Rome, political phases of, 125
Romulus and Remus, story of, 10
royalism, 151. *See also* monarchies
rulers, 81
    in the ancient Near East, 145–46
    democratic plainness and, 149
    religious, 146
    sexual conduct of, 188–89
    wealth of, 150, 198

Sabbath, 163–65
sacrifices, 38, 77, 95, 110, 114–15, 126, 184–85, 209
salvation, civic, 7, 108, 134
science
    advances in, 111
    institution of, 69
    religion as, 110–11
scripture, political content in, 6
second commandment, 3, 62, 70, 118, 121, 123, 124, 127, 133, 206
    anti-sumptary legislation and, 149
    on concentration of wealth, 178
    communitarian correctives in, 160
    David undermining, 128
    executive branch and, 137, 149
    government's executive branch and, 19
    intent of, 149
    international affairs and, 143
    legal tradition of, 150
    presumption underlying, 150

religious idols and, 151
religious paganism and, 150
transgressions against, 146–47, 151
secular-sacred separation, 17, 22–23, 32, 107, 122–30
self-government
    readiness for, 17
    as theme in Bible, 106–7
servant leadership, 27
seventh commandment, 3, 120, 144
    intent of, 190
    international affairs and, 143
    linked with the first commandment, 191
    public policy and, 191–93
    strict construction and, 192–93
Sinai, political constitution and, 16
Sinuhe, story of, 10, 176
sixth commandment, 3, 121
    citizens' rights and, 175
    civic killing and, 176–77
    enforcement of, diluted, 177
    freedom of expression and, 178
    humane treatment and, 186
    international affairs and, 143
    international relations and, 186
    and land for Israel, 181
    narrow interpretation of, 175
    national census and, 182
    prescribing neutralism and pacifism, 180
    punishment and, 185
    right to life and, 183–84
social killing, 184
social welfare policies, 70–71, 165, 172, 206
socio-historical method, 104
sorcery, 107
source analysis, 104
South Africa, 7
sovereignty, 133
    individual, 18
    people retaining, 82
    sharing of, 73
speech
    freedom of, 29, 54, 138–39, 178
    law and, 17
standing, political meaning of, 92

Syria, governance and, 11

tabernacle, 36–37, 44, 59, 64
taxation, 59, 114–15, 207
temple, civic uses for, 40, 59–60, 64–65, 98, 113
Ten Commandments. *See also individual commandments*
  as catechism, 2
  civil government and, 2–3, 19
  cultural movement invited by, 204
  democratic republicanism in, 105
  doctrinal reform and, 2
  enacting governmental form outlined in, 67–68
  faithfulness to, 19
  first table of, 2, 19, 174
  following secular document format, 19
  as foundational law for new democracy, 20
  individual morality and, 1, 2, 3
  intent of, 73, 140
  Israelite government and, 1
  Jesus' placing of, in context of democracy, 204
  justice and, 199–200
  liberal construction of, 77
  local governance and, 81–82
  misinterpretation of, 4–5
  modern Christian take on, 3
  national treasury system and, 61
  negative forms in, 206
  priests as guardians of, 37–38
  prologue to, 140–41
  purpose of, 1–4, 20, 138
  ratification of, 18–19
  responding to Israel's conditions, 118–21
  second table of, 120, 174, 204n6
tenth commandment, 3, 121
  audience for, 206–7
  on concentration of wealth, 178
  as commonwealth law, 208
  education and, 205–6
  Jesus' recasting of, 204
  land theft and, 196
  moveable assets and, 207

  privacy rights and, 208
  purpose of, 205
  welfare services and, 206
term of office, 28–29, 44, 53–55, 83, 92
theft, 197
theocratic image, 6
theo-politics, 6
third commandment, 2, 3, 119, 120, 134
  on commerce and property, 159–60
  debt and, 160
  economic organization and, 19
  freedom and, 159
  free enterprise and, 153–54, 165
  privacy rights and, 208
  responsibility and, 159
  societal activity and, 154–55
three crowns, 94–96
time, sanctification of, 164
tithes, 59, 114–15
Torah, 37–38, 68–69, 103. *See also Pentateuch*
tradition history, 104
tribes, 169
  central government and, 8
  chiefs of, 30, 41, 73, 81, 95
  cooperation between, 8, 18, 26
  emergency law for, 18
  governance and, 11, 81–82, 133
  individual sovereignty and, 18
  mutual support of, 19–20
  northern, seceding from southern, 13
  political organization of, 42
  self-determination of, 8
  voting and, 85–86
tribute, paid to other nations, 143
Tyre, 12

United States
  Articles of Confederation, 20
  Bill of Rights, 20
  coins in, 146
  Constitution of, 137, 139, 159, 160, 170, 185–86
  Declaration of Independence, 141
  early confederation of, 126
  histories of, 103, 105
  legislative branch supremacy in, 149

military power of, 183
national banking in, 59, 60, 64
national taxation in, 59
organization of, 67

violence
    ethic of, 176
    national government and, 179
voting. *See* elections

war power, 49–50, 72, 86, 174–75, 182
Washington administration, 67

wealth
    accumulation of, 119, 178
    redistribution of, 116
welfare policies, 70–71, 165, 172, 206
well-being sacrifice, 115
wisdom prophets, 108. *See also* prophets
women, rights of, 119–20
worship, law and, 17
worship politics, 151
worship practices, 110, 116
worship religion, 151

xenophobia, 6

www.ingramcontent.com/pod-product-compliance
Lightning Source LLC
Chambersburg PA
CBHW051635230426
43669CB00013B/2305